VETERANS UNCLAIMED BENEFITS

Veterans Unclaimed Benefits

The Insider's Guide

5th Edition

Michael Riedel

iUniverse, Inc.

New York Lincoln Shanghai

Veterans Unclaimed Benefits
The Insider's Guide

iUniverse, Inc.

For information address:
iUniverse, Inc.
2021 Pine Lake Road, Suite 100
Lincoln, NE 68512
www.iuniverse.com

ISBN: 0-595-29537-1

Printed in the United States of America

For over two centuries, Americans have fought and died to protect and defend the integrity and ideals of the Constitution of the United States of America. Since the American Revolution, over 45 million veterans have served, more than one million have died in the name of freedom. Many others have made enormous sacrifices, suffered greatly, and experienced unknowable loss so we all could live a better life in this world.

This book is dedicated to the many brave men and women who've paid the ultimate price for freedom while serving faithfully, with courage and honor.

MISSION

Our mission is to provide you with the most valuable, up to date, informative, one of a kind, information available on veterans benefits. We strive to support every veteran with clear and responsible data. This never before published information is designed to help you obtain the maximum in veteran's benefits from Federal, State, and local agencies. We are devoted to helping every veteran and dependent to the fullest.

Contents

▼

About This Book

Whether you are only interested in one VA benefit or absolutely every benefit that you're entitled to, this book is for you! *Veterans Unclaimed Benefits* provides you incredible insight and information that can be helpful to all veterans, survivors, and dependents. It is designed to give you quick access to the information you need while breaking through the confusion of government red tape and bureaucracy.

We hope you find this book easy to understand. It has been compiled to help you with any possible situation, but we do realize that each situation is as individual as each person. Because of this, we know your circumstances may need further explanation or personal assistance. Take the time to reread over any parts that are unclear to you at first, this can help in understanding the benefits and information better.

Introduction

Veterans' benefits have been around since Abraham Lincoln and the Civil War. President Lincoln realized the huge debt that was owed to the men and the families who sacrificed so much. Since then, the veterans of America have amassed a large array of benefits. Of course, things have changed over the years, but there remains a solid foundation of benefits for all veterans to take advantage of, you just have to know how. Veterans and their families need to know that there are excellent programs and benefits that still await them.

While some veterans, dependents, and widows have benefited from the programs and services the VA has to offer, most have not. According to statistics from 1990-2001, there are more than 25 million veterans in the U.S. Approximately 70 million people, or a quarter of the U.S. population are potentially eligible for VA benefits and services because they are veterans or family members of veterans[1]. Sadly, less than 5 percent of all veterans ever step foot into a VA medical center and astonishingly enough, almost 90 percent of all veterans don't apply

---

1. Source: Mathematica Policy Research, Inc., and VetPop2001.
   VetPop2001 relies on a combination of data from the 1990 U.S.
   Census, the U.S. Department of Defense, Office of the Actuary, and the
   Defense Manpower Data Center. It estimates the number of veterans
   defined by age, year, gender, race/ethnicity, degree of disability, period
   of service, length of service, and state. The US Department of Veterans
   Affairs funds this research.

for any benefits at all. A total lack of advertising on the part of the VA combined with the absence of an honest willingness to really help our nation's veterans has caused an infinite number of individuals to go without benefits.

The U.S. Government and especially the VA isn't doing nearly enough to help veterans and their families. Recent budget proposals have veteran's benefits, programs, and employees being reduced. VA medical centers alone have lost over 25,000 employees in the last 8 years while enrollment for medical care has more than quadrupled! To make things worse, benefit counselors at VA regional offices and medical centers nationwide are neglecting to inform veterans and their dependents of entitlement to *all* possible benefits. This is compounded by the overall confusion of the VA benefits system. This unacceptable treatment is costing veterans immeasurable benefits, it's costing them their livelihood.

Many veterans have never filed for any benefits simply because they don't know what they're entitled to. While others who have filed have been misinformed about all that they are eligible for. Still others have used VA programs and are actually receiving some type of VA benefits, yet they could be entitled too much more but don't know it. This is why *Veterans Unclaimed Benefits* is such a valuable resource tool for all veterans and their families.

The object of this book *is* to clearly explain all the benefits that have been designed for America's veterans and their dependents through the U.S. Department of Veterans Affairs, State veterans agencies, and county offices. We hope to simply and efficiently inform you about your benefits, provide you with all the facts, advise you on how to apply for all the benefits you're eligible for, and help you take advantage of things you don't even know exist.

▼

CHAPTER 1

THREE BIG SECRETS TO RECEIVING YOUR VA BENEFITS!

1. You must apply! Don't assume you're not eligible!

This is the biggest key to receiving your benefits! You won't receive anything unless you apply. Don't assume_anything. Unfortunately, the mistake of most veterans is that they don't apply for benefits at all. There seems to be a common misconception among vets that they're not eligible for anything, or that benefits are only for war veterans or combat veterans. Not true! No matter what your status, you must apply.

2. You must know and understand what you're applying for.

Veterans Unclaimed Benefits will help you learn about all VA benefits and programs, and what you possibly could be entitled to. And in certain cases, there is specific information you need to know in order to make the right kind of claim(s). For instance, some claims have a time limit on filing. Some claims can be granted even if denied previously. You just have to know exactly what to do and how to apply. Service connected disability claims from injuries or conditions resulting from military service are the most common and diverse types of claims, and *Veterans Unclaimed Benefits* will help you with all the important details.

3. You must follow up regularly on your claim status.

You know the old saying, "Look out for number one", remember it when dealing with the VA. The VA is notorious for long delays when processing any type of claim. You must be looking out for yourself every step of the way. You may find the occasional government worker who will do their best for you but it still may not be good enough. Call the VA often to see what is going on with your claim(s). Keep calling and calling so they know you're educated about you're situation and you're going to keep following up on your claim(s) until you receive a decision in a reasonable time. Be persistent and courteous, that combo will get you further than anything else.

CHAPTER 2

▼

VETERAN STATUS

Discharges • Basic Eligibility • Service Periods

Eligibility for most VA benefits is based upon discharge from active military service under honorable or general conditions and a minimum period served. Some benefits *require* an honorable discharge.

Dishonorable and bad-conduct discharges issued by general court-martial bar VA benefits. Veterans in prison and parolees may be eligible for certain VA benefits. VA regional offices must clarify eligibility of prisoners and parolees.

Veterans with disabilities incurred or aggravated during active military service *may* qualify for medical or related benefits regardless of time served and discharge characterization.

Any Veteran

Active Service: Full-time service as a member of the Army, Navy, Air Force, Marines, Coast Guard, Merchant Marines (WWII), or as a commissioned officer of the Public Health Service, the Environmental Services Administration or the National Oceanic and Atmospheric Administration.

Guard and Reserve Service: Completion of at least six years of honorable service in the Selected Reserves and the National Guard provides home loan benefits. Persons serving in the active Guard and Reserves under a six-year contract have education benefits. Twenty-year reservists have limited burial benefits.

Wartime Service Periods

Certain VA benefits and medical care <u>require</u> wartime service. Under the law, VA recognizes these war periods:

Mexican Border Period: May 9, 1916, through April 5, 1917, for veterans who served in Mexico, on its borders or in adjacent waters.
World War I: April 6, 1917, through November 11, 1918; for veterans who served in Russia, April 6, 1917, through April 1, 1920; extended through July 1, 1921, for veterans who had at least one day of service between April 6, 1917, and November 11, 1918.
World War II: December 7, 1941, through December 31, 1946, *(includes Merchant Marines).*
Korean Conflict: June 27, 1950, through January 31, 1955.
Vietnam Era: August 5, 1964, through May 7, 1975; February 28, 1961, for "in country" veterans who serve before August 5, 1964.
Gulf War: August 2, 1990, through a date to be set by law or Presidential Proclamation.

Special War Groups

The Defense Department has recognized active military service in 28 organizations during special periods that include World Wars I and II. Members of these groups <u>may</u> be eligible for VA benefits to include medical and pension benefits if the Defense Secretary certifies their service and issues a discharge under other than dishonorable conditions.

Application for a discharge certificate must be made on DD Form 2168 to the applicable service department. A form and instructions can be obtained by calling the VA at 1-800-827-1000. At the same time ask the VA for application forms for specific benefits (pension, home loan, etc.).

Service in the following groups has been certified as active military service for benefit purposes:

- Women Air Force Service Pilots (WASPs).

- Signal Corps Female Telephone Operators Unit of World War I.

- Engineer Field Clerks

- Women's Army Auxiliary Corps (WAAC).

- Quartermaster Corps female clerical employees serving with the American Expeditionary Forces in World War I

- Civilian employees of Pacific naval air bases who actively participated in defense of Wake Island during World War II.

- Reconstruction aids and dietitians in World War I.

- Male civilian ferry pilots.

- Wake Island defenders from Guam.

- Civilian personnel assigned to OSS secret intelligence.

- Guam Combat Patrol.

- Quartermaster Corps members of the Keswick crew on Corregidor during World War II.

- U.S. civilians who participated in the defense of Bataan.

- U.S. merchant seamen who served on block ships in support of Operation Mulberry in the World War II invasion of Normandy.

- American Merchant Marines in oceangoing service during World War II.

- Civilian Navy IFF radar technicians who served in combat areas of the Pacific during World War II.

- U.S. civilians of the American Field Service who served overseas in World War I.

- U.S. civilian employees of American Airlines who served overseas in a contract with the Air Transport Command between December 14, 1941, and August 15, 1945.

- U.S. civilians of the American Field Service who served overseas under U.S. armies and U.S. army groups in World War II.

- Civilian crewmen of U.S. Coast and Geodetic Survey vessels who served in areas of immediate military hazard while conducting cooperative operations with and for the U.S. Armed Forces between December 7, 1941, and August 15, 1945.

- Members of the American Volunteer Group (Flying tigers) who served between Dec. 7, 1941, and July 18, 1942.

- U.S. civilian flight crew and aviation ground support employees of United Air Lines who served overseas in a contract with Air Transport Command between Dec. 14, 1941, and Aug. 14, 1945.

- U.S. civilian flight crew and aviation ground support employees of Transcontinental and Western Air, Inc. (TWA), who served overseas in a contract with the Air Transport Command between Dec. 14, 1941, and Aug. 14, 1945.

- U.S. civilian flight crew and aviation ground support employees of Consolidated Vultee Aircraft Corp. (Consairway Division) who served overseas in a contract with Air Transport Command between Dec. 14, 1941, and Aug. 14, 1945.

- U.S. civilian flight crew and aviation ground support employees' of Pan American World Airways and its subsidiaries and affiliates, who served overseas in a contract with the Air Transport Command and Naval Air Transport Service between Dec. 14, 1941, and Aug. 14, 1945.

- Honorably discharged members of the American Volunteer Guard, Eritrea Service Command, between June 21, 1942, and March 31, 1943.

- U.S. civilian flight crew and aviation ground support employees of Northwest Airlines who served overseas under the airline's contract with Air Transport command from Dec. 14, 1941, through

  Aug. 14, 1945.

- U.S. civilian female employees of the U.S. Army Nurse Corps who served in the defense of Bataan and Corregidor in 1942.

Peacetime Service

Any veteran who served in the active military service who did not serve during a period of war as noted in this section, and who was discharged or released from that service under conditions other than dishonorable.

CHAPTER 3

▼

VA RECORDS

VA Claim Number

When you contact the U.S. Department of Veterans Affairs (VA) for benefits of any kind, you will be assigned a *VA file number* by which you are identified. This number is also called a *claim number* or "C" number. You will need to use this number anytime you contact the VA. Whether by phone, letter, or fax, you must reference this number in order to be properly identified. Once you're given a *file* or *claim number* that is how the VA will always recognize you. For some veterans, the VA uses their Social Security number as the claim number. Older veterans who filed claims with the VA decades ago were issued VA claim numbers that are separate from their social security number or military service number.

BENEFIT TIME TABLE

Benefit	Time Limit To File	Where To File
Service-Connected Disability Claim	No time limit	Any VA office
VA Medical Care Combat Illnesses	No time limit 2 Years	Any VA Medical Facility Any VA Medical Facility
One-time Dental Care	Within 90 days of separation	Any VA Medical Facility
Education, Vocational, or Readjustment Counseling	No time limit	Any VA office/Vet Ctr
Vocational Rehabilitation	12 years from first rating And subsequent ratings	Any VA office
Burial	Service-Connected burial has no time limit. Non-Service connected death 2 yrs. Headstone no time limit.	Any VA office
Montgomery GI Bill Education	10 years from discharge	Any VA office
GI Home Loan	No time limit	Any VA office
Service member's Group Life Insurance	Coverage terminates 120 Days after discharge	Any VA office
Veterans Group Life Insurance	Within 120 days of discharge	Any VA office

CHAPTER 4

▼

DISCHARGE PAPERS

Keeping • Replacing • Requesting • Correcting

Whether you were discharged yesterday or 40 years ago, you *must* have your discharge paper in order to receive VA benefits. This section is devoted to information about your discharge because it is so vitally important to your life as a veteran.

DD214 • Discharge Paper • Separation Paper

These terms all mean the same thing; verification of your military service. You received your discharge paper on your last day of active duty. This is your only proof that you served in the military, the VA will not accept anything else, safeguard this document. Veterans of the last 20 years or so have been given a Department of Defense Form 214 (DD214) as a separation paper. Prior to that, WDAGO Form 53-55 was used or separation papers were provided on other forms depending on your military branch and the time period you served. Your separation papers, WDAGO Form 53-55, or your DD214 is most commonly referred to as your *discharge paper*.

Do not confuse your discharge paper with the fancy colorful *certificate* you received from the military that says "honorable discharge" in big letters across the top. The "honorable discharge" *certificate* is for viewing purposes only; it has <u>no value</u> when it comes to verification of your military service.

Don't Make Assumptions

Your discharge is the key to obtaining all your veterans benefits. Don't assume that the government or the VA has easy access to your separation paper or DD214. Often veterans prolong contacting VA until they really need help. When the VA has to request a discharge from the National Personnel Record Center it could take 6-12 months. Sometimes it's found that records have been destroyed or there is no record at all of some veterans. This is why all veterans need to safeguard their discharge and all military records; it could be the only proof that you're a veteran.

Safe Storage of Your Discharge

It's up to you to take care of your discharge. The first thing the VA will ask for when you apply for benefits is your separation paper or DD214. Many times you may have to provide your discharge when applying for jobs, also. You never know when you might need to prove you've had weapons training or some other specialized area of training. Widows and dependents will also need to provide the discharge of a deceased or disabled veteran. Store your discharge in a safe place like a safe deposit box at your local bank where you can quickly and easily locate it.

Registering Your Discharge

You should also register your DD214 with your county recorder's office. Generally, there is no charge. The recorder's office will "*certify*" that the original discharge or DD214 was examined. By doing this you can obtain an official *certified* copy of your discharge whenever you need it. If you lose the original or if it's ever stolen or destroyed you can always get an official copy without having to contact the military. The VA will accept an official *certified* copy in place of the original discharge if it is certified from a government recorder's office.

NOTE: The VA cannot certify separation documents and DD214s. The VA also will not accept a *notarized* copy of a separation paper or DD214; it must be a *certified* copy.

Photo Copies

Generally, photocopies of official documents are not accepted for benefit purposes. On very rare occasions, the VA will honor a *photocopy* of a DD214 or separation document as proof of service where there are mitigating circumstances. Terminally ill veterans needing medical or nursing home care or a veteran needing burial benefits might be accepted. Ask for a VA supervisor to authorize your photocopy. But keep in mind this decision is totally subjective and what one supervisor might do another may not.

Replacement Copy

If you've never registered your separation paper or DD214 with a recorder's office or it's been lost, stolen, or destroyed, don't hesitate to apply for a replacement copy right now. Refer to chapter five of this book (Veteran's Records & Medals) for complete information on how to request and obtain your separation paper, DD214 or any other military records.

Important Note To All Veterans

Let your family members know where your discharge is. There may come a time when your health or your death will prevent you from telling your family where your discharge is. This could severely impair and slow down processing of medical, burial, or pension benefits and payments.

Discharge Review and Upgrade

Each of the military services maintains discharge review boards with authority to change, correct, or modify discharges or dismissals that are not issued by a sentence of a court martial. The board has no authority to address medical discharges. The veteran or, if the veteran is deceased or incompetent, the surviving spouse, next-of-kin or legal representative may apply for a review of discharge by writing to the military department concerned, using DD Form 293. This form can be obtained at any VA regional office.

If more than 15 years have passed since discharge, DD Form 149 should be used. Service discharge review boards conduct hearings in Washington, D.C. Traveling review boards also visit selected cities to hear cases. In addition, the Army sends teams to locations to videotape the testimony of applicants for later review by a board in Washington, D.C. Discharges awarded as a result of unauthorized absence in excess of 180 days make persons ineligible for VA benefits regardless of action taken by discharge review boards, unless the VA determines there were compelling circumstances for the absences. Boards for the correction of military records also may consider such cases.

Veterans with disabilities incurred in or aggravated during active military service may qualify for medical or related benefits regardless of separation and characterization of service. Veterans separated administratively under other than honorable conditions may request that their discharge be reviewed for possible recharacterization, provided they file their appeal within 15 years of the date of separation. Questions regarding the review of a discharge may be addressed to the appropriate discharge review board at the following addresses:

- **ARMY**—Army Discharge Review Board, Attention: SFMR-RBB, Room 200A, 1941 Jefferson Davis Hwy, Arlington, VA 22202-4504.

- **NAVY & MARINE CORPS**—Navy Discharge Review Board, 801 N. Randolph St., Suite 905, Arlington, VA 22203.

- **AIR FORCE**—Air Force Military Personnel Center, Attention: DP-MDOA1, Randolph AFB, TX 78150-6001.

- **COAST GUARD**—Coast Guard, Attention: GPE1, Washington, D.C. 20593.

CHAPTER 5

▼

VETERAN'S RECORDS & MEDALS

At some point in your life, you'll find that you need or want copies of your VA or military records. Under the Freedom of Information Act (FOIA) you can request and receive copies of your military and VA records. You should always keep a personal record of dealings with the government. Don't confuse paranoia with common sense. You know what I mean if you've ever had a disagreement with the government, the military, or the VA. This section will help you understand the value of your records, how to obtain them, and how to safeguard them.

Keeping Good Records

Keeping good records is a must for all veterans. You never know when you'll have to provide documentation or proof of something. At any time the VA, Social Security, the IRS, or some other agency of Uncle Sam could contact you with a question. The burden of proof will always lie with you. At the very least, keep a file at home of all your military and VA records. This includes all letters from VA, your enlistment documents, discharge paper, orders, citations, service medical records, military pay records to include all your leave and earnings statements, legal documents to include your will, marriage certificates, divorce decrees, etc. Keep everything of value; this goes for all your civilian records also. If you're not sure whether or not to keep something, than keep it.

DD214 • Discharge

This is the single most important document regarding your military service and your eligibility for VA benefits. You must safeguard your discharge paper in case you ever need it for something important. There are many reasons you might need your discharge paper in addition to using it for your VA benefits.

If you do not have your discharge paper and you need a copy, before you contact the military for a copy, call the VA and ask if they have a file on you. If they do have a file on you, chances are your DD214/discharge paper will be in it and you can receive a copy of it in 10 to 20 days.

This Is Important

When you call the VA at 1-800-827-1000 and ask for a copy of your discharge paper, you might be told you have to fill out Standard Form 180 (SF180) and mail it to the National Personnel Records Center (NPRC) in St. Louis, MO. This is standard practice for VA telephone representatives. If this happens to you—here's what you do: Ask the representative on the phone if you have a VA file located at RPC 376. This is the main VA records center where they hold inactive records. A telephone representative can make a computer request to RPC 376 and have a copy of your discharge mailed to you (if available from your record) in about 2 weeks. If you mail SF180 to the NPRC in St. Louis it takes about 6 months, sometimes longer. VA representatives routinely do not offer to do this because they don't want to take the time to do it.

Requesting Records From The Military and The National Personnel Records Center (NPRC)

If you've checked with the VA and they don't have your records, or the records you need, then your next step is to contact the military directly or the National Personnel Records Center. Standard Form (SF) 180 is the form you use. You can obtain this form by calling the VA office closest you at 1-800-827-1000. You might even be able to pick it up at a local or state VA office, or even better, get it off the Internet at www.va.gov/forms.

Charges for Copies

The military and the NPRC don't usually charge for copies of records, but they do reserve the right to. Depending on your request, you could be charged for the copying.

How Long Will It Take?

Requests to the military and the National Personal Records Center can take 60 days to 1 year. You can call (314) 538-4201 for a possible status request. Basically, you're at the mercy of the NPRC. If you haven't received your request in 3 months or so, and you're really desperate to get your records, you might try contacting a Senator or Congressional representative. Contact a VA regional office at 1-800-827-1000 for the phone numbers and addresses of Senators and Congressional Representatives.

Enlistment Documents

Retain your enlistment documents that prove you signed up for the GI Bill, college fund, incentives, bonuses, or a special occupation. You never know when the military, the Internal Revenue Service (IRS), or some other government agency may penalize you because of a computer error.

Leave and Earnings Statement (LES)

Your leave and earnings statement(s) can be incredibly crucial in proving you paid a debt you owed the military or proving you made contributions into the Montgomery GI Bill—Active Duty Chapter 30, or the Veterans' Educational Assistance Program (VEAP) Chapter 32. Some veterans have had to re-prove they already paid a debt or have lost thousands of dollars in educational benefits because the Department of Defense computers didn't update the VA computers with the correct information and there's no proof except your LESs. NOTE: Trying to obtain LESs from the military after your discharge can be very difficult and time consuming. Disposition and destruction of military pay records is probably one of the more efficient things the military does.

Requesting Records From VA Regional Offices

The record or file that the VA regional office has on you is dependent on whether or not you've ever contacted the VA before and filed any sort of claims for benefits.

For veterans who've filed for service connected or pension disability benefits before, VA records usually include some, most, or maybe even all of your military records, you never really know where your whole file is until you do some snooping around. The military and the federal archives don't automatically send your records to VA once you're out of the military.

VA Medical Centers

VA medical centers keep records on veterans for medical care received in that particular medical center. Veterans who've been treated at different VA medical centers around the United States should keep personal copies of their medical records.

Requesting Your Records

When requesting your own records from the VA, you have to first decide if you need to contact the VA medical center or the VA regional office. All requests for records must be in writing. Addresses for all medical centers and regional offices are located in chapter 25. Here are some examples of how to address a record request:

FOIA RECORDS REQEUST	FOIA RECORDS REQUEST
Los Angeles VA Medical Center	Houston VA Regional Office
1234 Main Street	1234 Main Street
Los Angeles CA 90210	Houston TX 78654

Here's a sample request letter:

Date: Jan 1, 2003

Dear VA,

I request a copy of my complete file to include all my military documents, medical records, and VA records.

Sincerely,
GI Joe

Print Name
Address
Any Town USA 90210
VA File Number: 123456789
Social Security Number: 123456789
Phone Number: (503) 555-5555

Only request the information you need, you don't have to ask for the whole record unless you need it. Most veterans' records will be in more than one place. You may have to send out more than one request depending on what information you want and your individual circumstances. Call the VA regional office nearest you at 1-800-827-1000 and ask someone to look up your records while they're on the phone with you. They can at least tell you where your VA file is so you know where to address your request. If you happen to address your request to the wrong VA office, it could take months of waiting before you receive any records.

How Long Will It Take

Requests to VA regional offices can take anywhere from 30 days to 6 months depending on the workload of the clerks handling the requests. VA regulations state information requests must be sent out within 10 days of receipt. If your request is taking longer than 10 days than call the VA every week and ask for an update. No matter what they told you the week before, call back every week and keep on them until they send it to you. The squeaky wheel gets the records, keep calling back.

Charges for Copies

The VA doesn't usually charge for copies of records, but they do reserve the right to. Depending on your request, you could be charged for the copies but generally, this is not done.

What If Someone Else Requests Your Records or Information?

Your records are protected under the Privacy Act of 1974. By law, the VA cannot release any information about you to anyone except the monthly amount the VA pays you (if any).

Requesting Records on a Deceased Veteran

Anyone can request a record(s) on a deceased veteran. Deceased records are no longer protected under the Privacy Act. If you call to request a record, make sure you have as much information on the veteran as possible (i.e. full name, VA claim number, SSN, service number, date of birth, date of death, service dates, etc.).

Correction of Military Records

The request for a correction of a military record is submitted on DD Form 149. You would not request a discharge upgrade using this form unless more than 15 years have passed since your discharge. For information on discharge upgrades, refer to chapter four of this book. Any VA regional office will have the form. The secretary of a military department, acting through a board for correction of military records, has authority to correct any military record, when necessary, to correct an error or remove an injustice. DD Form 149 is most commonly used to correct misspelled names or incorrect social security numbers.

A correction board may consider applications for correction of a military record, including review of discharges issued by a court-martial. The veteran, survivor or legal representative generally must file a request for correction within three years after discovery of the alleged error or injustice. The board may excuse failure to file within the prescribed time if it finds it would be in the interest of the justice to do so. It is the responsibility of the applicant to show why the filing of the application was delayed and why it would be in the interest of the board to consider the application despite the delay. To justify any correction, it is necessary to show to the satisfaction of the board that the alleged entry or omission in the records was in error or unjust. Applications should include all available evidence, such as signed statements of witnesses or a brief of arguments supporting the requested correction. Contact the VA regional office at 1-800-827-1000 to have DD Form 149 sent. If it's within 15 years since your discharge and you're looking to apply for a discharge upgrade, ask for DD Form 293.

MEDALS AND DECORATIONS
Replacement Procedures

Medals and decorations awarded while in active military service will be issued upon request by the veteran or if deceased, by their next-of-kin. Send your requests to the appropriate service and addresses listed below.

Submit your request on Standard Form (SF) 180 if possible. Call the VA at 1-800-827-1000 and they'll send you the form. Attach a copy of your discharge paper (WDAGO Form 53-55 or DD Form 214) if you have it, or submit a very clear written request with the following information: Veterans full name, military service number, social security number, branch of service, dates of service (approximate if you have to), list of medals or decorations you want replaced. Make sure you sign your request.

ARMY

Active duty personnel—apply through their Commanding Officer.
Retired Personnel—apply through the CG, ARPERCEN, 9700 Page Blvd, St. Louis, MO 63132
All Others—apply through U.S. Army Reserve Personnel Center, ATTN: ARPC-VSE, 9700 Page Blvd, St. Louis, MO 63132-5100.

AIR FORCE

Active duty personnel—apply through the Major Air Commanders.
Not on active duty—apply to the National Personnel Records Center, Chief Air Force Branch, 9700 Page Blvd, St. Louis, MO 63132.

NAVY

Active duty personnel—apply through their Commanding Officer to the Chief of Naval personnel for issuance of medals.

- Inactive (enlisted) reservists—apply to Cognizant Commander of Naval Districts to the Chief of naval Personnel, (Attn: PERS-E24) Washington DC 20370

- Discharged personnel—apply to National Personnel Records Center, Chief Navy Branch, Rm 3475, 9700 Page Blvd, St. Louis, MO 63132-5100.

MARINE CORPS

All active duty personnel, discharged, retired or Fleet Marine Corps Reserves—apply to Marine Corps Liaison Officer, National Personnel Records Center, Chief Marine Branch, 9700 Page Blvd, St. Louis, MO 63132-5100.

COAST GUARD

All personnel—apply to National Personnel Records Center, Chief Coast Guard Branch, 9700 Page Blvd, St. Louis, MO 63132-5100.

MERCHANT MARINES

Awards given by the Secretary of Transportation—apply to Secretary of Transportation, 400 7th Street SW, Washington D.C. 20590.

CHAPTER 6

▼

ACTIVE DUTY

What you need to know before you discharge!

Leaving Active Duty

This is where it all starts. The key to understanding your veterans benefits and what they are begins by receiving accurate and useful information from the military.

When leaving active duty there are so many things to consider. This truly is a defining moment in a person's life. The decisions you make at this point in your life are incredibly crucial, whether you're retiring after 20 years or just finishing a four-year hitch. With or without the government and the VA you will be faced with some tough decisions.

Moving back home or to a new state, buying a house, looking for a job, or starting college are just a few things to consider. Receiving good and useful information from the military and the VA is a huge key in helping you to start out right.

Something that you've probably learned by now in dealing with the government and the military is that you never get the whole story, the complete picture, or all the facts. Don't get me wrong, I believe the military is a great place for many reasons, but like all other facets of the government, it's so huge, in-depth, and intertwined with red tape that you may get hurried when it comes to receiving the proper information when you out-process.

Before you leave the military you must have all your affairs in order if you truly want to take full advantage of all your veterans benefits and get the right start for you and your family.

Service Medical Records (SMRs)

Before you discharge make sure you've got a complete copy of your SMRs! Do not leave your final duty assignment without a copy. You will need them if you ever file a disability claim with the VA. Many times records are lost between the military and the VA and if you file a disability claim with the VA and they tell you the military lost your records you can't do anything about it. And, it could literally cost you hundreds of thousands of dollars in benefits and pay. Sometimes personnel officers will tell you that they'll mail you a copy. Do not agree to it unless you have no choice, get a copy *before* you out-process! Your SMRs will prove to be one of the most vital records you will ever need the rest of your life, make sure you obtain your SMRs before you discharge! I cannot emphasize this point enough!

Asking Good Questions & Getting Good Information

During out-processing, it helps to be proactive and somewhat aggressive when looking into your options and making decisions. Don't be afraid to ask questions of your base or post personnel office and all instructors at your final out-processing briefings. The information you receive can really make your life easier or make it more difficult depending on the information you receive.

Veterans Unclaimed Benefits is an excellent guide to help you learn about your benefits, make decisions, and ask good questions. I've found, from personal experience, that most out-processing briefings are much too brief and lack good information that can be used in taking your next step into civilian life. By getting into the habit of asking a lot of questions, you'll find that the information you receive is more detailed and accurate. Or, you'll be able to find out that you need to look somewhere else for accurate information. Ask good questions and pay attention.

Bad Information

What can you do when you're misinformed, given bad information, or not informed about a benefit you're entitled to? Not much, you could lose the benefit, money or both. There is no recourse you can take against the military or the VA. Military and VA representatives are not held legally accountable for their actions and guidance and you're left holding the bag.

The worse part is finding out now about benefits and programs that you could have been told about years earlier. Much of the time you have no recourse, the frustration can be overwhelming.

A common scenario that takes place after discharge is one where a veteran contacts the VA for information through phone calls or in person, experiences long waits and busy signals, receives different answers from VA representatives, is sent confusing letters, and consequently must endure unexplainable frustration.

I've counseled literally thousands and thousands of veterans, many of whom told me they received bad information from the military. Of course they didn't know it until I explained the benefits they were entitled to now and how everything really worked.

Foolish Assumptions

Do yourself a big, big favor and don't ever assume anything about your VA benefits. Read this book thoroughly, file for some benefits, and see what kind of answer you receive from the VA. Many people have found out, only when it's too late, that they made an assumption about their benefits and it cost them. Always be prepared.

Avoid Rushing to Out-process

Make sure you jump through all the hoops when out-processing and leaving active duty. Don't skip any briefings and make sure you pay attention and ask questions. It will pay off down the road.

When I left the Air Force my TAP briefing and out-processing was not handled properly. Of course I didn't know this at the time because I didn't know anything about VA benefits and I was in a hurry to get out. I believed the instructors giving the briefings knew what they were doing. I now know the information provided was poor but it was convincing enough at the time and I was in a hurry. I had other plans to get home fast, kiss the ground, enjoy my freedom and find an employer that wanted to pay me lots of money.

Transition Assistance Program & VA Benefits

The Transition Assistance Program (TAP) and Disability TAP (DTAP) briefings are supposed to be mandatory for all out-processing personnel. Most personnel do receive the briefings but unfortunately much of the time they lack good information. Often, military instructors aren't trained properly on VA benefits.

Instructors providing TAP and DTAP briefings don't work for the VA and the VA does not train them. They usually were given a crash course on VA benefits. Uncaring actions of government and military offices are detrimental to all veterans. Information tends to be passed on from vet to vet as you've probably found out.

Sometimes you'll find that an actual VA employee will be briefing you on your benefits when you out-process. But this doesn't mean there's any assurance that your briefing will be fully intact of all that you need to know. In order for a person to be counseled properly on their VA benefits, a one on one needs to take place and a lot of questions need to be asked of you. That's probably the biggest problem with the VA and the military, there is not enough personal interest shown to each individual to accurately help them.

I've had interviews with veterans that told me they never applied for benefits before because they were told that they weren't eligible at the TAP or final discharge briefing. This kind of situation can end up costing a veteran thousands of dollars in benefits because he/she didn't file a claim earlier or never files at all. It could end up costing other possible State and local benefits, also. If it sounds like I'm going on-and-on, I am. It needs to be made clear, don't believe anything until you see it in writing with your name on it. At the very least, a veteran should contact the closest VA Regional Office *immediately* after discharge at 1-800-827-1000. Read this book and ask a lot of questions.

Exit Bonuses

Discharge incentives, special benefit pay and separation payments have been a big part of the military over the past ten years, or so, beginning with the reductions in force in the early 1990's. It doesn't mean that every GI being released receives money, only certain ones. Like everything else it depends on a service member's personal situation.

To facilitate the downsizing of the armed forces, two new sections were added to Title 10 of the United States Code. The purpose of these sections is to encourage service members who would otherwise face possible involuntary separation or denial of reenlistment to separate voluntarily. Service members have the option to receive payment under one of two incentive programs: Special Separation Benefit (SSB) or Voluntary Separation Incentive (VSI).

To qualify for either of these exit bonuses, the service person must have served on active duty for more than six (6) years but fewer than twenty (20) years as of December 5, 1991; served at least five (5) years of continuous active duty immediately before separation; and agree to serve in the Ready Reserve. If exit bonuses are discontinued, any VSI recipients and early retirees with monthly or annual payments will continue to get their money on schedule.

If you're eligible for an exit bonus, the military branch will officially notify you in writing.

Special Separation Benefit (SSB)

SSB is a onetime, lump sum payment made on a service member's last day of military service. The amount received is determined by taking the amount of basic pay that was paid for a service member's last year on active duty multiplied by 15 percent. That figure is then multiplied by the number of years on active duty. SSB recipients must enlist for at least three years in the Ready Reserve.

IMPORTANT: If a SSB recipient is eligible to receive VA disability compensation, than all VA compensation is withheld until the total amount of the SSB payment is recouped.

If SSB recipient qualifies for military retirement as a reservist the SSB amount must be repaid to the government before retirement benefits will be paid.

If they later qualify for a retirement as a federal civilian and use their military time to compute the amount of their civil service retirement, then they must pay a portion of their SSB into the civil service retirement fund.

All are considered concurrent benefits and cannot be paid simultaneously.

Voluntary Separation Incentive (VSI)

VSI is an annual payment made on the anniversary of the service member's last day of active duty. The very first payment is made on the service members last day of active duty. Veterans receive VSI payments each year for twice the number of years that they spent on active duty.

Like other exit bonuses, the VSI formula begins with the amount of basic pay that the veteran earned during his or her last year on active duty. That figure is multiplied by 2.5 percent. The figure derived from that calculation is then multiplied by the number of years the person spent on active duty.

VSI recipients must agree to serve in the Ready Reserve for as long as they receive the exit bonus. The pay they receive from the military for drill periods and two-week annual trainings on active duty is unaffected by their VSI.

If these former service members qualify for military retirement as reservists, their obligation to serve in the reserves ends without affecting their annual VSI payments. Some money will be withheld every month from their reserve-retired pay, until they've paid back the entire VSI amount.

VSI recipients who qualify for retirement as federal civilians don't have to pay a portion of the VSI they have received into the civil service retirement fund, as happens with SSB recipients. If a VSI recipient dies before receiving the full amount of the exit bonus, annual payments will continue to his or her survivors.

Separation Pay

Separation pay is a one-time, lump-sum bonus paid to some people who are forced out of the military involuntarily. To calculate the payment, the amount of basic pay earned by the veteran during the last year on active duty is multiplied by 10 percent. The product of that calculation is then multiplied by the number of years the person spent on active duty. Separation pay members must spend at least three years in the Ready Reserve

Separation pay is broken down two ways—full separation pay and half separation pay. Those with half separation pay, as the name implies, receive half the bonus determined by the usual formula for separation pay. It applies to specific veterans who have "black marks" on their military records but who still receive discharges that are honorable or general.

Full separation pay goes to service members with good military records who are prevented from continuing in uniform due to (usually) an overabundance of people with the same military skills. There are no limits on maximum payments.

Eligibility

To be eligible for separation pay, service members must have at least 6 years of total active duty time, with at least 5 years of continuous active duty, and less than 20 years total time.

Ineligible

Ineligible for half or full separation pay are veterans who can receive military retirement pay, service members who have spent only their initial obligated period or initial enlistments on active duty, and people receiving dishonorable discharges, bad conduct discharges, or discharges rated as "other than honorable."

Early Retirement

Since the early 90's, active duty members have been able to retire after serving more than 15 years but less than 20 years. Individuals are selected for early retirement; there are no applications or volunteer program.

Figuring Payment

The computation of the monthly payment of early retirees begins with the person's basic pay and does not consider housing allowances, bonuses, or special pay. The beginning figure used is the average of the service member's last three earning years on active duty. That average figure is multiplied by 2.5 percent of each year the person spent on active duty. Then, that figure is reduced by one-twelfth of a percentage point for each month that a person's active duty service falls short of twenty years.

Early retirees are provided the same retirement benefits as are 20-year retirees. They have lifetime access to commissaries and base exchanges. They have space-available access to on-base clinics and hospitals, and are eligible for CHAMPUS or Tricare, the military's health insurance programs until they're eligible for Medicare.

Spouses, dependent children, and some other dependents qualify for many of the same benefits. Early retirees can also sign up for the Survivor's Benefit Plan (SBP), which pays a surviving spouse and/or family members when a retiree dies. Regarding a service-connected death, SBP is offset by VA Dependency and Indemnity Compensation (DIC) dollar for dollar. If the veteran's death is service-connected, survivor's can choose which benefit is best for them. SBP is taxed while DIC is not.

Final Physical

Insist on a final physical! Medical issues documented from the physical exam could prove to be very important in the future. Decades from now, your family's financial future may depend on VA benefits based on that physical. MAKE SURE YOU GET ONE!

If your military service created or aggravated medical problems, you could be entitled to compensation from the VA. VA compensation can begin years after discharge, there is no time limit to file, but there does need to be evidence of a disability. A minor problem to a young veteran at discharge could grow over the years into a disability that prevents you from earning an income when you're 50.

Very Important!

If you do have any physical or mental issues upon discharge, contact the VA and submit a service-connected disability compensation claim using VA Form 21-526. By applying for compensation early, your military medical records are transferred to VA for good. This can prove to be invaluable if later in life (even decades) you find you have dealings with the VA for disability reasons. This is where it is very dangerous to assume you WON'T have any problems later in life.

Severance Pay

If you receive severance pay for a disability or injury caused in service, you MUST file a service-connected disability claim with VA. Severance pay is taxed, VA compensation IS NOT TAXED! Also, if you have taxes withheld from severance pay before you leave service, and later the VA grants service-connection, you can have all the taxes refunded back to you. Disabilities recognized by the VA as service-connected cannot be taxed. Contact the IRS if you deserve to have taxes refunded.

Bottom Line: Do not hesitate in contacting the VA once you've separated from military service. Read this book, educate yourself, ask questions, and take advantage of what you're entitled to.

Honorable Discharge

An honorable discharge is very important in regards to your VA benefits. If you receive less than an honorable discharge you will lose entitlement to your Chapter 30, Montgomery GI Bill Active Duty education benefits, and possibly your VA Home Loan benefits.

The Next Step

There are so many benefits awaiting you once you leave military service, but do you really know what they are and how to claim them? How do you know if your situation will be handled properly? As we've already covered, just one piece of bad information can literally cost you thousands of dollars in benefits not to mention valuable time, effort and frustration.

The information ahead will help you leave the military under control of your situation and arm you with information to help you take advantage of your veteran's benefits.

Before You Leave—Check List

Obtain a complete copy of your Service Medical Records (SMR)
Obtain a copy of your dental records
Obtain copies of your base personnel file and your unit personnel file
Keep all your military school certificates and diplomas

Your Federal, State, and Local Veterans Benefits

The following is a basic checklist for service members leaving the military.

Reemployment Rights
Job Finding Assistance
Federal Job Assistance through the Veterans Readjustment Appointment
Transition Assistance Program
Operation Transition
Small Business Loans
Farm Loans
Social Security Benefits
No Fee Passports
Disabled Veterans Outreach Job Program
Unemployment Compensation and Benefits
Service Connected Disability Compensation
Nonservice Connected Disability Pension
Home Loan
Health Care and Medical
Education
Life Insurance
Commissary and Exchange Privileges
Death Gratuity Payment
Burial
State Benefit Programs

CHAPTER 7

▼

DEALING WITH THE VA

Chances are, your first contact with the VA will be over the telephone. How you're treated and the information you're provided over the phone is paramount in regards to how you will perceive what is being done to help you.

Calling the VA for help and answers to questions can quite literally become an exercise in futility. Much of the time you may endure a busy signal. When you actually do get through, the VA employee may not be trained very well. This is a very common problem throughout the whole VA system.

> Recent information has shown that as much as 30% or more of the calls to VA regional offices have been blocked. This means the lines are so busy that no one can get through! This has been an ongoing problem over the years. Financial resources are not being allocated to add phone lines; and new employees are not being hired and trained to manage existing lines properly.

If you find a competent VA rep, ask him or her if it's okay if you ask for them every time you call. Tell them you're willing to wait for a call back even if it takes a day or two. It's worth it to get accurate help and information

3 Minutes!

Many questions need to be asked of each person that calls to accurately assess their situation. Most VA counselors don't take the time to ask all the necessary questions because of pressure to handle each call in an average of 3 minutes. That's the VA standard; each call should average 3 minutes. What kinds of things do you think you can get accomplished in 3 minutes? How about the most asked question of all, "What benefits am I eligible for?" To properly handle this question it's going to take some time. Each person's situation is different and each needs to be handled individually. By forcing employees to limit their calls to three minutes, the VA has literally decided that it's not important for VA counselors to take the time to inform America's veterans accurately, with the respect they've so greatly earned.

Employee Promotions Are Largely Based on Number of Phone Calls Taken and Claims Processed!
VA Oversees Their Own Quality Assurance, They Answer to No One and Police Themselves!
Customer Service is RARELY Monitored for Quality, Accuracy or Satisfaction!

A large number of phone calls and claims are routinely mishandled or denied simply because VA employees want to accumulate work credits and qualify for bonuses and promotions. This is a serious problem that exists on a daily basis! There is constant pressure on VA employees to produce statistics even if it's at the expense of the veteran. It's tragically ironic. Veterans are given bad information or turned away with a denial of their claim so an employee can count another statistic to show they've "helped" or processed another veteran's issue. With "good numbers or statistics", VA employees are promoted and paid more. This is all at the expense of America's veterans and their livelihood. This has gone on far to long and the VA knows it. This lack of attention and action on the part of the Secretary of Veterans Affairs and VA Central Office upper management to address this serious problem shows they're not genuinely interested in helping each and every veteran, dependent or survivor with the respect they deserve.

Working to deny claims seems to be easier for some VA claim representatives and rating board members than working to grant a claim. Based on the pressure to produce and meet case count each day, many VA employees lose sight of why they really have a job at the VA. The result: Employees routinely deny issues or make it so difficult for the veteran that they just give up pursuing their claim or calling back.

What You Can Do

Be courteous and nice to VA employees; even if you've had bad experiences in the past. It will not help by being difficult or rude. Get the employee's name and team number before you do anything else. More often than not, when you have a person's name and you're nice to them, they'll provide you with the proper attention you deserve. If you question the information given to you by the VA representative, you may want to acquire the services of a Veterans Service Officer from an established Service Organization (see chapter 23) to review the VA's instructions.

Letters of Complaint and Thank You

If you run into problems with VA employees, don't be afraid to write a letter of complaint. This works much better than the other popular method of "let me speak to your supervisor." Letters to VA regional offices that are addressed to the DIRECTOR will trickle down through management channels. It may only take one well-written letter to get the attention of the right person who will look into your situation. Employees don't like having negative attention drawn to them. Write "thank you" letters as well when someone goes out of their way to help you. It's very important to acknowledge service that goes above and beyond.

Fastest Action to Your Complaint

If you want the fastest action on your complaint write your Senator. Make sure your issue warrants intervention by a Senator's office. Use your best judgment, if you're not sure, go ahead and call your Senator, that's what they are there for. All Senate offices have veterans representatives that will help with your problem. Advise the representative of all the information on your situation; be very specific. If you don't have the phone number or address of your Senator, look in the phone book or call your state veterans office for the number (see chapter 25).

Why You Should Complain

If veterans don't complain about poor treatment and service, then nobody will know there's a problem. It's that simple.

There are many benefits and programs to take advantage of, and your patience in corresponding and interacting with VA employees will be beneficial. Be persistent, ask a lot of questions and don't give up.

Other Options
Secretary of Veterans Affairs

You can also write to the Secretary of Veterans Affairs at the following address:
Secretary of Veterans Affairs

810 Vermont Avenue NW
Washington, D.C. 20420

President of the United States

Lastly, complaints to the President of the United States ARE heard and answered. But, it takes 4-6 months for these letters to trickle down through the channels to be addressed. It's recommended to write and not call the White House.
President of the United States
The White House
1600 Pennsylvania Avenue NW
Washington, DC 20500

White House Electronic Communications:

President George W. Bush: president@whitehouse.gov
Vice President Richard Cheney's E-Mail:
vice.president@whitehouse.gov

CHAPTER 8

▼

MEDICAL BENEFITS

Hospital • Out Patient • Pharmacy • Nursing
Home • Domiciliary

The VA healthcare system has undergone a reformation in the last couple years. The goal is to provide a more balanced approach to medical care for veterans. The reform changes the old VA system to resemble that of the private medical industry. The biggest factor affecting the level of care for veterans and eligibility determinations continues to be appropriations and funding from Congress. Each VA medical center and associated outpatient clinics and vet centers are funded differently. The care you receive at one VA medical center or clinic may not be the same at the next. The VA is trying to organize a uniform level of care.

This new VA health care plan may be for you if:

- You're not covered by medical insurance;

- You're having trouble getting health coverage;

- You would like to supplement your present health care coverage.

Medical services provided by the VA include: Adult day health care, diagnostic services, domiciliary care, homeless program, mental health care, nursing home care, nutritional services, rehabilitation, patient education, pharmacy services, primary care, smoking cessation, specialty clinics, substance abuse programs, surgical services and women's health needs.

In this section, we will focus on the basics of the VA health care system, what you can expect, and ways to use existing VA programs to help with your health care needs. We admittedly don't have all the answers as each veteran's health issues will vary along with their given priority level of care, what VA facility they're being treated at, as well as other determining factors.

A big part in VA healthcare reform is the new emphasis on preventive medicine and primary care. The VA used to only focus on healing a veteran's current medical condition(s), now the VA is helping to promote, preserve and restore health. Also new is the fact that a primary care facility and physician is assigned to the veteran.

Military Service Requirement

For veterans who entered active duty before September 7, 1980, there is no minimum length of service requirement. However, veterans who entered active duty on or after that date must complete 24 months of continuous service except for service-connected disabled veterans. Reservists and members of the National Guard called to active duty must complete the full period for which they were called to active duty. Members of the National Guard and Reservists whose only service was active duty for training purposes are not routinely eligible for VA medical care.

Enrollment

It may come as a surprise to some veterans that care in a VA medical center is not free to all veterans. To receive health care, veterans generally must be enrolled with the VA medical system. A veteran may apply for enrollment at any time. You can begin by calling the toll free enrollment line at 1-877-222-8387, or the VA medical center nearest you, not the VA regional office. Some veterans are not required to enroll, but to permit better planning of health resources nationwide, all veterans are urged to enroll.

When You Enroll

You will be scheduled for a health appraisal appointment (can take up to 6-12 months), which consists of a physical exam, prevention screening, any needed laboratory work and initial medications. You will be assigned a primary care provider at that time. All future appointments will be made with your assigned primary care provider.

NOTE: Services that you may be paying for now under non-VA private care (high co-payments, prescriptions, etc.), may be provided by the VA at a lower cost or possibly free depending on your individual circumstances. Start the enrollment process immediately to speed the approval.

Application

All veterans can get an application, VA Form 10-10 EZ, by visiting, calling or writing any VA location of care or any veterans' benefits office. Or you can apply over the phone by calling the Application Toll-Free Hotline at 1-877-222-8387. Veterans can also submit the completed form in person or by mail to any VA healthcare facility. When you apply, it's best to have your separation paper (DD214) available. If you mail your application, only send a copy of your separation paper (DD214).

VA forms are also available at the VA forms website at http://www.va.gov/forms.

Medical Facilities

An important aspect of enrollment is for veterans to identify which VA location of care they choose as their preferred facility. This can be a community-based outpatient clinic or a VA medical center.

The preferred facility is where veterans receive their primary care. If, for any reason, a selected facility is unable to provide the health care needed by an enrolled veteran, then that facility will make arrangements for referral to another VA facility or to one of the VA's private sector affiliates to provide the required care. Veterans are eligible for a comprehensive health care package that is completely portable across the entire VA health care system.

Application information is stored in a central database at the Health Eligibility Center in Atlanta, Georgia. Individual veteran enrollment and eligibility data can be accessed by VA medical facilities nationwide. Because of central database capabilities:

- Veterans can receive care at any VA health care facility while traveling.

- The veteran does not need to reapply at a different VA location of care if they move.

- For minor changes, a veteran simply has to notify VA staff at their preferred healthcare facility that will in turn electronically update the database in Atlanta.

Uniform Benefits Package

Once a veteran is enrolled and has identified their preferred facility, they'll receive a VA patient data card (to be used at any VA medical facility) and a *Uniform Benefits Package*. This will be provided to all enrolled veterans regardless of the veteran's priority group (see below). Public Law 104-262 calls for the VA to furnish hospital care and medical services that are defined as "needed". The VA defines "needed" as care or service that will promote, preserve and restore health. This includes treatment, procedure, supply or service. The decision of need will be based on the judgment of the veteran's health care provider and in accordance with generally accepted standards of clinical practice. VA health care services include such things as:

- Preventive services including: immunizations, screening tests, health education and training classes

- Inpatient hospital, medical, surgical and mental healthcare, including care for substance abuse

- Primary care

- Outpatient medical, surgical and mental healthcare, including care for substance abuse

- Diagnosis and treatment

- Comprehensive rehabilitative care and service

- Durable medical equipment

- Respite and hospice care

- Urgent and limited emergency care in VA facilities

- Palliative care

- Drugs and pharmaceuticals including: medically necessary, over-the-counter drugs, that are approved by the VA

Some enrolled veterans may be eligible for some services that are not part of the *Uniform Benefits Package*. Veterans must still qualify for them on a case-by-case basis, and special restrictions apply to each. These services include:

- Reconstructive non-elective, non-cosmetic surgery

- Limited nursing home care

- Limited domiciliary care

- Limited non-VA hospitalization or health care services for veterans with special eligibility

- Limited dental care

- Readjustment counseling

- Adult day healthcare

- Home healthcare and services

- Homeless programs

- Sexual trauma counseling

Some health care services that will not normally be covered by the *Uniform Benefits Package* include abortion, membership in health clubs or spas for rehabilitation, special private duty nursing and gender alteration. Drugs and medical devices not approved by the Food and Drug Administration are not covered, except under special circumstances.

Eligibility

Eligibility for health care is based on many factors and could be limited based on what Congressional appropriations allow. Enrollment will occur based on priority groups.

Priority Groups

The priority groups are as follows, ranging from 1-8 with 1 being the highest priority for enrollment. Under the Medical Benefits Package, the same services are generally available to all enrolled veterans.

As of January 17, 2003, VA is not accepting new Priority Group 8 veterans for enrollment (veterans falling into Priority Groups 8e and 8g.)

Priority Group 1

Veterans with service-connected disabilities rated 50% or more disabling

Priority Group 2

Veterans with service-connected disabilities rated 30% or 40% disabling

Priority Group 3

Veterans who are former POWs
Veterans awarded the Purple Heart
Veterans whose discharge was for a disability that was incurred or aggravated in the line of duty
Veterans with service-connected disabilities rated 10% or 20% disabling
Veterans awarded special eligibility classification under Title 38, U.S.C., Section 1151, "benefits for individuals disabled by treatment or vocational rehabilitation"

Priority Group 4

Veterans who are receiving aid and attendance or housebound benefits
Veterans who have been determined by VA to be catastrophically disabled

Priority Group 5

Nonservice-connected veterans and noncompensable service-connected veterans rated 0% disabled whose annual income and net worth are below the established VA Means Test thresholds
Veterans receiving VA pension benefits

Veterans eligible for Medicaid benefits

Priority Group 6

Compensable 0% service-connected veterans
World War I veterans
Mexican Border War veterans
Veterans solely seeking care for disorders associated with:
Exposure to herbicides while serving in Vietnam; or
Exposure to ionizing radiation during atmospheric testing or during the occupation of Hiroshima and Nagasaki; or
For disorders associated with service in the Gulf War; or
For any illness associated with service in combat in a war after the Gulf War or during a period of hostility after November 11, 1998.

Priority Group 7

Veterans who agree to pay specified co-payments with income and/or net worth above the VA Means Test threshold and income below the HUD geographic index
Subpriority a: Noncompensable 0% service-connected veterans who were enrolled in the VA Health Care System on a specified date and who have remained enrolled since that date
Subpriority c: Nonservice-connected veterans who were enrolled in the VA Health Care System on a specified date and who have remained enrolled since that date
Subpriority e: Noncompensable 0% service-connected veterans not included in Subpriority a above
Subpriority g: Nonservice-connected veterans not included in Subpriority c above

Priority Group 8

Veterans who agree to pay specified co-payments with income and/or net worth above the VA Means Test threshold and the HUD geographic index

Subpriority a: Noncompensable 0% service-connected veterans enrolled as of January 16, 2003 and who have remained enrolled since that date

Subpriority c: Nonservice-connected veterans enrolled as of January 16, 2003 and who have remained enrolled since that date

Subpriority e: Noncompensable 0% service-connected veterans applying for enrollment after January 16, 2003

Subpriority g: Nonservice-connected veterans applying for enrollment after January 16, 2003

*Catastrophically Disabled: Individuals who have a severely disabling injury, disorder, or disease which permanently compromises their ability to carry out the activities of daily living to such a degree that they require personal or mechanical assistance to leave home or bed or require constant supervision to avoid physical harm to self or others.

Depending on Congressional appropriations and available resources, the VA will determine which priority groups will be enrolled each year. VA will not enroll more veterans than for whom benefits can be provided. This may mean that the VA enrolls fewer veterans and may be required to dis-enroll some veterans as well. Dis-enrolled veterans will be notified in writing of this decision and advised of their appeal rights.

Special Registry Exams
Gulf War—Agent Orange—Atomic Radiation—Sexual Trauma

Veterans who served in the Gulf War or who claim exposure to Agent Orange or atomic radiation or are receiving counseling for sexual trauma are provided with free, comprehensive medical examinations, including laboratory and other diagnostic tests deemed necessary by an examining physician to determine health status. Results of the examinations, which include review of the veteran's military service and exposure history, are entered into special, computerized databases, called registries. These databases assist VA in analyzing the types of health conditions being reported by veterans. Registry participants are advised of the results of their examinations in personal consultations. Veterans wishing to participate should contact the nearest VA health-care facility for an examination.

Financial Assessment

Veterans who are not service-connected disabled and are seeking enrollment based on their inability to pay for medical care must provide the VA with information on their family income and assets. This information will be used to determine if the veteran's income status falls below the VA threshold. This is called a "means test". The threshold is adjusted annually and announced in January. Income from a spouse and dependents are also considered.

VA has the authority to compare income information provided by the veteran with information obtained from the Social Security Administration and the Internal Revenue Service (IRS).

Private Health Insurance

If you have private health insurance <u>keep it</u>. DO NOT give up any existing health care coverage you have. VA health care is dependent on the level of Congressional appropriations, not on premiums paid by enrolled veterans. Veterans with private insurance or other public coverage such as Department of Defense, Medicare, or Medicaid may find VA enrollment to be a good complement to their other coverage.

By law, the VA is required to bill health insurance carriers for treatment provided to veterans for nonservice-connected conditions. This means the VA must bill any health insurance plan providing coverage for you, including policies held by you or your spouse. Some private insurance companies will apply any VA medical care charges toward satisfaction of your annual deductible.

Co-Payments

Depending on individual circumstances some veterans are required to make co-payments for their care and/or medications. Most veterans who have disabilities, injuries or conditions that *are not* related to military service and veterans who are rated 0% service-connected disabled (noncompensable), are required to complete an annual means test. This measures their family's income and assets.

A veteran is *exempt* from the medication co-payment requirement if:

- He or she is 50% service-connected disabled or greater

- The medication is for a service-connected disability only

- If their annual household income is at or below the VA threshold, or

- He or she is a former POW, WWI veteran, or a VA pensioner

Cost of Co-payments—Four Basic Types

The means test co-payment is for medication; outpatient, inpatient and long term care treatment. The amount of the co-payment can change annually.

- **Medication**—Congress established Prescription co-payment charges. The charge is $7 for each 30 day or less supply of medications provided on an outpatient basis for nonservice-connected conditions.

- **Outpatient**—The co-payments will be based on primary care visits ($15) and specialty care visits ($50).

- **Inpatient**—Congress determined the appropriate inpatient co-payment should be the current inpatient Medicare Deductible Rate ($840 in 2003) for the first 90 days that you remain in the hospital plus a $10 per diem charge.

- **Long Term Care**—VA charges for Long Term Care Services vary by type of service provided and the individual veterans ability to pay.

Emergency Care

Urgent and limited emergency care services are available to enrolled veterans at VA health care facilities or non-VA health care facilities at which the VA has a sharing agreement or contract. Only veterans with special eligibility may obtain emergency care, at VA expense, in a non-VA facility where VA does not have a sharing agreement or contract.

Call your primary VA medical facility and ask about your personal situation and emergency care. Make sure you understand what you would and wouldn't be responsible for in case of an emergency. Don't wait until an actual emergency to find out, chances are, you'll be pulling money out of your own pocket to pay a bill.

Private Care at VA Expense

Care in private facilities at VA expense is provided only under certain circumstances, namely, when VA has a contract agreement for certain services or when a veteran who is service-connected disabled and too far away *(usually 50 miles or more)* from a VA facility to receive "needed" care.

Fee Basis Medical Care

Certain veterans who meet specific eligibility criteria are entitled to receive routine, outpatient, medical care from non-VA physicians at the expense of the VA. Eligible veterans are required to apply in advance for this authorization. When a veteran has been authorized to see a private physician, a VA Outpatient Medical Care Authorization ID Card *(VA Fee Basis Card)* will be issued. This card is subject to a $125 per month limitation and does not cover dental treatment, emergency room treatment, or inpatient hospitalization in a private facility nor does it cover the costs of eye examination, psychiatric care, physical therapy, or chiropractic care without specific preauthorization.

Call your preferred VA medical facility for information on application for a Fee Basis Card.

Travel Pay for VA Medical Care

Veterans may be eligible for payment or reimbursement for travel costs to receive VA medical care. Travel payments are subject to a deductible of $3 for each one-way trip and an $18 per month maximum payment. Two exceptions to the deductible are travel for a compensation or pension examination and travel by special modes of transportation, such as an ambulance or a specially equipped van.

Beneficiary travel payments may be made to the following:

- Veterans whose service-connected disabilities are rated 30 percent or more.

- Veterans traveling for treatment of a service-connected condition.

- Veterans who receive a VA pension.

- Veterans traveling for scheduled compensation or pension examinations.

- Veterans whose income does not exceed the maximum VA pension rate.

- A veteran whose medical condition requires use of a special mode of transportation, if the veteran is unable to defray the costs and travel is pre-authorized. If the medical condition is a medical emergency, travel need not be pre-authorized when a delay would be hazardous.

Alcohol and Drug Dependence Treatment

Veterans eligible for VA medical care may apply for substance abuse treatment. Contact the nearest VA medical facility to enroll for care.

Readjustment Counseling • Vet Centers

Readjustment counseling is provided at vet centers to help veterans resolve war-related psychological difficulties like post traumatic stress disorder (PTSD) and to help them achieve a successful postwar readjustment back to civilian life. Assistance includes group, individual and family counseling. Some veterans may receive counseling from private-sector professionals who are on contract with the VA. A listing of vet centers can be found in the back of *Veterans Unclaimed Benefits* in the State Benefits Section.

Dental Care Benefits

VA dental care remains to be one of the more strictly regulated benefits the VA maintains. The Chief Dental Service may authorize outpatient dental treatment, or his professional designee for veterans classified in the following applicable conditions:

- Those whose dental conditions or disabilities are service-connected and compensable in degree may apply at any time and receive as many treatments for these conditions as are needed.

- Those whose dental conditions are service-connected, but not compensable in degree, and which are shown to have been in existence at time of discharge or release from active service must apply for outpatient dental care within 1 year after discharge or release. They may receive treatment only on a one-time completion basis, acceptable within the limitations of good professional standards.

- Those whose service-connected noncompensable dental conditions resulted from combat wounds or service injuries may apply at any time and receive as may treatments as are needed for these dental conditions.

- Former prisoners of war (POW) with service connected noncompensable dental conditions may apply at any time and receive as many treatments as are needed for these dental conditions.

- Those having non-service connected dental conditions or disabilities which are found by the VA to be directly related to and aggravating a service connected condition may apply at any time and receive as many treatments as necessary to alleviate the aggravation of the service connected condition.

- Disabled veterans who are receiving training under Vocational Rehabilitation and who need dental treatment in order to prevent interruption of their training may apply for the treatment as needed.

- Spanish-American War veterans and Indian War Veterans who need dental treatment may apply for and receive this type of treatment as needed.

- Dental services for persons hospitalized or domiciled pursuant to provisions of VA Regulations will be furnished such dental services as are professionally determined necessary to the patients' overall hospital or domiciliary care.

Eligibility Note:

Wartime veterans must have been separated or discharged under conditions other than dishonorable before they may be considered for outpatient dental treatment under applicable conditions above.

POW Dental Care

Those who were prisoners of war for 6 months or more, as determined by the concerned military service department may be authorized for any needed dental treatment.

Additional Groups Eligible for Dental Care

Veterans with compensable service connected dental conditions.

Veterans who apply within one year of discharge for treatment of service incurred dental conditions.

Veterans with non-compensable service connected dental conditions caused by trauma.

Those with service connected medical conditions that are professionally determined by the VA to be aggravated by a dental condition.

Certain veterans of conflicts prior to World War I whose dental conditions are presumed to have been service connected.

Outpatient Pharmacy Service

Outpatient pharmacy services are provided free to:

• Veterans receiving medication for treatment of service-connected conditions.

• Veterans whose income does not exceed the maximum VA pension.

Other veterans may only be charged $7 for each 30-day supply.

Home Town Pharmacy Program

This program provides eligible service connected veterans, who have been issued an outpatient medical and identification card, with Pharmacy service by community pharmacies. Drugs and medicines may be furnished on prescriptions of a licensed physician as specified therapy in treatment of a service-connected disability.

When the prescribing physician determines that it is necessary for the veteran to have his prescription filled promptly, he may take it to any pharmacy. Apply at your closest VA medical center.

Homeless Veterans

The VA provides health and rehabilitation programs for homeless veterans. Health Care for Homeless Veterans programs provides outreach and comprehensive medical, psychological and rehabilitation treatment programs. Domiciliary Care for Homeless Veterans programs provides residential rehabilitation services. The VA has a growing number of Compensated Work Therapy/Therapeutic Residence group homes, special daytime, drop-in centers, and Comprehensive Homeless Centers.

VA Medical Programs for Older Veterans

The veteran population is aging rapidly and the VA is trying to keep pace with expanded programs for older veterans. Medical centers should be contacted individually to find out specific resources and programs available at that facility. There are different eligibility criteria for each type of care listed here, and there must be resources available as well for placement. Here are some of the programs and benefits the VA medical system has in place for elderly veterans:

- *Nursing home care:* VA nursing home care units are based at VA medical centers to provide skilled nursing care and related medical or psychosocial services.

- *Domiciliary care:* VA supported state homes provide domiciliary care, or residential rehabilitation and health maintenance centers, for veterans who do not require hospital or nursing care but are unable to live independently because of medical or psychiatric disabilities.

- *Hospice care:* Program provides pain management, symptom control, and other medical services to terminally ill veterans as well as bereavement counseling and respite care to families.

- *Respite care:* Program designed to relieve the spouse or other caregiver from the burden of caring for a chronically disabled veteran at home.

- ***Geriatric Evaluation Management (GEM) Programs:*** GEM programs provide comprehensive healthcare assessments, therapeutic interventions, rehabilitative care and appropriate discharge plans.

- ***Noninstitutional Long-Term Care:*** Care includes hospital-based home care, adult day health care, home health aide services and community residential care programs.

- ***Alzheimer's Disease Programs:*** Veterans with dementia participate in all aspects of the healthcare system, including outpatient, acute and extended care programs.

Nursing Home Care

Nursing care in VA or private nursing homes may be provided for veterans who are not acutely ill and not in need of hospital care. *If space and resources are available, the VA may provide VA nursing-home care, it's not guaranteed in any way.* Veterans who have a service-connected disability that causes the need for nursing home care are given first priority. *Nonservice-connected* disabled veterans (pensioners) and 0% noncompensable *service-connected* veterans requiring nursing-home care for any *nonservice-connected* disability must submit an income eligibility assessment form, VA Form 10-10EZ, to determine whether they will be billed for nursing-home care. Income assessment procedures are the same as for hospital care.

Applicants who *may* be provided nursing-home care without an income eligibility assessment include:

- Veterans with compensable service-connected disabilities

- Veterans who were exposed to herbicides while serving in Vietnam

- Veterans exposed to ionizing radiation during atmospheric testing or in the occupation of Hiroshima and Nagasaki

- Veterans with a condition related to an environmental exposure in the Persian Gulf

- Veterans who are former prisoners of war

- Veterans on VA pension

- Veterans of the Mexican Border period or World War I

- Veterans who are eligible for Medicaid

Only 6 Months of Nursing Home Care

Veterans who need nursing home care may be transferred, at VA expense, to private nursing homes from VA medical centers, nursing homes or domiciliaries. VA-authorized care normally may not be provided in excess of 6 months, except for veterans who need nursing-home care for a service-connected disability or veterans who were hospitalized primarily for treatment of a service-connected disability.

Direct admission to private nursing homes at VA expense is limited to:

- Veterans who require nursing care for a service-connected disability after medical determination by the VA.

- Veterans who are rated 70% or greater service connected disabled for any condition(s).

- Patients in military hospitals who require a protracted period of nursing care and who will become a veteran upon discharge from the Armed Forces.

- Veterans who have been discharged from a VA medical center and are receiving home health services from the VA.

IMPORTANT LONG-TERM CARE INFORMATION
VA • Medicare • Medicaid • HMOs • Private Insurance

Long-term care (LTC) is the permanent need for facility (nursing home, foster home, assisted living, etc.) or in-home care. Long-term care is the single biggest issue older veterans (and all older people) will take into their retirement years. How do you plan on paying for it? *Do not assume* the VA will provide long-term care! Chances are, unless a veteran meets very specific criteria, he or she *will not be eligible*.

The long-term care issue is an enormous problem for the government and it is only getting worse. The impending long-term care need that will come from the baby boomers reaching retirement age is massive, and the government knows Medicaid doesn't have enough money to cover all the costs. That is why the government has built in some pretty good tax advantages for individuals who purchase private long-term care insurance. The following information should be taken into consideration when planning your long-term care needs:

VA Long-Term Care

As noted above, the VA will only help veterans who meet very specific criteria and need nursing home care only. *The VA does not help with any other type of long-term care.* Due to the limited options the VA offers, do not plan on the VA providing you or your loved one long-term care. If you can afford it and you qualify health wise, we recommend you buy private long-term care insurance.

HMO Long-Term Care Coverage

Most HMOs do not offer any long-term care coverage. If not, and if you can afford it, and you qualify health wise, we recommend you buy private long-term care insurance. However, recently some HMOs have stepped into the long-term care arena and have begun to offer some LTC options. If your HMO offers LTC coverage, make sure you

FULLY understand what your options are. Much of the coverage is limited by type and place of care, cost, etc. We strongly urge you to do your homework and explore all options available to you. Even though you have HMO health coverage, you may need to sit down with a professional and look at private long-term care insurance as a separate issue.

Medicare Coverage

Contrary to popular belief, Medicare *does not* provide or pay for long-term care. Medicare does pay 100% of *skilled* nursing home costs for the first 20 days of eligibility. Thereafter, *if your stay is approved*, you pay a $105 daily deductible and Medicare pays the balance. At $105 per day, your monthly out of pocket expense is $3150. If you can afford it and you qualify health wise, we recommend you buy private long-term care insurance.

Medicaid Coverage

Medicaid is welfare. This is a state run program. Federal and state funding (from your tax dollars) combine to form the Medicaid "pot of money". You must be almost flat broke to qualify for this program. To qualify, Medicaid requires that you spend down all resources to approximately $2000. Resource limits vary depending on whether you're applying as single or married and which spouse (or both) needs care. Once you qualify for Medicaid, much of the time you won't have a say in what facility you're placed in, and you'll have to share a room with one or more other residents, usually four to a room. If you can afford it and you qualify health wise, we recommend you buy private long-term care insurance.

Private Long Term Care Insurance

We *strongly* recommend that you purchase private long-term care. insurance. This is the only sure way you can have piece of mind knowing you'll be taken care of when the time comes. But not all long-term care insurance policies are the same. We recommend you contact your current agent or a broker to explore your long-term care options. Many companies have policies on the market that pay the same to the insured no matter what the need (nursing home, in-home care, assisted living, etc.). You work with an agent to devise a plan that specifically suits your financial, family, and emotional needs. Do your homework and choose a company that's financially sound and has a good reputation. You want to make sure they'll be there for you when you need them.

Domiciliary Care

Domiciliary care provides rehabilitative and long-term, health maintenance care for veterans who require minimal medical care but who do not need the skilled nursing services provided in nursing homes. VA may provide domiciliary care to veterans whose annual income does not exceed the maximum pension rate for their circumstances or to veterans the Secretary of Veterans Affairs determines have no adequate means of support. Many homeless veterans reside in VA domiciliaries around the nation. The following states have one or more VA domiciliaries:

ARIZONA—Prescott, **FLORIDA**—Bay Pines, **GEORGIA**—Dublin, **KANSAS**—Wadsworth, **MISSISSIPPI**—Biloxi, **NEW YORK**—Bath, **OHIO**—Dayton, **OREGON**—White City, **S. DAKOTA**—Hot Springs, **TENNESSEE**—Johnson City & Mountain Home, **TEXAS**—Bonham & Temple, **VIRGINIA**—Hampton, **WEST VIRGINIA**—Martinsburg, **WISCONSIN**—Wood.

Call the VA at 800-827-1000 and ask for the number to the domiciliary closest to you to find out about availability and application procedures. Prior approval must be made before a veteran can be admitted.

Hearing Aids & Eye Glasses

One of the most asked questions of the VA is "How do I get hearing aids and eyeglasses from the VA?" Veterans will receive hearing aids and eyeglasses under the following conditions:

- The VA rates them as having a service-connected disability of 50% or more.

- It has been less than one year since a veteran was discharged from the military service for a disability that the *military determined* was incurred or aggravated in the line of duty, and which the VA has not rated.

- If a veteran is seeking care from the VA for a service-connected disability only.

In addition, veterans *must* be receiving health care or services from the VA. If they do not have a service-connected disability rating of 10% or greater, hearing aids and eyeglasses will only be provided in special circumstances, *and not for generally occurring hearing or vision loss associated with aging.*

Hearing Loss & VA

Generally occurring hearing loss is very common in elderly veterans, especially WWII veterans and any veteran who has had exposure to high levels of destructive noise or sound without hearing protection. Many infantryman and combat veterans can tell you that much of the time (if not all of the time) hearing protection was not provided by the military. That fact alone will not help you to receive hearing aids or to receive a service connected disability rating. The VA says there has to be proof your hearing loss is directly related to military service by medical record. Basically, your medical records (private or VA) need to show you sought treatment for a hearing disability (loss) either in military service or within one year of discharge. If that is not the case then you need to seek service connection for any disability you incurred through military service in order to get hearing aids.

What You Can Do

Contact your closest *VA medical center* and enroll under the VA health-care system. A primary care physician will be assigned to you. Continue any private health care coverage you might have. Then contact your closest *VA regional office* and file a claim for a service-connected disability or for VA pension. If granted service connection at 10% or greater, not only will you receive eyeglasses and hearing aids but you'll receive at least $104 per month as well. Pensioners could possibly receive eyeglasses and hearing aids if prescribed by their VA primary care doctor.

> **Example:** Veteran calls the VA medical center and wants hearing aids and eyeglasses. He's been out of the military service for 50 years and has never filed for any benefits before. He's told he's not eligible because he's not a service-connected veteran. He then calls the VA regional office files a service-connected disability claim for migraine headaches because he's had migraines ever since his second year in the Army. He's been receiving private medical treatment and prescriptions for his migraines ever since he left service and never thought about contacting the VA. With all the medical evidence in place, the veteran is rated 10% service-connected disabled for migraines and is now eligible for $104 per month, eyeglasses, and hearing aids.

This seems like a long road to travel down, but in the end, it's worth it. Keep in mind; obviously not all veterans will have disabilities that will be found to be service connected.

Women Veterans Services

Each VA medical center has a Women Veterans Coordinator to help guide women veterans through the available programs. Women have their own set of unique health care needs and the VA is trying to accommodate women and provide services for a growing veteran population. Expanded services for women veterans include:

- Counseling for sexual trauma on a priority basis

- Post traumatic stress disorder

- Complete physicals

- Pap smears

- Mammography—Breast exams

- General reproductive healthcare information

- Family planning

- Birth control

Women with unique medical issues should contact the Women Veterans Coordinator at the nearest VA regional office and VA medical center. The regional office coordinator can help file claims for specific women related issues.

CHAMPVA Medical Care for Dependents and Survivors

CHAMPVA, the VA Civilian Heath and Medial Program, shares the cost of medical care for dependents and survivors of veterans. If not eligible for TRICARE (the medical program for civilian dependents provided by the Department of Defense (DOD)) or Medicare, Part A, as a result of reaching age 65, CHAMPVA is a health care program for eligible surviving spouses and dependent children of a veteran who:

- Died as the result of a service-connected disability or who, at the time of death had a total disability.

- Has a permanent and total service-connected disability.

- Died in the line of duty, and not due to misconduct.

ARE YOU LIVING WITH
INJURIES OR PHYSICAL OR
MENTAL MEDICAL CONDITIONS
THAT WERE
CAUSED BY MILITARY
SERVICE?

FILE YOUR
CLAIM NOW!

CHAPTER 9

▼

FAX CLAIM

Why a FAX claim?

To establish the earliest possible date of claim for benefit purposes. A FAX claim can also extend a time limit on submitting an application for time sensitive benefits. In most cases a FAX claim will be considered an "Informal" claim. The VA may not begin to assist you until they have a FORMAL claim (application) with an original signature.

What do I do?

Call the Federal VA at 1-800-827-1000 and tell them you want to file an INFORMAL claim by FAX. Be specific about what you want to claim. If you're not sure, tell the representative on the phone your situation. The representative will then clarify what type of benefit you are actually filing for. *Tell the VA Rep that you want to FAX in a claim for "XXXXX" benefit and that you'd like written confirmation sent back by FAX that your claim was received.* This will be your ONLY proof you faxed the VA a claim on a specific date and that date will stand as your date of claim if awarded benefits. If the VA loses your FAX and you don't have a copy from the VA rep, you're out of luck on proving your date of claim. *That could cost you up to and over $5000 in cash and benefits!*

VA representatives are not in the habit of telling veterans about FAX claims because it takes more time and it means more paperwork for them. But if you ask that an Informal FAX claim be made then they have to help you. *Insist on it and make sure you get the NAME and team number of the VA representative helping you!*

What kind of claims can I file by FAX?

Any claim for benefits through the VA can be made by FAX but most FAX claims are for service-connected compensation and for non-service disability pension to include widow's pension.

What happens?

If necessary, you'll be sent an application for the benefit you're claiming, which you should complete and return to the VA as soon as possible. Many times just a written statement will act as your complete claim for benefits. If so, then the VA is required to assist you in developing any further evidence necessary to complete your claim. Keep the copy of the FAX claim for your records in case you need it.

Can someone besides the veteran file the FAX claim?

The person making the claim (claimant) needs to sign the FAX claim, but of course anyone can FAX it for the claimant. Frequently spouses, family members, and friends FAX in claims for veterans or widows.

Any time limits?

After you FAX your claim you have one year to respond to the initial response the VA sends you (after receiving your FAX) before your claim dies. If you do this, benefits (if awarded) could be backdated up to a year. Just make sure you respond to any VA requests/letters AS SOON AS POSSIBLE to keep your claim rolling.

Example:

You might find that you're eligible for a benefit worth $850 per month. If you FAX in a claim to the VA on Jan 31, 2003, than VA must use Jan 31, 2003 as your date of claim. If no FAX claim was sent, than the VA uses the date they received your formal application in the mail as a date of claim. If they receive your application anytime in February 2003, then you've just lost one month of entitlement and $850. This goes for any monthly dollar amount, it could be $103 or it could be $5000 OR MORE! Multiply that by the number of months you may have thought about filing your claim and you're talking about a lot of money!

Unbelievably, most veterans don't return their applications right away. Some veterans wait months, and some even wait over a year to return an application.

PLEASE NOTE!

The VA must receive a formal claim *(if necessary, an actual application with your signature)* from you within one year of your FAX claim or the FAX claim is no longer valid and you could lose a whole year of benefit money!

Claim Overlooked

Sometimes when claims are completed and a decision is made, the FAX claim is overlooked. Pay attention to the date of claim the VA uses when they tell you you've been awarded benefits. It must match the date of your FAX to VA or they've made a mistake. Simply tell them the correct date of claim *(the date you originally Faxed in)* from your copy of the receipt of the FAX claim you were sent from the VA Representative. They will change the date and pay you the difference. BUT ONLY IF YOU HAVE CLEAR DOCUMENTATION! MANY TIMES THE VA LOSES FAX CLAIMS—SO MAKE SURE

YOU ASK THE VA REP FOR CONFIRMATION OF RECEIPT OF YOUR FAX CLAIM!

How do I use a FAX claim to extend the time limit on a benefit about to expire?

FAX claims are also used to extend the time limit on a situation or save a date of a benefit that is about to expire.

For instance, if newly discharged veterans file for service connected disability compensation anytime within one year of their date of discharge, benefits (if granted) are retroactively backdated to the date of discharge for pay purposes. If the one-year time limit expires, benefits (if granted) are only payable from the date the application is received.

You can send in a FAX claim 364 days after your discharge and tell the VA you're claiming service connection for a disability incurred in the military. You have one year from the date of that FAX to submit your formal application!

In another example, burial claims for reimbursement have a 2-year limitation. The VA must have an application on file within 2 years of the date of death of the veteran or a claim can no longer be made. That could cost a family up to $1500 or more in reimbursement! But, if you call the VA and send in a FAX claim for burial reimbursement, you have 1 year from the date of your fax to get the application into the VA. Technically, you could call in on the last day of eligibility for any benefit and make a claim, thus, adding a year to the filing period. This will work for any benefit with a time limitation. See the Veterans Benefits Timetable in chapter three.

Types of FAX Claims

The date of claim is the important issue here. File ANY claim as soon as a situation arises. This goes for veterans already receiving benefits also. Here are some examples of types of claims that can be made with a fax:

- **Service Connected Disability Claim:** Any injury, condition, or illness you believe is related to your military service. Includes: Special conditions, reopened claims, reevaluations, claims for increase, claims for unemployable veterans, permanent and total disability ratings, etc.

- **Veterans & Widows Pension Claims:** Original, reopened, Aid and Attendance, Housebound, In-Home Care, Nursing Home Care, Foster Home, & Residential Care

- **Burial Benefits Reimbursement**

CHAPTER 10

▼

SERVICE-CONNECTED DISABILITY COMPENSATION

If you became disabled physically or mentally while on active duty, received treatment (military or private) for your condition while on active duty, continue to have the condition since you've been discharged, and your condition is shown to be at a degree the VA believes is worthy of compensation *(according to regulation and a <u>subjective</u> review by a medical rating board specialist)*, then you could be eligible for service connected disability compensation. Active duty includes active duty for training (ADT) through the National Guard or Reserves.

There is no minimum service period necessary to be eligible. You could have been injured or disabled on your first day in basic training.

Time Limit

There is no time restriction on filing a compensation claim. Some people file their first claim when they're 80 years old.

Description of Benefit

Service connected disability compensation is a monthly payment for eligible veterans, 10% or higher who have a disability, illness or condition that was *incurred* in military service or was *aggravated* by military service. It is also paid to certain veterans disabled from VA health care. Benefits are tax-free!

Service connected is how the VA describes your disability or condition once the VA officially acknowledges that your disability began in military service or was aggravated by service.

- *Incurred* means your disability or condition began or was diagnosed by a doctor for the first time while in the military.

- *Aggravated* means you had the disability or condition before you entered military service (the military may or may not have known about it) and the condition was aggravated and became worse due to your military service.

NOTE: Veterans can be rated 0% service connected and receive free medical care but no monthly payment.

Medical Care

Compensation is a benefit that entitles you to receive free medical care for your military service related condition through VA medical facilities and <u>sometimes</u> private medical facilities. Many times, if you live 60 miles or more from a VA Medical Facility, you can be granted FEE BASIS private medical benefits. Discuss this option with the attending VA Medical Center.

Are You Eligible?

Eligibility and determination of service connection is decided by a review of your claim and all the information with your claim from you, the military, and private and VA doctors. The VA Rating Board at your Regional Office will decide if you are service connected disabled or not. You must be discharged under other than dishonorable conditions.

Monthly Benefit Payments

You could be eligible for a monthly benefit payment ranging from $104 to $2318 OR MORE depending on your disability percentage, number of dependents, and the specifics surrounding your disability or disabilities. The following pay chart became effective 12-01-02. Payments are tax free!

Percentage	Monthly Amount *(Single)*	Monthly Amount *(Married)*
10%	$104	Not Applicable
20%	$201	Not Applicable
30%	$310	$347
40%	$445	$495
50%	$633	$695
60%	$801	$876
70%	$1008	$1095
80%	$1171	$1271
90%	$1317	$1429
100%	$2193	$2318

You're paid even more if you have dependent children OR parents. Your benefit amount could be even higher, sometimes up to and above $5000 monthly depending on your disabilities. You may be paid additional amounts, in certain instances if:

- You have severe disabilities or loss of limb(s)

- You have a seriously disabled spouse (housebound or in need of daily Aid and Attendance)

The Application Process—What To Expect

- First the VA will review your application and everything you've submitted.

- Based on the disabilities you claim, the VA will gather evidence from the military or medical sources to support your claim.

- Next, you'll most likely be set up for a VA exam at a VA medical facility.

- Exam results are then forwarded to the VA Regional Office.

- Your entire claim is sent to the rating board for review and a decision.

- A Veterans Service Representative then inputs your decision into the VA computer system and a formal decision letter is sent to you.

Be Prepared!

This whole process can take 6 to 24 months depending on what you've claimed, whether records from the military or other sources are available, and how long it takes your claim to move through the VA system. Don't let this discourage you from filing a claim; you're entitled to your benefits!

How To Apply

Call the VA and file a FAX claim first! The VA will send you an application if necessary (VA Form 21-526). You must complete and return it within one year to hold your date of claim from your FAX. THIS IS EXTREMELY IMPORTANT FOR PAY PURPOSES. Return the VA Form 21-526 immediately to get the VA working on your claim as soon as possible. Make sure you sign, date, and provide a phone number on the application.

Please review the Special Claims Section following this section. You may have a special condition that needs special attention and evidence to be submitted with the application (VA Form 21-526).

NOTE: If you applied for benefits in the past and the VA granted or denied benefits, you don't need to file another VA Form 21-526. The VA needs a signed statement from you explaining what disabilities you want to claim, why you're claiming the disabilities, how your disabilities have changed since you first filed, and where you have been treated for the disabilities. See Reopened Claims Chapter.

What to Submit With Your Application (VA Form 21-526) Very Important

Even if you don't have some of the information listed here that should be submitted with your claim, don't let that delay you in submitting your application (VA Form 21-526). Your application is the most important part to the VA claim. All other information that is needed can be added later or as it comes along. Get your claim in ASAP.

Discharge Paper or DD214

You must submit the original or a certified copy of your discharge paper or DD214. This will clearly establish your status as a veteran. If you don't have your discharge paper don't worry. Go ahead and submit your claim without it. The VA will try and verify your service through their computer system and/or through contact with the National Personnel Records Center (NPRC).

Service Medical Records (SMR)

If you have a copy of your SMRs, let the Regional Office know you have them but <u>don't</u> send them in with your claim unless you're asked for them. The VA will only need your copy if they are unable to locate your <u>originals</u> from the military. If you do send a copy of your SMRs to the VA, make sure you keep another copy in your possession. The VA routinely loses records.

Private Medical Records

Attach photocopies of <u>any and all</u> private medical records that pertain to your claim, even if you were treated in a private hospital while on active duty. Don't assume the military kept the private records together with your military records. ALWAYS OBTAIN AND RETAIN PRIVATE MEDICAL RECORDS!

Continuity of Treatment

If it's been more than a year since you were discharged from service, the VA wants <u>you</u> to show continuity of medical treatment for your condition. In other words, the VA wants proof that you do have this condition, that it is continuing to be a problem, and that you have sought treatment since discharge for the condition. This will show proof of an ongoing condition.

Even if you did not seek treatment (which many vets don't, they just "live with" the condition) you must still file your disability claim. The VA can still grant service-connected compensation if the record clearly shows you were injured in service and your condition is shown to exist today to a compensable degree.

If you've been treated by a private doctor(s) and don't have the records, the VA will request the records for you. All you have to do is fill out a release authorization (VA Form 21-4142) and give it to VA. Your doctor will send your records directly to VA at no charge to you. But keep in mind that having the VA obtain your private records can take up to a year or longer. We recommend you obtain the records yourself.

Get The Records Yourself!

If you want to speed the process up greatly, get copies of your private medical records yourself and submit them to the VA. Much of the time it takes the VA 6-12 months just to request private medical records.

VA Medical Records

If you've received treatment at any VA medical facility, provide a statement regarding the nature of your treatment, the location of the facility, and when you were treated. The Regional Office will obtain your VA medical records for you.

Dependency Records

When you're rated 30% service connected or higher, your compensation increases for having dependents. Attach the following types of records to your application: Marriage certificate(s), all divorce decrees for you and your spouse, and birth certificates. Submit photocopies to be safe. Some records must be original or certified copy. Call and ask; each VA office may do things differently.

Giving your original records to the VA is not advised. You can obtain certified copies of your important dependency documents from your County Recorder's Office in the County you reside in. The VA will accept certified copies as if they were the original(s).

Other Information Needed

Attach a separate statement from you describing *in detail* how your disabilities affect you. Describe how your daily life, work, personal relationships, athletics, hobbies, etc. are affected by your disabilities. Be very specific and explain thoroughly. The person rating your claim won't know some things if you don't put it in writing and tell them.

Also have family members, friends, coworkers, and anyone else who has first hand knowledge of your disabilities provide a statement. Once again, have them be very specific about how they observe your disabilities and how they affect you.

If you are still in touch with any military buddies who witnessed your disability occur or your problems afterwards, have them provide a statement, also. Make it detailed using exact dates, places, and times, if you can.

IMPORTANT
Direct Result Claim

A direct result claim is a claim where your original service connected disability directly causes another disability. Example: Your service connected left knee condition has caused you to have a right knee condition because you've been favoring your left knee on a regular basis. You've overcompensated for your injured left knee using your right knee more and making up for the weakness in your left knee. Thus, you now have a right knee condition that is a direct result of your left knee condition and should be claimed as service connected.

Apply this to your own situation and you may have cause to make a direct result claim. The possibilities are endless. Joint conditions such as knees, ankles, hips, etc., are very common direct result claims. A less common but valid claim may be one where a veteran's mental condition like post traumatic stress disorder (PTSD) causes a physical injury. Example: A veteran with PTSD is working in his yard when a low flying plane flies overhead. The veteran reacts instinctively and dives on the ground because of a "flashback" and dislocates his shoulder in the process. A claim can be made for a service connected shoulder condition as a direct result of PTSD.

Duty to Assist

The VA has a duty to assist you in gathering evidence in support of your claim. If you do not have the evidence that is needed by the VA to process your claim, than by law, the VA is supposed to help get the information as long as YOU provide enough basic information about the issue.

VA Exam(s)

Any necessary exams will depend on your claim and any previous medical treatment you have received. The rating board will decide if you need an exam(s).

The Medical Center schedules all exams. They notify you by mail to let you know when and what exams are scheduled. You're supposed to receive (at minimum) a two-week advance notice for these exams but very often notices are received only days in advance of an exam.

At your exam make sure you clearly explain your condition to the doctor. Be as specific as possible about your symptoms and concerns. Make sure the doctor writes down how your disability affects you. Remember, the information from your exam will go to the rating board for a decision. If the doctor doesn't know how you're really affected by your condition on a daily basis, it won't be part of your permanent record and your claim will not be evaluated correctly! Approximately 2-3 months after your exam the results will be sent to the Regional Office.

Don't Miss Your Exam

Make sure you do not miss an examination! Having an exam rescheduled takes months. If you cannot make an exam call the VA Medical Center to cancel and then call the VA Regional Office at 1-800-827-1000 to reschedule the exam. You cannot reschedule with the VA Medical Center.

Make sure your address is current with the Regional Office and the VA Medical Center.

Rating Board

A rating board member is not a doctor or a medical professional. A rating board member is a person who is trained by the VA to evaluate medical and claim evidence per the requirements set forth in VA regulations. One person, not an actual board, will evaluate your claim.

Decision

The rating board determines if eligibility is established, and then will determine to what extent your disability affects you. They do this by granting your benefits on a percentage basis, 0%–100% disabling based on Federal law and regulations set forth by VA.

Many claims are not easy to decide based on the VA regulations and require a fair amount of subjective reasoning. This is why you must submit as much evidence as possible in your favor. Don't forget to submit statements explaining in detail how your disability affects you. Much of the time the rating board member can be swayed if there is just enough evidence leaning in your direction.

Payment

If you are awarded service connected disability compensation, you will receive your monthly payment on the first of each month for the preceding month. Benefits due for January are received on the first of February. If the first falls on a weekend or a holiday you should receive your payment the first business day prior to the weekend or holiday.

Bottom Line

File your claim. Be thorough. Submit as much evidence as you can to support your claim. Keep your VA medical appointments. Respond quickly to requests by the VA for information from you. Keep the VA informed of address and phone number changes. Follow up regularly on the status of your claim. Be assertive.

Review Exam (After Your Grant of Service Connection)

If you're granted service connection for a disability, the VA will examine you regularly. Depending on your SC disabilities, the VA will examine you every 2-3 years. This examination is scheduled to see if your disabilities have gotten better. If the VA believes you're not as disabled as rated previously, then your VA disability rating will be reduced. That is the main reason the VA schedules you for an exam. If your disabilities have gotten worse the VA won't take action to increase your benefits. You have to make a claim on your own for reevaluation of a disability that has gotten worse. See Reevaluations section.

Reimbursement of VA Medical Co-Payments

Some veterans begin receiving VA medical treatment for a condition before a grant of service-connection is made. If you've paid co-payments for medical care and or prescriptions regarding a disability that was pending a decision for service connection, and was/is later granted service connection, you can receive a reimbursement of your co-payments from the VA medical facility where you were treated. All you have to do is mail or take your disability rating showing your service connected conditions to the VA medical facility and they will refund your co-payments.

Related Benefits

Service connected disabled veterans may be eligible for any benefit listed below or all of them. Each related benefit listed below has its own criteria for eligibility.

- **Priority Medical Care**
  All service-connected veterans receive priority medical care for their service-connected disability. Veterans rated 50% disabled or greater may receive priority care for nonservice-related conditions, also.

- **Annual Clothing Allowance**
  Veterans, who because of a service connected disability, wear or use a prosthetic or orthopedic appliance (including a wheelchair) which tends to wear out or tear clothing, and veterans, who because of a service connected skin condition use a medication that causes irreparable damage to outer garments, are eligible for payment of an annual clothing allowance. To qualify for annual payment, eligibility must be established as of August 1 of the year for which payment is claimed. The annual August payment as of 1999 is $588.
  What appliances are included? Appliances such as an artificial limb, rigid extremity brace, rigid spinal or cervical brace, wheelchair, crutches or other appliance prescribed for the claimant's service connected disability. Soft and flexible devices, such as an elastic stocking are not included.
  What medications are included? Any medication, prescribed buy a physician for a service connected skin condition that causes permanent stains or otherwise damages the veteran's clothing.
  To make a claim for the clothing allowance, call the VA and file VA Form 21-8678.

- **Vocational Rehabilitation**
  College fully paid for! Service connected veterans rated 20% or higher who were discharged under other than dishonorable conditions, could receive rehabilitation services and assistance to overcome an employment handicap or to improve their capacity for independent living in their family and community. Approved training courses include college or university programs, vocational and trade schools, or apprenticeship programs. Other approved programs are available also. To file for Vocational Rehabilitation, visit or call the Federal VA at 1-800-827-1000 and submit VA Form 28-1900. Also, see Chapter 16, page 70 of this book.

- **State/Local Veterans Benefits**
  Depending on your service connected disability status, you could be

eligible for many state and local veterans benefits such as a property tax exemption, monthly education benefits, free hunting and fishing license, disabled auto plates, just to name a few. Once you receive your disability rating from the Federal VA Regional Office, contact your State VA office and your local County VA Office (if you have one) for all your benefits. See the State Benefits Section of this book.

- **Grants for Special Adapted Housing**
  Eligible veterans with service-connected disabilities may be entitled to a grant up to $48,000 for the adaptation of their home, or reimbursement of a home already acquired because of the nature of their disabilities. Apply through the Federal VA using VA Form 26-4555.
  Supplemental Financing: Veterans with available loan guaranty entitlement may also obtain a guaranteed loan or a direct loan from VA to supplement the grant to acquire a specially adapted home.

- **Federal & State Employment Preference**
  Service connected disabled veterans have a preference in obtaining Federal Employment jobs over nonveterans. Call your Federal VA Regional Office at 1-800-827-1000 and ask to speak with Human Resources for more information on your employment rights.

- **Service-Disabled Life Insurance**
  Life insurance for service connected disabled veterans. You must apply within 2 years of the date the VA notified you of your disability grant. You may qualify for up to $10,000 life insurance coverage even if a commercial company has rejected you for insurance. If you become totally disabled or unable to work for 6 months or more, your Government Life Insurance premiums could be waived entirely.

- **Automobile Grant and Adaptive Equipment**
  For eligible veterans, the VA will pay $9,000 to help purchase a vehicle for a veteran, and also pay for the equipment and installation of specially adapted equipment

Helpful Information & Tips

- If you file within one year of discharge from service, your benefits (if granted) will be retroactive to your date of discharge.

- Compensation payments are tax free and exempt from claims of creditors.

- You are paid a higher monthly amount for dependents if rated 30% or higher.

- If you're rated 30% or higher, you can receive additional monthly amounts if your spouse is housebound or needs regular aid and attendance of another person for daily functions.

- Reimbursement of VA Medical Co-Payments

- Your payments will be affected by any of the following circumstances:
  - You reenter military service.
  - You are receiving or start receiving military retired pay.
  - You receive or begin to receive drill pay as a Reservist or National Guard member.

- Your benefits are subject to future adjustment upon receipt of evidence showing any change in the degree of your disability.

- If you are unable to secure and follow a substantially gainful occupation because of your disabilities, you may be entitled to receive benefits at the rate for total disability (100%).

CHAPTER 11

▼

SPECIAL CLAIMS

Disability Compensation

Special claims is how *Veterans Unclaimed Benefits* describes specific service connected conditions, disabilities, and illnesses that have affected veterans and that need special attention in the collection of evidence to establish service connection for these types of disabilities. Here are some types of special disabilities and conditions in which to make a claim. Also, in this section there are complete descriptions of what to look for and how to make a claim for each particular special disability or condition.

Types of Special Claims:

- **Former Prisoner of War (POW):** Many disabilities, conditions, and diseases are a direct result of being a POW.

- **Post Traumatic Stress Disorder (PTSD):** Traumatic events in the past trigger emotional symptoms and conditions in the veteran some time after the actual event(s).

- **Agent Orange Exposure:** Vietnam veterans were exposed to Agent Orange or other herbicides that contained Dioxin. This exposure has and is causing horrible diseases and conditions in some Vietnam veterans.

- **Chronic Diseases:** There is a presumption of service-connection for some diseases that manifest to a degree of 10% or more within one year of discharge. Other diseases can be rated service-connected even if diagnosed 1 or more years after military service.

- **Asbestos Related Disabilities:** Asbestos exposure can cause chronic respiratory conditions as well as cancers. High exposure to asbestos is noted in U.S. Navy veterans and shipyard workers.

- **Gulf War Syndrome:** Thousands of Gulf War veterans are suffering from chronic symptoms of fatigue, joint pain, memory loss, headache, gastrointestinal and respiratory symptoms, rashes and other problems known as "Gulf War Syndrome."

- **Individual Unemployability:** When your *service-connected* condition keeps you from gainful or regular full time employment, you can be paid at the 100% rate when you're not rated 100%.

- **Permanent and Total Disability Rating:** A total disability rating is a window to more benefits.

- **Cold Exposure Disabilities:** Benefits and health care is extended to veterans suffering from the effects of exposure to extremely cold environments and frostbite. A new VA criterion finally includes injuries to any body part due to cold exposure, not just cold injury to feet.

- **1151 Claims:** From Title 38 United States Code 1151. Compensation for disability for death resulting from VA hospitalization, medical or surgical treatment, or examination.

- **Spina Bifida—Children of Vietnam Vets:** Vietnam veterans' children born with Spina Bifida will be provided medical benefits, vocational training and direct compensation.

- **Special Compensation for Combat Service Disabled Retirees:** "Special Compensation" for severely disabled length of service retirees of the Uniformed Services.

This section is dedicated to special claims because the VA does not always inform you about the possibility of these conditions. VA representatives are told to limit the questions they ask you and not to solicit claims from veterans. Somehow you're supposed to automatically know what to claim without knowing the law or rules surrounding these disabilities.

You could easily be suffering from symptoms and problems relating to a special condition and you don't even know it. Take the time to ask questions of a VA representative in order to receive the answers that will help in determining what exactly needs to be done to help your individual condition. The information in this section should help you a great deal in making a claim for a special condition that is service connected.

Just like any other service connected disability evaluation, *eligibility* and determination of special service connected conditions is decided by applying specific rules and laws in each individual case for each specific condition(s).

How to File a Special Claim

You must call the VA and file a fax claim first (see chapter nine). Tell the VA representative you want to file a service connected disability claim for "tell them your special condition". The representative will send you an application, VA Form 21-526, and any supplemental applications that apply to what you're claiming. Many of the disabilities and conditions listed in this section will require that a questionnaire and/or supplemental information be provided in order to process your claim. They will send you the required forms and questionnaires.

Return everything to the VA ASAP! Verifying the information you provide sometimes can be incredibly time consuming. Use the following information to help you file a claim if any of these conditions or disabilities applies to you.

PRISONER OF WAR (POW) Disabilities

Today, it is presumed that a former POW's disease or condition(s) are service-connected if the veteran was interned or detained for at least 30 days and their condition or disease has grown or manifest to a degree of 10% or more *at any time after discharge or release from active military service.*

The following POW diseases or conditions are recognized:

- Avitaminosis

- Beriberi (including beriberi heart disease, ischemic heart disease)

- Chronic dysentery

- Helminthiasis

- Malnutrition (including optic atrophy associated with malnutrition)

- Pellagra

- Any other nutritional deficiency

- Psychosis

- Any anxiety state

- Dysthymic disorder (depressive neurosis)

- Organic residuals of frostbite

- Post traumatic osteoarthritis

- Irritable bowel syndrome

- Peptic ulcer disease

- Peripheral neuropathy

POST TRAUMATIC STRESS DISORDER (PTSD)

As the name "post traumatic stress" suggests, traumatic events may trigger emotional symptoms some time after the actual events. Post traumatic stress is a normal set of reactions to an event that is outside the range of usual human experience and that would be markedly distressing to almost anyone. Sometimes, it becomes a disorder (PTSD) with the passage of time, when feelings or issues related to the trauma are not dealt with, but suppressed by the individual. This can result in problems for the individual in readjusting to community life following the trauma. PTSD is most commonly associated with military combat but can also be associated with eyewitness accounts, accidents or personal assault. A delayed stress reaction may surface after many years and may include some or all of the following symptoms:

- Anger, irritability, and rage

- Anxiety reactions

- Chronic depression

- Difficulty trusting others

- Emotionally constricting or numbing

- Guilt over acts committed or witnessed, the failure to prevent certain events, or merely having survived while others did not

- Hyper alertness and startled reactions

- Impacted grief

- Intrusive thoughts and memories

- Isolation and alienation from others

- Loss of interest in pleasurable activities

- Low tolerance to stress

- Problems with authority

- Problems with self esteem

- Sleep disorders and nightmares

- Substance abuse

PTSD does not need to have its onset during combat. For example, vehicular or airplane crashes, ship sinking, explosion, rape or assault, duty on a burn ward or graves registration unit, large fires, flood, earthquake, and other disasters would evoke significant distress in most involved persons. Prisoner of War (POW) status may also satisfy the requirements of an in-service stressor depending on the individual situation.

Establishing PTSD as a Service Connected Disability

Three major factors are needed to establish PTSD as a service connected disability:

1. **A diagnosis of PTSD by a physician (psychiatrist).**

2. **Military records that verify the stressful event occurred.**
   This can be verified in different ways. Through service medical records, personnel file or 201 file, or the most common is reviewing your discharge paper to see if you were assigned a combat military occupational specialty (MOS) and to see what awards and

decorations you received. Combat MOS's include but are not limited to:

Armor
Artillery
Infantry

The following <u>individual</u> decorations denote combat participation and are considered an established stressor for PTSD claim purposes:

Air Force Cross
Air Medal (Merit or Valor)
Air Force Commendation Medal (Merit or Valor)
Army Commendation Medal (Merit or Valor)
Bronze Star Medal (Merit or Valor)
Combat Action Ribbon
Combat Infantry Badge
Combat Medical Badge
Distinguished Flying Cross
Distinguished Service Cross
Joint Service Commendation Medal (Merit or Valor)
Marine Corps Expeditionary Medal
Medal of Honor
Navy Commendation Medal (Merit or Valor)
Navy Cross
Navy Expeditionary Medal
Parachutist Badge with Bronze Service Star
Purple Heart
Silver Star

The following <u>unit level</u> decorations denote combat participation:

Presidential Unit Citation (Army), (Navy), and (Air Force)
Air Force Outstanding Unit Award (Valor)
Air Force Organizational Excellence Award (Valor)

Republic of Vietnam Gallantry Cross Unit Citation Badge with Bronze Star

Valorous Unit Award

Even if you received one of the medals listed above, you will still have to complete a PTSD questionnaire. The receipt of the medal sets the foundation to confirm the stressing event occurred and you were involved.

3. **Having a social worker verify that PTSD reduces your ability to function in social or work settings, thus creating a link between your in-service stressor and current symptoms.**

Personal Assault

Personal assault is an event of human design that threatens or inflicts harm. Examples of this are: rape, physical assault, domestic battering, robbery, mugging, and stalking. If the military record contains *no documentation* that a personal assault occurred, alternative evidence might still establish an in-service stressful incident. Behavior changes that occurred at the time of the incident may indicate the occurrence of an in-service stressor. *If this relates to you, don't delay in filing your claim!*

Evaluations

To determine a diagnosis of your condition and how it affects your daily work and social activities, the VA will schedule you to meet with a psychiatrist and a social worker. You should be aware that the questions they would have to ask you are very sensitive in nature and may cause you some emotional distress. As difficult as it may be, it is extremely important that you respond to those questions as openly and as completely as you can. Without accurate and detailed information, it will be difficult for VA examiners to properly diagnose and assess your current condition.

Questionnaires and Forms

Also, the VA will have you complete a *PTSD Questionnaire* in order to give the VA needed information to verify the stressful event(s) that you experienced while you were on active duty. This is for combat and non-combat PTSD claims. Answering these questions could be a difficult and emotional experience for you. If that is the case, have someone help you with the questions. If it's too difficult to write down your answers than you might want to record your PTSD Questionnaire answers on audiotape. Then have someone transcribe it and type it out for you along with any other claim-related statements. Sign and date the statement and submit it to the VA.

The Most Important Factor in Your Claim

The single most important factor in the VA's ability to successfully research PTSD claims is how fully and completely you describe the stressing experiences. Make sure you describe *everything in full* on your PTSD Questionnaire. A stressful incident described in detail using who, what, when, and where, will likely be within the VA's capability to verify by using the various available records. Using complete detail is the key.

Vet Centers • Readjustment Counseling

Vet Centers are designed to provide readjustment counseling to help veterans resolve war-related psychological difficulties and to help them achieve a successful postwar readjustment to civilian life. Whether you file a service-connected disability claim for PTSD or not; or if you are denied compensation, you can still utilize VA Vet Centers.

Assistance includes group, individual and family counseling. If you served on active duty in a combat theater during World War II, the Korean Conflict, the Vietnam Era, the Persian Gulf War, or the campaigns in Lebanon, Grenada, Panama or Somalia, then you are eligible for counseling. Veterans who served in the active military during the Vietnam Era are eligible, even if they were not in a combat theater.

Counseling is also provided to veterans for difficulties due to sexual assault or harassment while on active duty. In areas distant from Vet Centers or VA medical facilities, veterans may obtain readjustment counseling from private-sector professionals who are on contract with the VA. To locate a contract provider, contact your nearest Vet Center.

Filing a Claim

Call the VA; get their FAX number and FAX in a claim for your PTSD condition (see FAX Claim Section). Don't delay in filing an application and any additional forms and questionnaires needed by the VA. Be thorough. Filing a claim for PTSD can be done simply by submitting the following to the VA:

- VA Form 21-526—(Application for Compensation)

- Discharge Paper (DD214)

- PTSD Questionnaire (VA will provide for you)

- Submit any medical records you have to support your claim

AGENT ORANGE DISEASES

Agent Orange was an herbicide used in Vietnam to defoliate trees and remove cover for the enemy. Agent Orange spraying missions were conducted in Vietnam between January 1965 and April 1970. Shipped in orange striped barrels, Agent Orange was a reddish-brown liquid containing two herbicides, the most common being dioxin. Over 2.6 million military service members served within the borders of South Vietnam.

The VA presumes or acknowledges that all veterans who served within the borders of Vietnam were exposed to Agent Orange. Many conditions and diseases that are now causing veterans health problems are linked to Agent Orange exposure.

All Agent Orange disability claims are based on military service in Vietnam. Service in Vietnam also includes service in the waters off-shore Vietnam, or service in other locations if the condition of service involved duty or visitation in Vietnam. Plainly put—you must have stepped foot on the ground in Vietnam and their must be a record of it. DD214 or TDY orders are the most common records used. Sometimes other records like ship's logs, or medical records will be the only indication and proof that you actually stepped foot in Vietnam. Navy veterans assigned to a ship have the hardest time proving they were in Vietnam due to a lack of documentation of classified missions on boats running the rivers of Vietnam. Many USAF personnel flew to and from Vietnam with no orders either simply due to mission needs and routine duty that wasn't documented formally.

Medical Treatment

The VA provides free medical treatment, on a priority basis, to veterans for health problems that may be related to Agent Orange exposure.

File Your Claim Due to Exposure to Agent Orange

If you have any of the following cancers, conditions, or diseases you should file a service connected disability claim for YOUR CONDITION, secondary to exposure to Agent Orange.

These are the diseases that VA currently presumes resulted from exposure to herbicides like Agent Orange. The law requires that some of these diseases be at least 10% disabling under VA's rating regulations within a deadline that began to run the day you left Vietnam. If there is a deadline, it is listed in parentheses after the name of the disease.

- **Chloracne** or other acneform disease consistent with chloracne. (Must occur within one year of exposure to Agent Orange).
- **Diabetes Mellitus, Type II**
- **Hodgkin's disease**

- **Multiple myeloma**
- **Non-Hodgkin's lymphoma**
- **Acute and subacute peripheral neuropathy**. (For purposes of this section, the term acute and subacute peripheral neuropathy means temporary peripheral neuropathy that appears within weeks or months of exposure to an herbicide agent and resolves within two years of the date of onset.)
- **Porphyria cutanea tarda**. (Must occur within one year of exposure to Agent Orange).
- **Prostate cancer**
- **Respiratory cancers** (cancer of the lung, bronchus, larynx, or trachea).
- **Soft-tissue sarcoma** (other than osteosarcoma, chondrosarcoma, Kaposi's sarcoma, or mesothelioma).

Chronic Lymphocytic Leukemia

On January 23, 2003, the National Academy of Sciences' Institute of Medicine issued its report, "Veterans and Agent Orange: Update 2002." The report concluded that there is "limited/suggestive evidence" of an association between exposure to the herbicides used in Vietnam and chronic lymphocytic leukemia (CLL). Based on that report, and all available evidence, the Secretary of Veterans Affairs determined that there is a positive association between CLL and the herbicides used in Vietnam.

On March 26, 2003, VA published a proposed rule in the Federal Register, which will add CLL to VA's list of diseases associated with herbicide exposure. This will create a presumption of service connection for Vietnam veterans with this disease. This change will not take effect until a final regulation is published.

Agent Orange Registry Exam

Veterans with questions related to illnesses associated with exposure to Agent Orange should definitely contact the Agent Orange Registry

Coordinator at the nearest VA Medical Center for information and to schedule an exam.

Veterans are eligible for a complete physical examination. If a VA physician suspects a disease might be related to Agent Orange, VA will provide free medical care. Those who participate in the examination program become part of an Agent Orange Registry and receive periodic mailings from VA about the latest Agent Orange studies and new diseases being covered under VA policies.

For the Agent Orange Registry physical examination, call your local VA hospital or clinic listed in the in the back of *VETERANS UNCLAIMED BENEFITS* under state listings. To file a compensation claim for a current disability related to Agent Orange, call 1-800-827-1000 and inform the VA you want to file a claim. They will send you the application and necessary forms. Send a FAX claim first to protect your date of claim—SEE BELOW.

Filing a Claim

Send a FAX claim first. Filing a claim for a specific condition related to exposure to Agent Orange can be done simply by submitting the following to the VA:

- VA Form 21-526—(Application for Compensation)

- Discharge Paper (DD214)

- A short statement attached to VA Form 21-526 stating: "I claim the following condition(s) to be related to my exposure to Agent Orange". Then list your condition(s).

- Submit any medical records you have to support your claim

CHRONIC DISEASES

Service-connection can be granted for diseases that manifest or grow to a degree of 10% or more within an allotted time period *after discharge,* depending on the disease. Most conditions or diseases must manifest to a 10% degree or higher within one year of discharge. Some diseases have longer time periods ranging from 3 years to 30 years and even a lifetime. These time periods are commonly referred to as presumptive periods because it is presumed that the disease or condition had begun in military service if diagnosed at a 10% degree or higher within the certain time period for that specific disease or condition.

IMPORTANT

If you have a condition or disease that was diagnosed after you were discharged from service, you still may be eligible for service-connected disability compensation. File a claim.

> ***Example (True Story):*** A veteran calls the VA and asks if he has any disability or medical benefits available. He needs help financially because he cannot work any longer due to the fact that he has multiple sclerosis (MS). The veteran had been out of the military for 12 years and had been living with multiple sclerosis for 8 years. That means he was diagnosed with MS 4 years after discharge. Because multiple sclerosis has a 7-year presumptive period for VA service-connected disability purposes, I told the veteran he needed to file a claim for service connection for multiple sclerosis. He provided private medical evidence to show the date he was diagnosed with MS and how his MS affects him now. He was granted service connection at the 100% rate and began receiving monthly tax-free checks for $1989. Many other benefits were made available to him as a service connected veteran at the 100% rate.

What's sad about this story is that this veteran had called the VA years before looking for help but the phone counselor at the time didn't help him file a claim because his MS started after he was discharged. This bad information cost this veteran over $2,000 per month for over 3 years, or roughly $72,000 (TAX-FREE!). There was no recourse to receive any back pay since no claim had been filed.

The following is a list of CHRONIC DISEASES that are recognized by the VA for service connection purposes if the disease had/has grown or manifested to a compensable degree (10% or higher) within the applicable presumptive period for that disease. If you have a diagnosis of any of these conditions, make sure you file a service-connected disability claim ASAP! This list IS NOT all-inclusive. File a claim if you have any doubts about your condition.

- Anemia, primary

- Arteriosclerosis

- Arthritis

- Atrophy, Progressive muscular

- Brain hemorrhage

- Brain thrombosis

- Bronchiectasis

- Calculi of the kidney, bladder or gallbladder

- Cardiovascular-renal disease, including hypertension

- Cirrhosis of the liver

- Coccidioidomycosis

- Diabetes mellitus

- Encephalitis lethargica residuals

- Endocarditis (this term covers all forms of valvular heart disease)

- Endocrinopathies

- Epilepsies

- Hansen's disease

- Hodgkin's disease

- Leukemia

- Lupus erythematosus, systemic

- Myasthenia gravis

- Myelitis

- Myocarditis

- Nephritis

- Other organic diseases of the nervous system

- Osteitis deformans (Paget's disease)

- Osteomalacia

- Palsy, bulbar

- Paralysis agitans

- Psychoses

- Purpura idiopathic, hemorrhagic

- Raynaud's disease

- Sarcoidosis

- Scleroderma

- Sclerosis, amyotrophic lateral

- Sclerosis, multiple

- Syringomyelia

- Thromboangiitis obliterans (Buerger's disease)

- Tuberculosis, active

- Tumors, malignant, or of the brain or spinal cord or peripheral nerves

- Ulcers, peptic (gastric or duodenal)

ASBESTOS—RELATED DISABILITIES

Asbestos exposure can cause chronic respiratory conditions as well as cancers. High exposure to asbestos is noted in U.S. Navy veterans and shipyard workers. World War II Navy veterans who served in a shipyard or on board a ship that are diagnosed with respiratory cancers or conditions are almost automatically granted service-connection (SC) for their condition(s). Of course any veteran whose record shows exposure to asbestos can possibly receive SC benefits.

The following is a list of the most common asbestos-related disabilities.

- Interstitial pulmonary fibrosis (asbestosis)

- Pleural effusions and fibrosis

- Pleural plaques

- Mesotheliomas of pleura and peritoneum

- Lung Cancer

- Gastrointestinal Tract Cancer

- Larynx and Pharynx Cancer

- Urogenital System Cancer (except the prostate)

PERSIAN GULF WAR DISABILITIES & CONDITIONS

The VA will pay service-connected compensation to a Persian Gulf War veteran who exhibits *objective indications* of <u>chronic disability</u> resulting from an illness or a combination of illnesses manifested by one or more signs or symptoms such as those listed below.

The VA regulations state that such disability or disabilities must have manifest either during active military, navel, or air service in the Southwest Asia theater of operations during the Persian Gulf War, or to a degree of 10% or more not later than <u>December 31, 2006</u>. That means some Gulf War veterans could have disabilities that aren't showing yet.

Theater of Operations

The Southwest Asia theater of operations includes Iraq, Kuwait, Saudi Arabia, the neutral zone between Iraq and Saudi Arabia, Bahrain, Qatar, the United Arab Emirate, Oman, the Gulf Aden, The Gulf of Oman, The Persian Gulf, the Arabian Sea, the Red Sea, and the airspace above these locations.

According to the VA, disabilities that have existed for 6 months or more and disabilities that exhibit intermittent episodes of improvement and worsening over a 6-month period *will be considered chronic*.

Signs or Symptoms

Signs or symptoms, which may be manifestations of undiagnosed illness, include, but are not limited to:

- Fatigue
- Signs or symptoms involving skin
- Headache

- Muscle pain

- Joint pain

- Neurologic signs or symptoms

- Neuropsychological signs or symptoms

- Signs or symptoms involving the respiratory system (upper or lower)

- Sleep disturbances

- Gastrointestinal signs or symptoms

- Cardiovascular signs or symptoms

- Abnormal weight loss

- Menstrual disorders

Qualifying Illnesses *(Gulf War Syndrome)*

Compensation may be paid for the <u>signs or symptoms</u> listed below. If you're a Gulf War veteran and a doctor diagnoses one or more of the following signs or symptoms by December 31, 2006, to a 10% or higher compensable degree, and the condition is shown for at least 6 months or longer you could be eligible for service-connected disability compensation. The following list is not exclusive, other signs or symptoms could qualify you for service connection. These are the most common:

- Abnormal Weight Loss

- Cardiovascular signs or symptoms

- Fatigue

- Gastrointestinal signs or symptoms

- Headache

- Joint Pain

- Menstrual Disorders

- Muscle Pain

- Neurologic signs or symptoms

- Neuropsychological signs or symptoms

- Signs or symptoms involving skin

- Signs or symptoms involving the respiratory system (upper or lower)

- Sleep Disturbances

INDIVIDUAL UNEMPLOYABILITY (IU)

If your *service connected* condition keeps you from gainful or regular full time employment, you can apply for evaluation for Individual Unemployability (IU). This benefit will pay you at the 100% rate if approved. A grant of this benefit doesn't increase your current disability percentage; it acknowledges that your current disability level (60%, 70%, 80% or 90%) is keeping you from gainful employment.

Once you complete and return VA Form 21-8940, the VA will contact previous employers for information and review your medical history. You may be scheduled for an exam to determine your disability level and/or to get a medical opinion. If you apply and are denied you still might receive an increase in your disability percentage. You can reapply at any time.

PERMANENT AND TOTAL (P&T) STATUS

A veteran who is 100% service-connected disabled, or is rated less than 100% but has been granted Individual Unemployability can apply for Permanent and Total Disability status.

What does permanent and total status mean to me?

Here are the following benefits when rated P&T:

- No more VA exams to determine if you're getting better.

- Piece of mind knowing the VA isn't going to lower your disability payment.

- Educational assistance for your spouse and dependent children (up to $485 p/month).

- Commissary and exchange privileges.

- CHAMPVA health care eligibility for your spouse and dependent children.

- Possible DIC benefits for your surviving spouse (includes much more, see Survivor's Benefits section)

How to Apply

If you're 100% SC disabled or receiving IU and you feel your condition will not get better; file for a Permanent and Total disability rating. There is no form used to apply. Simply send the VA a statement; "I request to be evaluated for permanent and total disability status. My condition is permanent and is not going to change." That's it! Good luck.

COLD EXPOSURE DISABILITIES

A 1998 ruling acknowledges cold-related injuries to include any body part affected by cold exposure. Conditions that may be related to cold exposure include:

- Peripheral Neuropathy

- Circulatory Problems

- Skin Cancer in Frostbite Scars

- Chronic Night Pain

- Arthritis of Exposed Parts

- Fungal Infections

Apply using VA Form 21-526. Attach a separate statement describing your condition(s), how long you've been affected, and whether or not you've received any VA medical or private treatment.

1151 DISABILITY OR DEATH CLAIM

Have you ever wondered what you can do if something bad ever happens to you while being treated at a VA Medical Center or under VA care? You or your surviving spouse have a couple options.

A rule allows for monthly compensation to be paid for disability or death resulting from VA hospitalization, medical or surgical treatment, or examination. If you have a disability that is a direct result of VA medical treatment, you may want to file an 1151 claim. Or, if treatment causes your death, your surviving spouse may want to file. Your other option would be to "sue" for damages. You can't really file suit against a VA medical center but you can file a claim for damages.

To file an 1151 claim all you need to do is submit a signed statement to the VA explaining in great detail what your medical issue is. Explain what happened while being treated and the ill consequences that you are suffering. Be very specific. It will be treated like a service-connected disability claim. All the evidence regarding the incident will be evaluated and a regional office rating board member at a local level will make a decision. If denied you can appeal.

If you choose not to file an 1151 claim and want to pursue damages against the VA, you may want to consult an attorney. One of the first things` you would need to do would be to contact the VA District Counsel at the closest VA regional office to where the injury took place and request a *Standard Form 95, Claim For Damage, Injury, Or Death*.

SPINA BIFIDA BENEFITS
Monthly Payments

Spina bifida patients who are children of Vietnam veterans are eligible for vocational training, health care, and a monthly allowance. The monthly allowance is set at three levels, depending upon the degree of disability suffered by the child. The three levels are based on neurological manifestations that define the severity of disability: impairment of the functioning of the extremities, impairment of bowel or bladder function, and impairment of intellectual functioning. Level 1 monthly rate is $228, level 2 monthly rate is $792, and level 3 monthly rate is $1,354.

Healthcare for Spina Bifida Patients

In addition to monetary allowances, vocational training and rehabilitation, the Department of Veterans Affairs (VA) also provides VA-financed healthcare benefits to Vietnam veterans' birth children diagnosed with spina bifida. For the purpose of this program, spina bifida is defined as all forms or manifestations of spina bifida (except spina bifida occulta), including complications or associated medical conditions related to spina bifida according to the scientific literature.

Healthcare benefits available under this program are limited to those necessary for the treatment of spina bifida and related medical conditions. Beneficiaries should be aware that this program is not a comprehensive healthcare plan and does not cover care that is unrelated to spina bifida.

Administration of the program is centralized to VA's Health Administration Center (HAC) in Denver, Colorado. HAC is responsible for all aspects of the spina bifida healthcare program, including the authorization of benefits and the subsequent processing and payment of claims. All inquiries regarding healthcare benefits should be made directly to HAC.

SPECIAL COMPENSATIN FOR SEVERELY DISABLED UNIFORMED SERVICES RETIREES

Public Law 106-65, dated October 5, 1999, (Title 10 U.S.C.1413) provides a "special compensation" for severely disabled length of service retirees of the Uniformed Services. This benefit will be administered by the Department of Defense (DoD). VA does not pay this benefit.

Who is eligible?

Length of service retirees who became severely disabled (70%, 80%, 90%, 100% or Individual Unemployability (IU)) within four years from their date of retirement are eligible for this benefit. Those retired for disability are not eligible.

Who will determine entitlement?

DoD will determine who is entitled to this payment based on data provided by the Department of Veterans Affairs (VA). The eligible retiree is entitled to this monthly benefit on or after October 1, 1999.

How much is this "Special Compensation?"

The amount of Special Compensation will be determined according to the current disability rating (for the month of entitlement) as reported by the VA to DoD:

- $100 for a disability rating of 70 or 80 percent.

- $200 for a disability rating of 90 percent, and

- $300 for a disability rating of 100 percent or (IU).

Do I have to file a claim?

No. DoD will automatically start paying eligible retirees identified electronically. However, DoD may contact retirees if additional information is required to determine entitlement.

When will this new benefit be paid?

VA, Defense Finance and Accounting Service (DFAS), Coast Guard and National Oceanic and Atmospheric Administration, and Public Heath Service are currently working together to match electronic records and develop a current and ongoing list of potentially eligible veterans. DoD has projected that the first payments will be made in early 2000. The awards will be retroactive to October 1, 1999.

Is this new benefit taxable?

Yes. Special Compensation paid under 10 USC 1413 is taxable income within the meaning of section 61 of the Internal Revenue Code.

Will there be an adjustment to my VA award?

There will be no adjustment of VA awards. It is to be paid from funds appropriated for pay and allowances of the recipient member's branch of service. Eligible retirees in receipt of VA disability compensation may receive this benefit in addition to their VA disability compensation.

▼

CHAPTER 12

EXTRA
SERVICE-CONNECTED
INFORMATION

Reevaluations • Total Ratings •
Unemployability Hospitalization Pay •
Co-Payments • Voc Rehab

If you have a service connected (SC) disability rating and you believe it doesn't accurately reflect the level of disability you're experiencing, then you can and should request a reevaluation of your disability from the VA.

REEVALUATIONS

Your VA record needs to correctly reflect your disability level. In turn, you deserve to be compensated accordingly regarding your SC disability. This could mean hundreds of dollars, maybe even a thousand or more per month above what you are receiving currently from the VA.

How to Claim a Reevaluation

Often, SC disabled veterans don't even realize they can have their disabilities reevaluated. The process is surprisingly simple. You can make a request for a reevaluation at any time you feel your disability has worsened. All you have to do is write the VA a statement (use any blank piece of paper, you don't need a form) expressing your disability or disabilities have become worse and you request a reevaluation. You need to state what your SC disability is, how it's changed since the last exam, and how it affects you (be very specific, i.e., daily problems, work problems, what you can and can't do, etc.). The VA should schedule you for an exam. That can take anywhere from 60 days to 8 months.

Make sure you advise the VA regional office when you make this claim for a reevaluation that you note all medical care received from VA or private physician since your last VA disability <u>rating</u>. Some times the VA may ask for your private medical records before they will schedule an exam.

SAMPLE LETTER TO VA

DATE: JAN 1, 2003

TO: VA
FROM: GI JOE
            VA Claim # 12-345-6789

REQUEST FOR REVALUATION

Dear VA,

My service connected left knee condition has gotten worse. I can no longer walk up and down stairs as my knee gives out. I can't drive my old truck anymore because I can't push in the clutch. I've fallen many times over the past few months and now use a cane. I've started to overcompensate and use my right leg and knee more. Now my right knee has

---

started hurting also. Because of my condition, I've had to quit my job as a UPS deliveryman.

All my medical treatment is received at the Portland VA medical center. I have not received private medical treatment.

OR

I have enclosed all my medical treatment records from my private doctor. I have also been treated at the Portland VA medical center. Please schedule an exam to determine my new disability level.

Thank you,
GI JOE

When you're at the VA exam make sure you CLEARLY EXPLAIN your condition to the doctor. You need to make sure the doctor knows exactly how your disabilities affect you. If the doctor doesn't write down your problems, it won't be part of your record and you might not receive an increase in your SC disability rating.

HOSPITALIZATION PAY—21 DAY RULE—100% DISABILITY PAY

If your service-connected disability causes you to be hospitalized, you may be entitled to 100% disability pay for a continuous hospitalization stay for *treatment or observation in excess of 21 days*. If you are continuously hospitalized in excess of 21 days for a service-connected disability, call the VA regional office nearest you at 1-800-827-1000 and make a phone claim for a hospital stay in excess of 21 days. Tell them the VA facility providing your treatment and the regional office can obtain the necessary medical documentation for payment.

TEMPORARY TOTAL RATINGS

If your service-connected (SC) condition temporarily worsens to a degree to where you are unable to pursue post hospital employment for a minimum period of at least 30 days, you may be entitled to a temporary total rating of 100%.

Most temporary total ratings come from service-connected surgeries. Post surgery recovery periods of convalescence are many times 30 days or more. Depending on your SC condition and the surgery, you may have a period of convalescence of 1 year or more. You must make a phone claim through the VA regional office at 1-800-827-1000 as soon as your surgery is completed! The VA regional office will obtain the necessary medical documentation from a VA medical facility. If your surgery or treatment is through a private doctor then provide the VA with copies of the hospital summary, treatment notes, and/or written confirmation by your doctor on the period of convalescence necessary. Because you are unable to work and not earning an income, VA regulations state that temporary total ratings are to be processed in 30-45 days.

> Important Note: *You must file your claim for a temporary total rating within 1 year of the date of your SC surgery or circumstances that caused you to be unemployable for a period of time. You lose your right to file if the 1-year time limit passes.*

INDIVIDUAL UNEMPLOYABILITY

If you believe your SC disabilities are keeping you from permanent full-time employment than you must file a claim for *Individual Unemployability* on VA Form 21-8940. This form is absolutely necessary to process this claim. If granted, you can receive VA SC disability pay at the 100% rate even if your disabilities are not technically rated at 100%. Call 1-800-827-1000 and ask for the form to be sent; return it ASAP.

VA MEDIAL CO-PAYMENTS

Some veterans begin receiving treatment for a condition before a grant of service-connection is made. If you've paid co-payments for medical care and or prescriptions regarding a disability that was pending a decision for service connection, and was/is later granted service-connected, you can receive a reimbursement of your co-payments from the VA medical facility where you were treated. All you have to do is mail or take your disability rating showing your service connected conditions to the VA medical facility and they will refund your co-payments.

DIRECT RESULT CLAIMS

A direct result claim is a claim where your original service connected disability directly causes another disability. Example: Your service connected left knee condition has caused you to have a right knee condition because you've been favoring your left knee because it was injured. You've overcompensated for you injured left knee using your right knee more and making up for the weakness in your left knee. Thus, you now have a right knee condition that is a direct result of your left knee condition and should be claimed as service connected.

Apply this to your own situation and you may have cause to make a direct result claim. The possibilities are endless. Joint conditions such as knees, ankles, hips, etc., are very common direct result claims. A less common but valid claim may be one where a veteran's mental condition like post traumatic stress disorder (PTSD) causes a physical injury. Example: A veteran with PTSD is working in his yard when a low flying plane flies overhead. The veteran reacts instinctively and dives on the ground because of a "flashback" and dislocates his shoulder in the process. A claim can be made for a service connected shoulder condition as a direct result of PTSD.

VOCATOINAL REHABILITATION REVIEW

Veterans who receive increases in existing service-connected disabilities are eligible for a review of their disability situation for possible entitlement to vocational rehabilitation. Even if the 12-year limit has expired, *any increase in a SC disability is grounds for a review for vocational rehabilitation if the veteran chooses.*

CHAPTER 13

▼

REOPENED DISABILITY CLAIMS

If you've ever been denied service-connected disability benefits or non-service-connected disability pension, and you want to file your claim again, then you will be filing a *Reopened Disability Claim*.

What Is a Reopened Claim?

A reopened claim is where a veteran's claim had previously been denied and is reopened with new evidence.

Review Original Rating Decision

Most successful reopened claims start with reviewing the rating attached to the *original* disability claim denial. The rating decision describes what evidence is needed to grant a positive decision in the veteran's favor. If you don't have your original rating you should call the VA and ask to have a copy sent to you. Usually they can help with a simple request like that, but you may be asked to submit a formal request in writing for a copy of your original rating.

You don't have to pursue a reopened claim by using the original rating decision, but it's helpful. You can always submit any evidence you believe will change the decision of your claim.

New Evidence

Read the rating decision carefully. Obtain the necessary evidence listed or noted in the original rating decision. It usually entails submitting new medical evidence but sometimes might mean obtaining, never before seen, military service medical records or other military documents. You may want to solicit the help of a Veterans Service Organization.

VA Medical Co-Payments

Some veterans begin receiving treatment for a condition before a grant of service-connection is made. If you've paid co-payments for medical care and/or prescriptions regarding a disability that was pending a decision for service connection, and later was granted service-connected, you can receive a reimbursement of your co-payments from the VA medical facility where you were treated. All you have to do is mail or take your disability rating, showing your service connected conditions, to the VA medical facility and they will refund your co-payments.

Appeals

If you feel the original decision on the claim is wrong, you can file an appeal of the decision. You must file your appeal within one year of the date of the original decision. Filing an appeal means you believe the claims stands on its own merit and are requesting an outside review of the facts through the Board of Veterans Appeals (BVA).

Filing An Appeal

You start the appeal process by sending the VA a statement that you "disagree with VA decision dated 01/01/01." See Chapter 14 regarding appeals.

CHAPTER 14

▼

APPEALS & HEARINGS

Veterans have the right to appeal decisions made by a VA regional office or medical center. Any decision can be appealed. Typical issues appealed are disability compensation, pension, education benefits, recovery of overpayments, medication co-payment debts and reimbursement for medical services that were not authorized.

Most appeals concern service-connected (SC) disability claims, so we are focusing our attention on SC appeals. *You can appeal any part of a decision or the whole decision.* For instance, you may be granted service-connected compensation at the 10% rate but you believe it should be 20% or higher. When you file your appeal be very specific about your disagreements.

The Process & Time Limits

A veteran has one year from the date of the notification of a VA decision to file an appeal. The process is started by the veteran sending a signed and dated statement called a "Notice of Disagreement" to the VA office that made the decision. Just a simple note, which reads, "I disagree with the VA decision dated 01/01/00." Go on to explain exactly why you disagree with the decision. Pay close attention to all the evidence listed and how the decision-maker interprets the evidence in relation to the regulations. All the reasons and basis for a decision are provided in the VA rating decision. If you need help with your appeal, we suggest you contact a service organization. They have personnel that are specifically trained in helping veterans with appeals. And the best part is that their services are free. Of course, you can always obtain the services of a lawyer, if you choose.

Next, the VA will respond to you in 3 to 12 months with a "Statement of the Case" (SOC), which explains what facts, laws, and regulations were used in deciding your case. The SOC is almost a complete duplicate of the rating decision that accompanied your original decision. But the process says you must have a SOC. Along with the SOC will be a VA Form 9 or "Substantive Appeal". You must return the Form 9 *(to the VA regional office)* within 60 days of the mailing of the SOC or within one year from the date the VA mailed its original decision to you, whichever period ends later. Send back the VA Form 9 right away.

VA Form 9

The VA Form 9 is extremely important to your appeal. On the form (and on an attached signed statement if needed), make sure that you CLEARLY state the benefit(s) you are seeking and point out any mistakes you think the VA made when deciding your claim.

Board of Veterans Appeals (BVA)

If you don't have any new evidence to submit with your VA Form 9 than your appeal is ready to be sent to the Board of Veterans Appeals in Washington, D.C. The BVA will add your appeal to their docket in the order in which they receive it along with the other appeals from around the nation. You'll be assigned a docket number and placed in line. Average wait time for a decision is anywhere from 18 months to 3 years. To learn the current status of your appeal call (202) 565-5436.

Remanded Appeals

A remand is an appeal that is returned to the local VA regional office after an initial review (but no decision) by the BVA. This is done because the BVA finds that the original review of evidence and decision on the part of the local VA regional office regarding the case was not done properly or is lacking in detail. When a case is remanded back it comes with a list of actions the local VA regional office must accomplish. After performing the additional work, (which can take 1 month to 1 year), the regional office *may* issue a new decision. If a claim is still denied, the case is returned to BVA again for a final decision.

Approximately 30-40% of all cases appealed to the BVA are remanded back to the original VA regional office. This is another reason that an appeal can take years to be accomplished.

New Evidence

You can submit new evidence at any time to help substantiate your claim. If you submit new evidence with your VA Form 9 *before* your appeal goes to BVA, the VA will issue you a Supplemental Statement of the Case (SSOC). The SSOC addresses the new evidence you submitted. If you disagree with the SSOC, you have 60 days to submit a statement explaining why you disagree with it.

If you submit new evidence *after* your claim has been sent to BVA, then the new evidence will sit and wait at the VA regional office until the BVA makes a decision based on the evidence of record with the file. Once the file and claim are returned, a VA regional office rating board member will then review the new evidence regarding the appeal and a new decision will be made on the new evidence. That decision is separate from the original decision, and if disagreed with, would start a new appeal all over again. Sounds like fun doesn't it?

There's Another Way

If you disagree with a decision that the VA has made, you have another option *before* you decide to appeal. This option can save you time and helps you avoid the appeal process altogether. This option is only good if you plan on submitting new evidence regarding the original claim. If you do plan on submitting new evidence, then move down and start reading the section below on new and material evidence.

If you don't have any new evidence to submit, and you still disagree with the VA decision, then file your appeal immediately starting with a "Notice of Disagreement" statement signed by you. Your appeal will go to the BVA on the merits of all the original evidence. A BVA member in Washington D.C. can make another subjective decision based on the exact same evidence as the first decision. Hopefully, the decision you disagree with will be overturned in your favor.

New & Material Evidence

Instead of filing an appeal right away, you can reopen your claim immediately by sending in *new and material evidence* regarding the decision. *New* means it is not merely the same or duplicate of other evidence on record, and *material* means it is relevant to your claim. By sending in new and material evidence (without appealing), it is treated as a reopened claim. To justify a reopening of a claim on the basis of new and material evidence, there must be a reasonable possibility the new evidence, when viewed in the context of all the evidence; both new and old would change the outcome of the decision. When you submit new evidence within one year of the decision that you disagree with, if approved, the grant on the new evidence would go back to the original date of your claim. The VA regional office will take probably 2 to 6 months to decide on new evidence, whereas, an appeal would take a minimum of 18 months before you hear on a decision. The good part is that you can still appeal to the BVA anytime as long as it's within one year of the notification on the original decision. Use your time wisely and respond quickly to any VA requests.

BVA Hearings

If you do appeal, you have the right to present your case in person and appear before the BVA in Washington, D.C., at your VA regional office (with a traveling BVA Board), or through a videoconference hearing.

If you go to Washington, D.C. you have to wait 18 months to 3 years for the hearing. If you wait to see the BVA Traveling Board you sometimes have to wait up to 2-3 years. The wait for the BVA Traveling Board can also be very short depending on where you live and what the schedule of the Board is. Could be 4 months or could be 3 years. Your best bet is definitely the videoconference hearing. If you really want to speak with a BVA Board member, you usually can expect to meet with them in 30 to 120 days from the date you request the videoconference hearing. The videoconference hearing is in "real time" through a live video hook up. You most likely would go to your closest VA regional office where they would have a special room set up to handle videoconference hearings. It is suggested that you seek representation from a service organization before you attend the hearing. If you want to speak to the Board of Veterans Appeals in person, and you don't want to wait years, schedule a videoconference hearing anytime by calling your VA regional office at 1-800-827-1000.

US Court of Veterans Appeals

A VA claim may be appealed from the Board of Veterans' Appeals to the US Court of Veterans Appeals. This court is independent of the Department of Veterans Affairs. Only claimants may seek a review by the court; the VA may not appeal board decisions.

120 Days

The appeal must be filed with the court with a postmark that is within 120 days after the Board of Veterans' Appeals mails its final decision.

How To Appeal a BVA Decision

To appeal a Board decision to the Court, you must file an original Notice of Appeal directly with the Court at:

United States Court of Veterans Appeals
625 Indiana Avenue, NW, Suite 900
Washington, DC 20004

If you filed a *motion to reconsider* with the Board within the 120-day time frame and that motion was denied, you have an *additional* 120 days to file the Notice of Appeal with the Court. This 120-day period begins on the date the Board mails you a letter notifying you that it has denied your motion to reconsider. A "Notice of Appellate Rights" will be mailed to you if the Board denies your motion to reconsider your appeal.

If you appeal to the Court, you should also file a copy of the Notice of Appeal with the *VA* General Counsel at the following address:

Office of the General Counsel (027)
Department of Veterans Affairs
810 Vermont Avenue, NW
Washington, DC 20420

The original Notice of Appeal that you file with the Court is the only document that protects your right to appeal a *BVA* decision. The copy sent to *VA's* General Counsel does not protect that right or serve as your official filing.

The court does not hold trials or receive new evidence. The court reviews the record that was considered by the Board of Veterans' Appeals. Oral argument is held only at the direction of the court. Either party may appeal a decision of the court to the U.S. Court of Appeals for the Federal Circuit and to the Supreme Court of the United States. Appellants may represent themselves before the court or have lawyers or approved agents (service organization) as representatives.

To obtain more specific information about the Notice of Appeal, the methods for filing with the Court, Court filing fees, and other matters covered by the Court's rules, you should contact the Court directly at the (Indiana Avenue) address given above. You may also contact the Court by telephone at 1-800-869-8654.

The first day of the 120 days you have to file an appeal to the Court of Veterans Appeals is the day the Board's decision is postmarked, not the day the decision is signed.

Court Decisions

The court's decisions are published in West's Veterans Appeals Reporter, in the WESTLAW and LEXIS on-line services and on the court's electronic bulletin board. The bulletin board can be reached at (202) 501-5836. For information about case status or the court's rules and procedures, contact the Clerk of the Court, 625 Indiana Avenue NW, Suite 900, Washington, D.C. 20004, or call 1-800-869-8654 from 1pm to 4pm, EST.

APPEAL CHECKLIST

• Consider having a veteran service organization representative (ex: American Legion, Disabled American Veterans) assist you with your appeal.

• File your Notice of Disagreement and VA Form 9 ASAP!

• Be as specific as possible when identifying the issue or issues you want the Board to consider.

• Be specific when identifying sources of evidence you want the VA to obtain.

• Keep the VA informed of your current address and phone number.

- Be very clear (on your VA Form 9) about whether or not you want a BVA hearing, what kind, and where you want it held.

- Provide all the evidence you can that supports your claim, including medical treatment records or statements from a physician.

CHAPTER 15

▼

MISCELLANEOUS
VETERANS INFORMATION

Verification of Military Experience and Training

The Verification of Military Experience and training (VMET) Document, DD Form 2586, is provided to all eligible departing service members. The document helps service members verify previous experience and training to potential employers, write their resumes, prepare for job interviews, negotiate credits at schools, and obtain certificated or licenses. The military departments make the VMET document available by mail and on the Internet (http://www.dmdc.osd.mil/vmet), from which service members can view it online or print locally. Service members should receive their DD Form 2586 between 90-180 days prior to separation.

Job Finding Assistance

State employment offices help veterans find jobs by providing free job counseling, testing, referral and placement services. Veterans are given priority when referring applicants to job openings and training opportunities. Disabled veterans receive the highest priority in referrals. Employment offices also assist veterans by providing information about unemployment compensation, job markets and on-the-job apprenticeship training opportunities. Veterans should present a copy of their military discharge, DD Form 214 at the nearest state employment office.

Job Partnership Training Act

The job Partnership Training Act provides for a national job training program for disabled, Vietnam Era and recently separated veterans. Job training programs may be conducted through public agencies and private nonprofit organizations. Veterans should apply at the nearest state employment office.

Disabled Veterans Outreach Program

State employment offices locate disabled veterans and help them find jobs. Outreach staff members are usually disabled veterans themselves. Most staff members are located in offices of the state employment service but some may be stationed in VA regional offices and readjustment counseling centers (Vet Centers).

Unemployment Insurance

Weekly unemployment insurance may be paid to discharged service members for a limited period of time. State laws govern the amount and duration of payments. To apply, veterans should immediately contact the nearest state employment office after leaving military service and present a copy of their discharge.

Reemployment Rights

A person who left a civilian job to enter active duty in the Armed Forces may be entitled to return to the job after discharge or release from active duty. Reemployment rights are provided for those who served on active duty or reserve components of the Armed Forces. Certain requirements must be met.

If there are problems in attaining reemployment, the employee should contact the Department of Labor's Veterans Employment and Training Service (VETS) in the state of the employer concerned. This applies to both private sector and federal employees, including the Postal Service.

Federal Jobs for Veterans

The Veterans Readjustment Appointment (VRA) authority helps to provide veterans with jobs in the federal government. The VRA authority allows federal agencies to appoint Vietnam-Era and post-Vietnam Era veterans to jobs without competition. Such appointments may lead to conversion to career or career-conditional employment upon satisfactory work for two years. Veterans seeking VRA appointment should apply directly to the agency where they wish to work.

Disabled Veterans Affirmative Action Program

The Office of Personnel Management (OPM) administers the Disabled Veterans Affirmative Action Program (DVAAP). All federal departments and agencies are required to establish plans to facilitate the recruitment and advancement of disabled veterans. Career America Connection provides information regarding job opportunities at (912) 757-3000 or on their home page at www.usajobs.opm.gov.

Loans for Farms and Homes

Loans and guaranties may be provided by the U.S. Department of Agriculture to buy, improve or operate farms. Loans and guaranties are available for housing in towns generally up to 20,000 in population. Applications from veterans have preference. For further information contact farm Service Agency or Rural Economic and Community Development, U.S. Department of Agriculture, Washington, DC 20250, or apply at local Department of Agriculture offices, usually located in county seats.

Small Business Administration (SBA)

A number of SBA programs are designed to help businesses owned and operated by veterans. Available help from the SBA includes business training, conferences, counseling, surety bonding, government procurement and financial management assistance. SBA loans are made under its Loan Guaranty Program. A bank or other lending institution advances the loan amount with SBA guaranteeing up to 85 percent of the total amount. In each SBA field office a veterans affairs officer is designated as the contact person to assist veterans. Information about SBA's programs is provided at field offices. Check the phone book for the nearest SBA office or call 1-800-827-5722.

Waiver of Overpayments

If you find that you owe the VA money for some reason, and you understand why you owe the money, and you don't have the financial means to pay; you can request a waiver of the overpayment. Basically, you would file for a waiver of an overpayment if you do not dispute the overpayment but are unable to afford paying it off. The VA will have you complete a financial status report and make a decision based on your income versus your debts. They also have to decide if the cause of the overpayment was fraudulent or not. It's possible that if you have an extreme financial hardship, you won't have to pay back money you received.

Passports to Visit Overseas Cemeteries

"No-fee" passports are available for family members visiting overseas graves and memorial sites of World War I and World War II deceased veterans. Eligibility is reserved for surviving spouses, parents, children, sisters, brothers and guardians of the deceased who are buried or commemorated in American military cemeteries on foreign soil. For additional information, write to the American Battle Monuments Commission, Courthouse Plaza II, Suite 500, 2300 Clarendon Blvd, Arlington, VA, 22201, or phone (202) 761-0537.

Death Gratuity

Military services provide a death gratuity of $6,000 to a deceased service member's next-of-kin. The death gratuity is paid for the death in active service for retirees who died within 120 days of retirement as a result of service-connected injury or illness. Parents, brothers or sisters may be provided the gratuity, if designated as next-of-kin by the deceased. The gratuity is paid by the last military command of the deceased. If the beneficiary is not paid automatically, application must be made to the military service concerned.

Find Anyone Receiving VA Benefits

You can call the VA and potentially locate anyone who is receiving disability payments. The Privacy Act of 1974 protects veterans from having their personal information released. The VA can only release the monthly amount paid to the veteran by the VA. But, there is a way to contact veterans through the VA that doesn't jeopardize their privacy.

If you're looking for a veteran than do the following: Call the VA at 1-800-827-1000 and tell the telephone representative that you're trying to locate a veteran and you need a little help. Tell them that you'd like to have the VA forward a piece of mail for you to the veteran you're trying to reach. That way the veteran's privacy is not compromised and you still get your message to the veteran. Write a letter to the VA asking that your letter to the veteran be forwarded. Include a stamped envelope and the letter to the veteran you're trying to reach. You must leave the letter you want forwarded unsealed so a VA representative can read it and make sure it's appropriate. The VA can then forward your letter to the veteran.

CHAPTER 16

▼

VOCATIONAL
REHABILITATION

Education & Job Training for
Service-Connected Disabled Veterans

Vocational Rehabilitation *(chapter 31 benefits)* is a great program set up to really help service-connected disabled veterans. Any veteran who receives a disability rating from the VA should seriously consider education or job training under this program.

The vocational rehabilitation program is designed to provide all services and assistance necessary to enable service-connected disabled veterans to achieve maximum independence in daily living and, to the maximum extent feasible, to become employable and to obtain and maintain suitable employment.

Eligibility

Veterans and service members are eligible for vocational rehabilitation if they meet the three following conditions:

- They suffer a service-connected disability or disabilities in active service that is rated at least 20% disabling. Veterans with a 10% disability also may be found eligible if they have a serious employment handicap.

- They are discharged or released under other than dishonorable conditions or are hospitalized awaiting separation for a service-connected condition at least 20% disabling.

- They need rehabilitation to overcome an employment handicap caused substantially from a service-connected disability.

Periods of Eligibility

A veteran must complete a rehabilitation program within 12 years of a veteran's initial service-connected disability rating from the VA. This period may be extended if a medical condition prevented the veteran from training or if the veteran has a serious employment handicap. The VA may provide counseling, job placement and post-employment services for up to 18 additional months.

Evaluation & Counseling

A comprehensive evaluation to determine your need for rehabilitation services and assistance will be accomplished. The VA will provide you counseling to assist you to develop a rehabilitation plan designed to reach your goals. Counseling remains available throughout the program to assist you with problems that may arise. The VA will arrange evaluation and counseling appointments at convenient times for you. The VA will pay your travel expenses to and from these evaluation and counseling appointments.

Rehabilitation Services

If the VA finds you entitled, you may be authorized up to 48 months or more of rehabilitation services and assistance. You may receive necessary education and training in colleges and universities, vocational schools, apprentice and other on-the-job training establishments, as well as special rehabilitation facilities. The VA will provide counseling; medical care and treatment, employment assistance to get and hold a job, and other needed services. If a vocational goal is not currently feasible for you, the VA may provide services and assistance needed to improve your capacity for independent living.

Support & Payment

The VA will pay the costs of tuition and required fees, books, supplies and equipment needed for your program. The VA may also pay for special support, such as tutorial assistance, prosthetic devices, lip reading training and signing for the deaf. The VA will help the veteran to pay for at least part of the transportation expenses unique to disabled persons during training or the employment stages of the program. The VA also can provide an advance against future benefit payments for veterans who have financial difficulties during training.

The VA will pay a subsistence allowance each month based on the type of program, rate of attendance, and number of dependents a veteran has. This allowance is received in addition to any compensation or other disability benefits to which you are entitled.

Subsistence or training allowance, for a vocational rehabilitation training program

In some cases, a veteran requires additional education or training to become employable. A subsistence allowance is paid each month during training and is based on the rate of attendance (full-time or part-time), the number of dependents, and the type of training. The charts shown below reflect the rates as of October 1, 2002.

Chapter 31 Subsistence Allowance Rates As of October 1, 2002

The following Subsistence Allowance rates are paid for training in an Institution of Higher Learning

Number of Dependents
Number of Dependents   **Full Time**   **Three Quarter Time**   **One Half Time**

No Dependents
$454.96
$341.85
$228.74

One Dependent
$564.34
$423.87
$283.41

Two Dependents
$665.03
$497.21
$333.13

Each Additional Dependent
$48.48
$37.28
$24.87

Subsistence Allowance is paid for full time training only, in the following training programs:

Nonpay or nominal pay on-job training in a federal, state, local, or federally recognized Indian tribe agency; training in the home; vocational course in a rehabilitation facility or sheltered workshop; institutional non-farm cooperative.

Number of Dependents
Full Time

No Dependents
$454.96

One Dependent
$564.34

Two Dependents
$665.03

Each Additional Dependent
$48.48

The following rates are paid for Work Experience programs:

Non-pay or nominal pay work experience in a federal, state, local or federally recognized Indian tribe agency.

Number of Dependents
Full Time
Three Quarter Time
One Half Time

No Dependents
$454.96
$341.85
$228.74

One Dependent
$564.34
$423.87
$283.41

Two Dependents
$665.03
$497.21
$333.13

Each Additional Dependent
$48.48
$37.28
$24.87

Subsistence Allowance is paid for full time training only in the following training programs:

Farm cooperative, apprenticeship, or other on-job training:

Number of Dependents **Full Time**

No Dependents
$397.79

One Dependent
$481.05

Two Dependents
$554.39

Each Additional Dependent
$36.06

Subsistence Allowance is paid at the following rates for combined training programs:

Combination of Institutional and On-Job Training (Full-Time Rate Only):

Number of Dependents
Institutional Greater than one half
On-Job Greater than one half

No Dependents
$454.96
$397.79

One Dependent
$564.34
$481.05

Two Dependents
$665.03
$554.39

Each Additional Dependent
$48.48
$36.06

Subsistence Allowance is paid at the following rates for Non-farm Cooperative Training:

Non-farm Cooperative Institutional Training and Non-farm Cooperative On-Job Training—Full Time Rate Only:

Number of Dependents FT Non-farm Coop/Institutional FT Non-farm Coop/On-Job

No Dependents
$454.96
$397.79

One Dependent
$564.34
$481.05

Two Dependents
$665.03
$554.39

Each Additional Dependent
$48.48
$36.06

Subsistence Allowance is paid at the following rates for Independent Living programs:

A subsistence allowance is paid each month during the period of enrollment in a rehabilitation facility when a veteran is pursuing an approved Independent Living Program plan. Subsistence allowance paid during a period o Independent Living Services is based on rate of pursuit and number of dependents.

Independent Living subsistence allowance rates:

Number of Dependents
Full Time
Three Quarter Time
One Half Time

No Dependents
$454.96
$341.85
$228.74

One Dependent
$564.34
$423.87
$283.41

Two Dependents
$665.03
$497.21
$333.13

Each Additional Dependent
$48.48
$37.28
$24.87

Subsistence Allowance is paid at the following rates for Extended Evaluation programs:

A subsistence allowance is paid each month during the period of enrollment in a rehabilitation facility when a veteran requires this service for the purpose of extended evaluation. Subsistence allowance during a period of extended evaluation is paid based on the rate of attendance and the number of dependents.

Extended Evaluation program subsistence allowance rates:

Number of Dependents
Full Time
Three Quarter Time
One Half Time
One Quarter Time

No Dependents
$454.96
$341.85
$228.74
$114.35

One Dependent
$564.34
$423.87
$283.41
$141.70

Two Dependents
$665.03
$497.21
$333.13
$166.57

Each Additional Dependent
$48.48
$37.28
$24.87
$12.41

| 2003 Vocational Rehabilitation Rates • Monthly Subsistence Allowance | | | |
Type of Training	No Dependent	One Dependent	Two Dependents	Each Additional Dependent
A				
Full-Time	$454.96	564.34	665.03	48.48
3/4-Time	$341.85	423.87	497.21	37.28
1/2-Time	$228.74	283.41	333.13	37.28
B				
Full-Time	$454.96	564.34	665.03	48.48
C				
Full-Time	$397.79	481.0	554.39	36.06
D				
Full-Time	$454.96	564.34	665.03	48.48
3/4-Time	$341.85	423.87	497.21	37.28
1/2-Time	$228.74	283.41	333.13	24.87
1/4-Time	$114.35	141.70	166.57	12.41

*Type of Training

A. Institutional or unpaid work experience in a federal, state or local agency, or a federally recognized Indian tribe agency.

B. Unpaid on-the-job training in a federal, state or local agency, or a federally recognized Indian tribe agency; training in a home; vocational course in a rehabilitation facility or sheltered workshop; independent instructor; institutional non-farm cooperative.

C. Farm cooperative, apprenticeship, on-the-job training, or on-job non-farm cooperative. The VA payment is based on the wage received.

D. Independent living or extended evaluation.

Reestablishing Voc Rehab through SC Disability Increase

Veterans who receive increases in existing service-connected disabilities are eligible for a review of their disability situation for possible entitlement to vocational rehabilitation. Even if the 12-year limit has expired, any increases SC disability is grounds for a review for vocational rehabilitation if the veteran chooses.

VA Work Study Program

The work-study program allows you to perform work for the VA in return for an hourly wage. You are paid tax-free. You may perform outreach services under the supervision of a VA employee, prepare and process VA paperwork, work at a VA medical facility, or other approved activities. You must train at the three-quarter or full-time rate. Contact the Work Study Office at your closest VA regional office at 1-800-827-1000 for an application and more information on the program.

Combination of Benefits

Veterans approved for vocational rehabilitation and work-study will receive disability compensation, vocational rehabilitation subsistence allowance, work-study payments, and their education program paid in full by the government.

CHAPTER 17

▼

GI BILL EDUCATION PROGRAMS

Montgomery GI BILL • VEAP • Survivor's Education

If you do nothing else with your VA benefits, you'd better take advantage of your GI Bill education benefits! Where else can you trade $1200 for $50,000 or MORE! This is the number one reason young men and women should join the military!

The GI Bill has changed over the years but still remains a fixed foundation of military service and an incredible benefit. The options available through the different education and training programs provide students a wide variety of choices and curriculums to pursue in furthering their education. The following *Veterans Unclaimed Benefits* information should help ensure that you have few problems with your benefits.

Contacting the VA with Questions

If you choose to contact the VA with a question or problem, you have two options: You can call the VA Education Office at 1-888-442-4551 or the nearest VA Regional Office at 1-800-827-1000. Be prepared for overloaded, busy phone lines.

VA Education Assistance Programs

There are four VA education assistance programs.

- Montgomery GI Bill-Active Duty Educational Assistance Program, (Includes the Vietnam Era Education Program (Chapter 34) now combined with Chapter 30)   • *Chapter 30*

- Post-Vietnam Era Veterans' Educational Assistance Program (VEAP)   • *Chapter 32*

- Montgomery GI Bill-Selected Reserve Education Assistance Program   • *Chapter 1606*

- Survivors' and Dependents' Educational Assistance Program   • *Chapter 35*

Payment Information—All Programs

Depending on the education program you're eligible for, and the type of training you take, monthly VA education payments will differ. You will see different monthly rates on the following pages.

Basic Information
Schools and Programs of Education

The GI Bill is an assistance program. It is not intended to fully pay for a student's education. It is designed as a supplement to help students in any way needed. Once a student enrolls and pays for their tuition and other costs up front, out of their own pocket, the VA will send GI Bill payments to the veteran to use for whatever purpose the student deems necessary; i.e. rent, groceries, car expenses, anything!

The VA will only pay education assistance benefits to a student, if the student is in an approved program at an approved school or training facility and is attending satisfactorily.

Approved schools and programs throughout the United States will vary. The U.S. Department of Veterans Affairs (VA) usually relies on the State Department of Education's criteria for authorizing which schools and programs will be approved for VA purposes in any particular state. If the state you reside in recognizes the school or program for official education purposes than the VA should also. You can ask the school if it is VA approved or call VA at 1-800-827-1000 to find out. If the school isn't sure if it is VA approved, than it's probably not approved. To apply for VA approval the school or program official should contact the closest Federal VA Education Liaison Representative at 1-800-827-1000 to learn how to become VA approved.

Larger schools in the United States use a computer based program called VA Cert to certify a students status electronically to the VA for enrollment and student status purposes. This is necessary to help students receive correct payment.

Every approved school or training facility has a designated VA certifying official(s) commonly referred to as "vet clerks". Designated certifying officials are the only persons who can sign enrollment paperwork.

Time Limits

All education programs except the Vocational Rehabilitation Program have a 10-year time limit in which to use the benefit from your date of initial eligibility.

If you did not use your education benefits within the 10-year period your benefits have expired and cannot be used. In *very rare* circumstances, the 10-year period can be extended if you have a very good reason why you were not able to utilize the benefit during the 10 years. You have to write the VA and explain in detail why you couldn't use your benefits in the time allotted. You also must provide documentation regarding the reason, i.e. medical condition, hospital records, religious mission, etc.

Uncommon Sense

Once you start receiving benefits, you must maintain satisfactory attendance, conduct, and progress. If you do not meet the standards set by your school, the school's veterans official must notify the VA. The VA will stop your benefits if the school reports problems with any of the above. Notify the veterans' clerk at the school and the federal VA at 1-800-827-1000 if any of the following changes:

• Address changes

• Program changes

• Enrollment changes

• Place of training changes

• Attendance changes

Types of Training for All Programs (Chapter 30, 35, & 1606)

• Undergraduate and Graduate Training (Institutions of Higher Learning (IHLs) & State, Private, and community colleges and universities)

• Non-College Degree (NCD)/Certificate Programs

• Business, Technical or Vocational Schools

• Apprenticeship/On-the-Job (OJT) Training

• Cooperative Training

• Flight Training

- Independent Study Programs

- Foreign Training (Only programs leading to a college degree)

- Correspondence Courses Remedial, Deficiency, and Refresher Courses

School/Program Verification

For IHLs, NCD and certificate programs, business, technical, or vocational schools, cooperative training, and independent study programs, you should check with the school first to see if they are VA approved. You can also call the VA regional office in the state the school resides.

How To Apply

All students must apply for education benefits through the appropriate office. You can always apply through the veteran's clerk at your school. The veteran's clerk should know where the applications are to be sent. Use the following forms:

Chapter 30	•	VA Form 22-1990
Chapter 1606	•	VA Form 22-1990
Chapter 35	•	VA Form 22-5490

Chapter 30 and 1606 applications need to be mailed with a copy of DD214 to the VA Regional Education Center for your state. Chapter 35 applications need to mailed to the VA Regional Office having the veterans claim file.

Receiving Monthly Payments

After choosing a school and submitting your application to VA, ask the certifying official at your school to complete an enrollment certification. The certifying official will send the enrollment certification to the appropriate VA regional education office. VA will process the form and determine your eligibility to benefits.

College or University Training

If you are taking courses leading to a degree at a college or university, tax-free monthly payments are made to students after each month of training/attendance on the first day of the following month. EX: Payment received on June 1 is for the month of May. Benefit payments are based on training time (full-time, 3/4 time, 1/2 time, or less than 1/2 time). Several factors affect training time (credit or clock hour program, accelerated or non-accelerated, etc).

Vocational—Technical—Business School

If you are in a high school program or a certificate or diploma program at a business, technical, or vocational school, you will not receive payment until you have completed a verification form showing your attendance. You will receive a form each month and you must complete and return it to the appropriate VA regional office. After processing, VA will release a check.

Apprentice—OJT Program

If you are in an apprenticeship or on-job-training program, you will receive a form to report the hours worked each month. Sign the form and give it to the certifying official for the company or union. The certifying official must complete the form and send it to the appropriate VA regional office. After processing, VA will release a check.

Correspondence School

If you are taking a correspondence course, you will receive a form on which you should show the number of lessons you completed that quarter, i.e., March, June, September, and December. Send the form to the school for certification of the number of lessons serviced during the quarter. The school will send the form to the appropriate VA regional office. After processing, VA will release a check. Payments are based upon the number of lessons serviced by the school.

Flight School

VA sends flight schools a supply of blank monthly certification of flight training forms. The school completes the form by entering the number of hours, the hourly rate, and the total charges for flight training received during the month. Review and sign the completed form and send it to the appropriate VA regional office. After processing, VA will release a check.

VERIFICATION OF ENROLLMENT

Before payment can be made, a monthly verification of enrollment must take place on most programs. Depending on the type of training and the program the student is under, monthly attendance verification differs. Some programs and training types require the student to return a form to the VA or call in verification.

Advance Payments

Approved veterans can receive up to 2 months of education benefits in advance if requested. The school must be approved for advance pay, the student must be enrolled for at least 1/2 time training, and the request has to be submitted to the VA 30-120 days before the beginning date. Checks are sent to the school payable to the student.

6-Credit Hour Exclusion

You are entitled to an automatic 6-credit exclusion regarding your education benefits. What this means is, the first time (and only the first time) you change or reduce your enrollment to fewer credits by dropping a class or two, the VA will still pay you the maximum amount possible up to 6 credits for the whole term. This is automatic; you won't be notified, just paid. The first time this happens to many students they call the VA because they think they've been overpaid. The exclusion covers any change up to 6 credits. If you drop only 3 credits, you're paid for 3, not 6. If you drop 9 credits, you're paid for 6. This will also reduce your overall entitlement, so pay attention and make sure you have enough entitlement left when it comes time to graduate.

PROGRAM AND PAYMENT INFORMATION
CHAPTER 30 • Montgomery GI Bill—Active Duty

The Montgomery GI Bill—Active Duty (Chapter 30) program provides up to 36 months of educational benefits. You must have an honorable discharge and had your military pay reduced by $1200. The chapter 30 program does not grant a refund to veterans, only to designated family members in the case of a service person's death.

In general, if you serve your full enlistment on active duty and separate with an honorable discharge you will not have any problems receiving your benefits.

The following monthly payments under chapter 30 covers IHLs (colleges & universities), NCD courses, certificate programs, and business, technical, or vocational schools:

Effective 10-01-2003

3 OR MORE YEARS OF SERVICE		LESS THAN 3 YEARS SERVICE
Full-time	$985	$800
3/4 time	$738.75	$600
1/2 time	$492.50	$400
1/4 time	$246.25	$200

- Less than 1/2 time training pays: Tuition and fees not to exceed the 1/2 time rate.

- Quarter-time or less pays: Tuition and fees, not to exceed the 1/4 full-time rate.

Non-Receipt of Payment

If you do not receive your education payment by the fifth of the month than it's very possible your attendance was not verified. You can do this quickly by calling the VA and requesting it be processed immediately.

Kicker—Additional Money!

An additional amount, called a kicker, may be added to the monthly benefit for some veterans who served with specific Military Occupation Specialties (MOS). The monthly kicker ranges up to $1000 monthly in addition to your Montgomery GI Bill Chapter 30 benefits.

Extra Chapter 30 Money!

Under chapter 30, you have 36 months of original entitlement. In using your chapter 30 you may attend school full-time, three-quarter time, or half time for any given period. Changes in your attendance will change your remaining entitlement in different increments. After 2 years of school, you may have 20 months and 14 days of entitlement remaining. There is a little rule the VA has that says if a student has enough entitlement to start a term or semester; the VA will pay the student for the whole term or semester. What this means is that you could have only 1 day of GI Bill entitlement left to be utilized, and get paid for the whole term or semester. All you need is 1 day to start the term; if you organize your schedule right it could mean a possible extra $2900 or more in your pocket to help you with expenses.

Chapter 34/30—Vietnam Era Eligible

A military retiree who entered the service (or agreed to delayed entry) before 01/10/77 and was eligible to receive chapter 34 benefits on 12/31/89 may receive chapter 30 benefits. No $1200 contribution is required.

The following monthly payments under chapter 34/30 covers IHLs, NCD courses, certificate programs, and business, technical, or vocational schools:

Effective 10-01-03

	Single Veterans	One Dependent	Two Dependents
Full-time	$1173.00	$1209.00	$1240.00
3/4 time	$880.25	$906.75	$930.25
1/2 time	$586.50	$604.50	$620.00

Chapter 32 • VEAP—ONLY PROGRAM WITH REFUND!

Individuals must have initially entered active duty between 01/01/77 and 07/01/85 and enrolled and contributed to VEAP before 04/01/87. Veterans must have an *other than dishonorable discharge*. Many VEAP veterans separated from active duty after 09/30/90 had the opportunity to convert from chapter 32 to chapter 30. Veterans contributed up to $2700 with a 2 for 1 match from the VA ($8100 maximum). Additional kicker may have been made by the military.

VEAP payments vary depending on the type of training or education and the amount of the contribution of the veteran. Call the VA and ask what your amount would be. Your payment information should be set up on the VA computer system.

Benefit entitlement is 1 to 36 months depending on the number of monthly contributions. You have 10 years from your release from active duty to use VEAP benefits. If there is entitlement not used after the 10-year period, your portion remaining can be refunded but you must apply for the refund, it is not automatic!

Get Your Refund!

Use VA Form 4-5281. Contact the VA at 1-800-827-1000 and ask the Rep to send you the form. Read the instructions carefully, you must have your signature verified by an authorized person. There is no time limit on filing for a refund.

Chapter 1606 • Montgomery GI Bill Selected Reserve

Chapter 1606 is an educational program with 36 months of full-time entitlement for active members of the selected reserve. Selected Reserve components of the Ready Reserve include the Army Reserve, Naval Reserve, Air Force Reserve, Marine Corps Reserve, Coast Guard Reserve, Army National Guard, and Air National Guard. Chapter 1606 eligibility is determined by the Department of Defense (DOD) or by the Department of Transportation (Coast Guard), not by the VA. Basic eligibility requires a 6-year obligation to serve in the Selected Reserve and satisfactory participation in required Selected Reserve training.

The following monthly payments under chapter 1606 covers IHLs, NCD courses, certificate programs, and business, technical, or vocational schools:

Effective 10-01-02

Full-time	**$276**
3/4 time	**$207**
1/2 time	**$137**
<1/2 TIME	**$69**

APPRENTICESHIP AND OJT

Education benefits can be paid for apprenticeship and OJT (on-job-training) under chapters 30, 32, 35, and 1606. Make sure VA approves the training you want to take. A trainee must work 120 or more hours during a month to be paid the full VA training allowance for that month.

Rates:

The following are monthly rates for apprenticeship and OJT training:

- **Chapter 30:** Effective 10-01-03, individuals who complete a 3-year obligation, or complete 2 years on active duty and sign up for 4 years in the Selected Reserve, receive $675 the first 6 months, $495 the second 6 months, and $315 the remainder of the program. Individuals who complete a 2-year obligation receive $549 the first 6 months, $402.60 the second 6 months, and $256.20 the remainder of the program.

- **Chapter 32:** Benefits vary, but the most common full-time rate is $225 per month. Trainees are paid 75% of their full-time rate the first 6 months, 55% the second 6 months, and 35% the remainder of the program. If you don't know your full-time rate, call the VA and ask.

- **Chapter 35**: $495 the first 6 months, $370 the second 6 months, $246 the third 6 months, and $124 the remainder of the program.

- **Chapter 1606**: Effective 10-01-03, $207 the first 6 months, $151.80 the second 6 months, and $96.60 the remainder of the program.

Flight Training

VA benefits reimburse 60% of actual charges, not to exceed approved rates. Education benefits are paid for flight training at approved flight schools under chapters 30, 32, and 1606. Check with your VA regional office for a list of approved flight schools. Make sure the school is approved before you commit to lessons and payments.

Correspondence Schooling

Correspondence training benefits reimburse a student a percentage of a completed lesson's cost. Lessons are reimbursed at the following rates:

- Chapter 30—55%

- Chapter 32—100%

- Chapter 1606—55%

- Chapter 35—Entitlement charged at one month for each $680 paid. Remember, you're entitled to 45 months of benefits. That's a total of $30,600 of benefit.

Schools approved for correspondence training change periodically. The easiest way to find out if your school is approved is to call the school and ask to speak with the person who handles veterans' certifications. You may also call 1-888-442-4551 and ask an education case manager.

If the program is not approved you should contact the State Approving Agency (SAA) of the state in which the school is located. For a listing of all SAA's call 1-888-442-4551.

Tutorial Assistance

If you're having trouble with a course and need a tutor, you may qualify for tutorial assistance. Tutorial assistance is available if you are receiving VA educational assistance at the half-time or more rate and have a deficiency in a subject making tutoring necessary. You can be reimbursed up to $100 per month. The maximum allowed is $1200 total. There is no entitlement charge for the first $600 under chapters 30, 32, and 1606. There is not an entitlement charge at all under chapter 35. To apply, complete VA Form 22-1990t and give it to the certifying official in the office handling VA paperwork at your school.

Qualify for 48 Months of Benefits

You may receive a maximum of 48 months of education benefits by combining more than one VA education program. For example, you could use all 36 months of your chapter 30 benefits and then use 12 months under chapter 1606 if you have a 6-year commitment in the Selected Reserve.

Overpayment of Benefits

An overpayment is an incorrect benefit payment that is more than the amount to which you are entitled. The VA takes immediate and aggressive action to recover overpayments. You have the right to request a waiver of overpayment or verification that the amount is correct. If an overpayment is not repaid or waived, the VA may add interest and collection fees to your debt and take one of the following actions to recover the debt:

• Withhold future benefits to apply to your debt

• Refer your debt to a private collection agency

• Recover the debt from your federal income tax refund

• Recover the debt form your salary if you are a federal employee

• File a lawsuit in federal court to collect the debt

• Withhold approval of a VA home loan guarantee

Be Responsible

Bottom line—be responsible. If you have a debt, pay it in a timely manner. If you agree with and take responsibility for the debt, pay the debt back in full immediately if you can. If not, call the VA Debt Management Center (DMC) at 1-800-827-0648 and arrange a payment plan. Tell them what you can afford to pay monthly towards the debt. It may be easiest to withhold future education payments if you're continuing your education. If not, call the DMC.

VA Work Study Program

The work-study program allows you to perform work for the VA in return for an hourly wage. You are paid tax-free. This program is available to any student receiving VA education benefits that is attending school three-quarter time or more. An individual working under this program may work at the school veterans' office, VA Regional Office, VA Medical Facilities, or at approved State employment offices. Work-study students are paid at either the state or Federal minimum wage, which ever is greater. If you have questions on this program contact the Work Study Office at your closest VA regional office at 1-800-827-1000 for an application and for more information on the program contact the VA Regional Education Office at 1-888-442-4551.

Note: If you have an education overpayment, you may be able to participate in work-study in order to reduce or eliminate your overpayment.

Foreign Country Education

The VA may approve programs offered by foreign institutions of higher learning that lead to an associate or higher degree, or the equivalent. The VA Central Office (VACO) in Washington, DC approves foreign programs. Before enrolling at a foreign school, first determine if the VA approves the course or program. Send an Email to **co223b@vba.va.gov**, or you can fax your request to: (202) 275-2636.

You can also write VACO for information. Students must clearly identify the school and program you're interested in. VACO will tell you if it's approved. If it isn't, VACO will explain how to get it approved. VACO's mailing address is:

Director, Educational Service (225A)
VA Central Office

810 Vermont Avenue NW
Washington, DC 20420

CHAPTER 35 • SURVIVORS' AND DEPENDENTS EDUCATIONAL ASSISTANCE PROGRAM

This program provides education and training opportunities to eligible dependents of certain veterans. There is a full range of educational programs to take advantage of; this information will help you understand how the program works and basic eligibility rules. If you're eligible for DIC than you'll be eligible for Chapter 35 education benefits.

Eligibility

Commonly referred to as Chapter 35 benefits, the Survivors' and Dependents Educational Assistance Program provides financial aid for the education of dependent sons, daughters, and spouses of:

- Veterans who die of, or are permanently and totally disabled as the result of, a service-connected disability. The disability must arise out of active service in the Armed Forces.

- Veterans who died from any cause while such service-connected disability was in existence.

- Service persons missing in action or captured in line of duty by a hostile force.

- Service persons forcible detained or interned in line of duty by a foreign government or power.

Entitlement

Eligible spouses and dependent children may be entitled to receive up to 45 months of education benefits. You may receive a maximum of 48 months of benefits under more than one VA education program. For example, if you used 36 months of your own benefits as a veteran, and are eligible as a dependent, you could have 12 more months to use.

Time Limits on Eligibility

Spouses: Benefits end 10 years from the date the VA finds you eligible or from the date of death of the veteran. In certain instances, the VA can grant an extension of this period. This is possible if a physical or mental disability prevented you from using some portion of your education benefits. The physical or mental disability must occur during your 10-year period of eligibility.

Children: To receive benefits of attending school or job training under the program, you must be between the ages of 18 and 26. In certain instances, it is possible to begin before 18 and to continue after age 26. Marriage of a child is not a bar to this benefit. It's possible to receive an extension to your 31st birthday for extenuating circumstances (i.e. joining the military, religious mission, etc.).

Approved Training & Education Programs

You may receive benefits for a wide variety of training. A State agency or VA must approve each program offered by a school or a company. If you want to know if you can receive benefits for a particular program, contact the VA regional office in the State where you will train or attend school. Here are some types of training that are approved through the VA.

- Degree programs (associate, bachelor, master, and doctorate) through an approved college or university.

- Courses leading to a certificate or diploma from business, technical, or vocational schools.

- Apprenticeship or job training programs offered by a company or a union.

- Spouses can take correspondence courses.

- Farm cooperative courses.

- Foreign education programs only if leading to a college degree.

- Secondary school programs if you are not a high school graduate.

- Secondary school deficiency or remedial courses to qualify for admission to an educational institution.

Chapter 35 Payments

Education payments vary depending on what type of training you're taking. The most common is college or university schooling. You receive payments on the first of every month. All payments are tax-free.

Training Time	Monthly Rate
Full-Time	$680
Three-Quarter	$511
One-Half	$340

If you are training less than half-time, you receive the lesser of:

- The monthly rate based on the tuition and fees for course(s); or

- $340 for less than one-half time or $170 for one-quarter time.

Counseling Services

An eligible dependent can receive counseling services from the VA for the purpose of assisting the dependent in selecting an educational or vocational objective, developing a plan to achieve that objective, and overcoming any obstacles of successful completion of educational or vocational objective(s). Contact the Vocational Rehabilitation Office at 1-800-827-1000.

Education Loans for Surviving Spouses

Loans are available to spouses who qualify for educational assistance. Spouses who have passed their 10-year period of eligibility may be eligible for an educational loan. During the first two years after the end of their eligibility period, they may borrow up to $2,500 per academic year to continue a full-time course leading to a college degree or to a professional or vocational objective that requires at least 6 months to complete. The VA may waive the six-month requirement. Loans are based on financial need. Contact the Vocational Rehabilitation Office at your nearest VA regional office.

RESTORED ENTITLEMENT PROGRAM FOR SURVIVORS (REPS) • VERY IMPORTANT PROGRAM!

REPS is not a VA education program, but it is based on school attendance of certain eligible surviving children of deceased veterans. This program is administered and paid by the VA, using entitlement criteria from the Social Security Administration, and funded by the Department of Defense.

In 1981, certain Social Security benefits for survivors were terminated through Public Law (PL) 97-35. At the time, Senator Dan Quayle helped pass an amendment that replaced most of the lost or reduced benefits. This concerned surviving spouses and children of members and former members of the armed forces who died on active duty before August 13, 1981, or died as a result of a service-connected disability that was incurred or aggravated prior to August 13, 1981.

This is a little confusing, but it is an important benefit. Any veteran, who currently has a service-connected condition that began prior to August 13, 1981, and has dependents, should be aware. A surviving spouse and any dependent children (between 18-22 years old) will be eligible for REPS benefits if they meet program criteria, and if the veteran died from his service-connected condition that was acknowledged by VA prior to August 13, 1981.

This is important because it could mean a lot of extra money for eligible survivors. The monthly benefits are paid on the first of the month. Benefit amounts range anywhere from $175 to $950 per month depending on the circumstances. Claims are processed at the VA regional office in St. Louis, Missouri.

Eligible surviving spouses can receive REPS payments for dependent children in their care. The youngest child in their care must be between the ages of sixteen and eighteen. A surviving spouse becomes potentially eligible for REPS for their child when their child reaches age 16.

Eligible surviving school children of deceased veterans need to be at least 18 years old, unmarried and enrolled in a post secondary school full-time.

A student can receive Chapter 35 and REPS at the same time. A student can also take advantage of tax-free work-study benefits, as well. Apply through your closest VA regional office using VA Form 21-8924. Don't be surprised if there is some confusion when you ask about REPS benefits.

CHAPTER 18

▼

VA HOME LOAN
The Basics of Using a VA Guaranteed Home Loan

The main purpose of the VA home loan program is to help veterans finance the purchase of homes with favorable loan terms and at a rate of interest that is usually lower than the rate charged on other types of mortgage loans.

This is a reusable benefit and there is no time limit. Veterans can buy several homes using VA guaranties, but can only own one at a time.

VA Guarantee

VA guaranteed loans are made by a lender such as a mortgage company, savings and loan association, bank, or credit union. VA's guaranty on the loan protects the lender against loss if the payments are not made, and is intended to encourage the lender to offer veterans loans with more favorable terms. The amount of guaranty on the loan depends on the loan amount and whether the veteran used some entitlement previously. With the current maximum guaranty, a veteran who hasn't previously used the benefit may be able to obtain a VA loan up to $203,000 depending on the borrower's income level and the appraised value of the property.

Advantages of VA Home Loans

• No down payment is required in most cases.

• Loan maximum may be up to 100 percent of the VA established reasonable value of the property, however, loans generally may not exceed $203,000.

• Flexibility of negotiating interest rates with the lender.

• No monthly mortgage insurance premium to pay.

• Limitation on buyer's closing costs.

• An appraisal that informs the buyer of property value.

• Thirty-year loans with a choice of repayment plans: Fixed payments, graduated payments, or growing equity mortgage payments.

• An assumable mortgage, subject to VA approval of the assumer's credit.

• Right to prepay the loan without penalty.

• VA performs personal loan servicing and offers financial counseling to help veterans avoid losing their homes during temporary financial difficulties.

Requirements for VA Loan Approval

To get a VA loan, the law requires that:

- You must be an eligible veteran who has available home loan entitlement.

- The loan must be for an eligible purpose.

- You must occupy or intend to occupy the property as your home within a reasonable period of time after closing the loan.

- You must have enough income to meet the new mortgage payments on the loan, cover the costs of owning a home, take care of other obligations and expenses, and still have enough income left over for family support; and

- You must have a good credit record.

Steps to A VA Home Loan

- Apply for a Certificate of Eligibility. This certificate is needed by the lender to prove you're an eligible veteran. Contact the VA at 1-800-827-1000 for an application (VA Form 26-1880). You'll have to send the form and a copy of your discharge paper to a VA loan office for processing. The VA will tell you which loan office to send everything to.

- Choose a Lender. Contact a lender by phone and ask about getting pre-qualified for a home loan. The lender will tell you what documents you need to provide so they can tell you how much money they'll lend you for a house. Once you have this loan figure you can "shop around" for a house in your price range.

- Decide on a home and sign a purchase agreement.

- Order an appraisal from the VA (usually this is done by the lender). Most VA regional offices offer a "speed-up" telephone appraisal system. Call the VA at 1-800-827-1000 for details. If the lender is authorized by VA to do automatic processing, upon receipt of the

VA appraised value determination, the loan can be approved and closed without waiting for VA's review of the credit application. For loans that must first be approved by the VA, the lender will send the application to the local VA office, which will notify the lender of its decision.

- Close the loan and move in.

What Can A VA Loan Be Used For?

1. To buy a home.

2. To buy a townhouse or condominium unit in a VA-approved project.

3. To build a home.

4. To repair, alter, or improve a home.

5. To simultaneously purchase and improve a home.

6. To improve a home through installment of a solar heating and/or cooling system or other energy efficient improvements.

7. To refinance an existing home loan.

8. To refinance an existing home loan to reduce the interest rate and add energy efficient improvements.

9. To buy a manufactured (mobile) home and/or lot.

10. To buy and improve a lot on which to place a manufactured home which you already own and occupy.

11. To refinance a manufactured home loan in order to acquire a lot.

$6000 to Improve A Home

Improve a home by installing energy-related features such as solar or heating/cooling systems, water heaters, insulation, weather-stripping/caulking, storm windows/doors or other energy efficient improvements approved by the lender and the VA. These added features may be added with the purchase of an existing dwelling or by refinancing a home owned and occupied by the veteran. A loan can be increased up to $3000 based on documented costs or up to $6000 if the increase in the mortgage payment is offset by the expected reduction in utility costs. A refinancing loan may not exceed 90 percent of the appraised value plus the costs of the improvements.

Costs of Obtaining a VA Loan

Funding Fee—

- All veterans must pay a basic funding fee of 2.0 percent to the VA except service connected disabled veterans rated 10% or higher. A down payment of 5 percent or more will reduce the fee to 1.5 percent and a 10 percent down payment will reduce it to 1.25 percent.

- All eligible Reserve/National Guard individuals must pay a funding fee of 2.75 percent. A down payment of 5 percent or more will reduce the fee to 2.25 percent and a 10 percent down payment will reduce it to 2.0 percent.

- The funding fee for loans to refinance an existing VA home loan with a new VA home loan to lower the existing interest rate is 0.5 percent.

- Veterans who are using entitlement for a second or subsequent time who do not make a down payment of at least 5 percent are charged a funding fee of 3 percent.

Other Closing Costs

The lender may charge reasonable closing costs. These costs may not be included in the loan. The following items may be paid by the veteran purchaser, the seller, or shared. Closing costs may vary among lenders and also throughout the nation because of differing local laws and customs.

- VA appraisal

- Credit report

- Loan origination fee (usually 1 percent of the loan)

- Discount points

- Title search and title insurance

- Recording fees

- State and/or local transfer taxes, if applicable

- Survey

No commissions, brokerage fees or "buyer broker" fees may be charged to the buyer.

Eligibility Requirements

Veterans with active duty service that was not dishonorable, during World War II and later periods are eligible for VA loan benefits.

- World War II, Korean Conflict, and Vietnam Era veterans must have at least 90 days service.

- Peacetime veterans and active duty military personnel must have had more than 180 days' active service for peacetime prior to September 7, 1980, for enlisted, and October 16, 1981, for officers.

- Enlisted veterans with service that began after September 7, 1980, or officers with service beginning after October 16, 1981, must have served at least 2 years in most cases.

- Veterans with compensable service connected disabilities don't have to meet the above criteria.

Persian Gulf War

Reservists and National Guard members who were activated on or after August 2, 1990, served at least 90 days and were discharged honorably are eligible.

Selected Reservists and National Guard

Members of the selected Reserve and National Guard who have completed 6 years of service and have been honorably discharged or are still serving may be eligible. Eligibility for Reserves and National Guard individuals will expire September 30, 2003.

Remaining Entitlement & Restored Entitlement

Veterans who had a VA loan before may still have "remaining entitlement" to use for another VA loan. Over the years changes in the law regarding entitlement have caused confusion for veterans. Contact the VA loan office closest you by calling 1-800-827-1000 for clarification on your individual situation.

Veterans can have previously used entitlement "restored" to purchase another home with a VA loan if:

The property purchased with the prior VA loan has been sold and the loan paid in full, or, a qualified veteran-transferee (buyer) agrees to assume the VA loan and substitute his or her entitlement for the same amount of entitlement originally used by the veteran seller. The entitlement may also be restored one time only if the veteran has repaid the prior VA loan in full but has not disposed of the property purchased with the prior VA loan. Remaining entitlement and restoration of entitlement can be requested through the nearest VA office by completing VA Form 26-1880.

HUD/FHA VETERANS PROGRAM

The VA isn't the only Federal agency with home loan guaranties for veterans. The Department of Housing and Urban Development (HUD) has a HUD/FHA veterans program.

Although this isn't a VA program, veterans applying for a HUD/FHA loan need to obtain a special certification of eligibility from a VA regional office. Veterans must obtain VA Form 26-8261(a), "Request for Certificate of Veterans Status." After completing the application and returning it to a VA office, a qualifying veteran will receive a Certificate of Veterans Status. You can then proceed with a HUD/FHA loan.

POW/MIA WIVES

Effective December 24, 1970, the wives of American servicemen who are missing-in-action or are prisoners of war are eligible for GI loans to buy a home. To qualify, the active duty serviceman must be listed by his branch of service for more than 90 days as missing-in-action, captured in the line of duty by a hostile force, or forcibly detained or interned in the line of duty by a foreign government or power.

Only one loan may be granted under this provision. If not used, entitlement terminates automatically when the serviceman is no longer officially listed in one of the above categories. Use of a wive's entitlement won't reduce the veteran's entitlement.

CHAPTER 19

▼

LIFE INSURANCE
SGLI • VGLI • RH Disabled • VMLI • Hoax

Life insurance should be a part of everyone's financial portfolio, even if it's your entire portfolio. Don't leave your family struggling to survive financially in the untimely event of your death. Make sure your family can make a comfortable transition if anything ever happens to you. It's very important. At the very least, you should make sure you have a "burial" policy so your spouse or family isn't paying for a funeral they can't afford.

There are four VA life insurance programs available to individuals immediately leaving the military. Two regular and two disabled insurance programs are currently open for new policyholders. The programs aren't free; you're required to pay premiums to keep your coverage current. Like most of the other VA benefits covered in this book, VA life insurance programs have changed many times.

This is one area where calling the VA for information may prove to be beneficial. You can contact the VA Insurance Center in Philadelphia at 1-800-669-8477. You may have to wait on hold but the VA insurance representatives are best suited to help you in understanding what

VA life insurance means to you. You also may want to contact a VA insurance representative when you're discussing your insurance needs with a private sector company so a thorough comparison can be made regarding life insurance programs and policies. Costs of life insurance premiums are <u>very</u> competitive.

Important

When checking into whether or not to buy VA life insurance, check with a life insurance professional first. They can help you compare policies and prices. Much of the time, an insurance representative will help guide you to the right kind of policy regardless of who provides it. If you don't know whom to contact, start with the company or broker that handles your car insurance *(if you're satisfied with the service)*, or ask a good friend what company or broker they use. *Much of the time, private life insurance policies are less expensive than VA Government Life Insurance. Do your homework before you purchase the first policy you see.*

Insurance Programs Currently Available

- Service members' Group Life Insurance (SGLI)

- Veterans Group Life Insurance (VGLI)

- Service Disabled Veterans Insurance RH (SDVI)

- Veterans Mortgage Life Insurance (VMLI)

Service members group life insurance (SGLI)

SGLI coverage is automatically insured for $200,000 for the following groups:

- Active duty members of the Army, Navy, Air Force, Marines and Coast Guard

- Commissioned members of the National Oceanic and Atmospheric Administration

- Commissioned members of the Public Health Service

- Cadets and midshipmen of the service academies

- Members, cadets and midshipmen of the ROTC while engaged in authorized training

- Members of the Ready Reserves

- Reservists and National Guardsmen who've completed 20 years towards their military retirement but haven't started receiving retired pay yet. Retired payments begin on the service member's 60th birthday.

Individuals may elect to be covered for a lesser amount or not to be covered at all. Part-time coverage may be provided to members of the Reserves who do not qualify for full-time coverage. Premiums are deducted automatically from an individual's pay or are collected by the individual's service.

Some reservists and National Guardsmen are covered by SGLI part-time if they are on official military orders for less than 31 days on active duty or active duty for training. Coverage includes travel to and from training sites.

Rates

SGLI coverage is available in increments of $10,000 up to $200,000. The current monthly cost or rate is ninety cents per each $10,000 in coverage. A $200,000 policy would cost you $18.00 per month. This is where you shop around for private term policies. Make sure you compare like policies. Use the exact same coverage criteria when comparing policies.

Dual Coverage

Veterans sometimes meet eligibility criteria for insurance coverage under SGLI and VGLI due to a changing status from active duty to ready reserve to inactive ready reserve and back again. Combined coverage cannot exceed $200,000.

Beneficiaries

A beneficiary can be any person, firm, corporation, veteran's estate, or any legal entity. Make sure you complete the required forms to avoid legal complications.

Application

When people become eligible for SGLI, they are automatically enrolled at $100,000 of coverage. To obtain more or less coverage, or no coverage, you have to request it. Contact the nearest military personnel office to get the forms to change coverage amounts.

VETERANS GROUP LIFE INSURANCE (VGLI)

SGLI may be converted to VGLI, which is renewable five-year term coverage. This program is administered by the Office of Sevicemembers' Group Life Insurance (OSGLI), 213 Washington St., Newark, NJ 07102. VGLI is available to:

- Individuals with full-time SGLI coverage upon release from active duty or the Reserves

- Individuals with part-time SGLI coverage who incur a disability or aggravate a preexisting disability during a reserve period which renders them uninsurable at standard premium rates

- Members of the Individual Ready Reserve and Inactive National Guard

Individuals entitled to SGLI coverage can convert to VGLI by submitting the premium within 120 days of separating from active duty or the reserves. After 121 days, the individual may be granted VGLI provided initial premium and evidence of insurability are submitted with one year after termination of the individual's SGLI coverage. Individuals with full-time SGLI coverage who are totally eligible for VGLI may purchase the insurance while remaining totally disabled up to one year following separation.

Coverage

Coverage can be for as little as $10,000, as much as $200,000; or any amount in between. In between coverage amounts must be in $10,000 increments. Some veterans may face restrictions on the amount of coverage they can obtain. Premiums must be paid to keep the policy current. Premiums are determined by the age of the veteran and the amount of coverage. Participants who choose to pay in one lump sum each year receive a discount.

Beneficiaries

A beneficiary can be any person, firm, corporation, veteran's estate, or any legal entity. Make sure you complete the required forms to avoid legal complications.

Application

Veterans must apply for VGLI coverage. Note the application time limits and requirements:

- Apply within 120 days after discharge—You qualify easily by paying your first premium.

- Apply after 120 days but within one year of discharge by paying your first premium and possibly undergoing an examination.

Veterans should receive the proper forms to convert from SGLI to VGLI from their military personnel office or you can call the VA insurance office at 1-800-669-8477.

SERVICE DISABLED VETERANS INSURANCE • RH INSURANCE

This insurance is limited to veterans who were discharged from military service after April 24, 1951. A veteran who has a service-connected disability but is otherwise in good health may apply to the VA for up to $10,000 in life insurance coverage at standard rates within two years from the date the VA grants service-connection for that disability.

Veterans who are totally disabled may apply for a waiver of premiums. Additional coverage up to $20,000 is available for veterans eligible for this waiver. Premiums cannot be waived on the additional insurance.

Application

Apply by calling your closest VA regional office at 1-800-827-1000 and asking for the application. Or you can call the VA Insurance Center at 1-800-669-8477.

VETERANS MORTGAGE LIFE INSURANCE (VMLI)

VMLI can permit a family to keep its home if a veteran dies before the mortgage has been paid. VMLI is for veterans who have extreme service-connected disabilities. To be eligible for VMLI, a veteran must first be eligible for the VA's Special Adapted Housing program, which provides grants to veterans with severe disabilities requiring extensive modifications to their homes.

The amount of VMLI coverage a veteran can obtain is directly linked to the value of the home the veteran is buying. The insurance policy cannot be worth more than the amount due on the home. The insurance decreases with the decreasing mortgage principal. Monthly premiums are required and are calculated using an unusual formula including the veteran's age, principal due on the home, and the remaining length of the mortgage.

The maximum amount of VMLI available for those veterans granted a specially adapted housing grant is $90,000. If the mortgage is disposed of, VMLI may be obtained on the mortgage of another home.

Application

VMLI coverage is automatic unless you tell the VA you don't want it.

Other Insurance Programs

The U.S. government has offered insurance to its active duty service members and veterans since World War One. Many of the earlier insurance policies provide annual dividends to veterans. None of the government insured life insurance plans, now available to people who are leaving the military or have left the military since the 60's, pays annual dividends.

WWII GI Insurance Hoax

For over three decades an insurance hoax has continued to plague America's veterans. Every year this falsehood resurfaces through many well known and trusted channels. Notices are printed and publicized to inform WWII veterans of an insurance dividend that they must apply for to receive. It promises a possible couple of hundred dollars.

No matter where you read this dividend information or where you hear it, don't believe it. It's absolutely false. Call the VA insurance Center at 1-800-669-8477 to confirm.

CHAPTER 20

▼

VA PENSION
Non-Service Connected Disability Pension

This program is designed for *wartime veterans* and their families in financial need that meet VA disability requirements. As a veteran, you paid for this program a long time ago with your military service to your country during a time of need. This is a way for the country to repay you in your time of need. Please do not assume anything about this program. I've meet people who've flat out told me they weren't eligible for VA pension when in fact they were. Most people for some reason assume that they are not eligible. Even though they don't know the law or the rules surrounding the program. Don't assume anything and read through this whole section before you come to any conclusions. Regardless of your current financial situation, you may need this program now or in the future. This is a great option if an unforeseen illness or accident changes your life and you don't have the financial means to pay for it.

Pay close attention to medical costs and how the VA Pension Program can be manipulated by your medical costs either on a regular basis or just once a year. It almost works like a tax return. If you pay close attention to detail regarding your medical costs, you could possibly receive big financial reimbursements from the VA.

Veterans Disability Pension

VA pension is paid to nonservice-connected disabled war era veterans after evaluating disability level, family income, and out of pocket medical expenses. Acceptable medical expenses reduce income dollar for dollar to bring income down. Once income is below VA levels, the VA will pay pensioners the difference between their adjusted income and the VA limit. High medical expenses such as in-home care, foster care, and nursing home care costs can reduce income down to zero. If your income is zero you're paid the maximum pension rate. Rates are listed on the next page.

Eligibility

There is no age requirement, only the following. You may be eligible *(all must apply)* if:

- You were discharged from service under other than dishonorable conditions,

- You served 90 days or more of active duty with at least 1 day during a war period,

- You have disabilities (not military related) that keep you from working a full-time job,

- Your countable family income is below a yearly limit set by Federal law

- Age 65 and older veterans automatically meet basic disability requirements, only income needs to be evaluated.

War Periods

You must have served at least 90 days on active duty and at least 1 day of duty must have been during one of the wartime periods listed below. It <u>is not</u> a requirement that a veteran served in combat or participated in combat missions, any military service during a war period qualifies.

PERIOD	FROM	TO
Mexican Border War	05-09-1916	04-05-1917
World War I	04-06-1917	11-11-1918
Russian Service (WWI)	04-06-1917	04-01-1920
World War II	12-07-1941	12-31-1946
Korean Conflict	06-27-1950	01-31-1955
Vietnam—In Country Service	02-28-1961	05-07-1975
Vietnam War	08-05-1964	05-07-1975
Persian Gulf War	08-02-1990	Present

Disability Levels

VA pension has 3 disability levels, each with a different income limit and different disability criteria.

You can send in private medical records to establish your disabilities or the VA can examine you to confirm your disabilities.

If you're 65 or older, the VA automatically concedes *basic* disability level. *Housebound* or *aid and attendance* levels need medical documentation.

Basic Pension

Basic level pension is paid based on permanent and total disability as established by the VA.

Example: Veteran diagnosed with a heart condition and doctor advises veteran not to work permanently.

Housebound (HB)

Housebound level pension requires medical documentation showing the veteran is unable to leave their home/residence without the assistance of another person.

Example: Veteran has a stroke and chronic arthritis and needs a walker to get around safely; cannot drive, etc.

Aid & Attendance (A&A)

Aid and attendance level pension requires medical documentation showing that the services of another person are required to help the veteran accomplish the daily chores of living (feeding, dressing, bathing, etc.).

Example: Veteran moves into foster or nursing home; or vet hires in-home care provider for daily assistance.

The examples above are just that, examples. Individual circumstances will vary widely and you won't know if you're eligible for any level of pension unless you apply. The VA rating board will determine if you're eligible. This information gives you an idea of who may qualify.

Income Limits

Listed below are pension income limits for all levels of pension disability. The VA sets annual income limits depending on how many dependents a veteran has. The chart below shows the pension annual limits broken down to monthly amounts.

MONTHLY PENSION INCOME LIMITS

STATUS	BASIC	HB	A & A
Single Veteran	$807	$987	$1347
Veteran with One Dependent	$1057	$1237	$1597

The VA counts family income for pension purposes.

Family Income

All available income less immediate family medical expenses paid out of pocket. The VA counts almost all sources of income to include earned income, wages, other pensions, insurance, Social Security, interest from stocks, bonds, CD's, investment properties, and net worth (not including your primary place of residence). The VA does not count SSI or AFDC as income but it still must be reported on the application.

Medical Expenses

Income can be reduced dollar for dollar by acceptable medical expenses. This may bring your income below the listed limits and the VA can then pay you the difference. This is generally paid in 12 equal monthly payments rounded down to the nearest dollar. If your medical expenses are higher than the limit(s) listed, your income could be considered to be zero and you would be paid the maximum amount listed. The VA is only concerned that you paid for your medical costs yourself and you were not reimbursed by any other source.

Example

A single veteran lives alone on his Social Security of $1000 monthly. He has a stroke and must move into a foster home because he can no longer live alone safely. He can feed himself but cannot bath or dress himself without assistance. The cost of the foster home is $2000 monthly. The veteran is approved for VA pension with aid and attendance (A&A). Because the foster home expense is more than his $1000 Social Security, his income is considered zero and he is paid $1,220 monthly to help cover the cost of his foster home care.

Other issues like receipt of Medicaid, or state veterans foster or nursing care can play a part in whether or not a veteran will receive pension.

Medical expenses are broken down into two groups: 1) <u>Ongoing monthly medical expenses</u> (i.e. Medicare, health insurance, foster home care, nursing home care, in-home care costs, etc.). 2) <u>Annual medical expenses</u> (i.e. prescriptions, doctor visits, ambulance bills, medical equipment bills, lab tests, etc.).

Annual Reimbursement Check

Any annual medical costs that cannot be considered ongoing can be claimed at the end of each year for a reimbursement check. You have to have already paid the medical bill yourself to get reimbursed. *All you do is list all your paid medical expenses on VA Form 21-8416 during the year as you pay them.* At the end of the year you mail in the form and the VA will reimburse you in about 1-4 months. A small deductible is used in calculating your reimbursement check. Single veterans have an *annual* deductible of about $484 and married veterans about $634. Any amount above the deductible will be reimbursed back to you.

Note: You are not eligible for any reimbursement if the VA is paying you the maximum amount payable under your circumstance.

Money for You Even When You're Not Eligible

You could be ineligible for monthly pension because your income is over the limit. Keep track of all your annual medical expenses on VA Form 21-8416 and mail it in at the end of the year to see if it reduces your income enough to receive an annual pension check in the form of a reimbursement. Many people receive thousands of dollars in reimbursement once every year. See the examples below and keep track of all your PAID medical expenses.

Examples of Medical Expenses

The following are *examples* of medical expenses to claim for reimbursement on VA Form 21-8416. List anything you believe is a medical expense, not just what on this list. The VA will determine if your reported medical expense is acceptable for pension purposes. Here are some examples:

Abdominal Supports
Acupuncture
Ambulance Hire
Anesthetist
Arch Supports
Artificial Limbs and Teeth
Back Supports
Braces
Cardiographs
Chiropodist
Chiropractor
Convalescent Home
Crutches
Dental Service
Dentures
Dermatologist
Eyeglasses
Food Prescription
Gynecologist
Hearing Aids & Batteries
Home Health Services
Hospital Expenses
Insulin Treatment
Medical Insurance

Invalid Chair
Lab Tests
Lip Reading Lessons
Neurologist
Nursing Services
Occupational Therapist
Ophthalmologist
Optician
Optometrist
Oral Surgery
Osteopath
Pediatrician
Physical Examinations
Physical Therapy
Podiatrist
Prescriptions and Drugs
Psychiatrist
Psychoanalyst
Psychologist
Psychotherapy
Radium Therapy
Sacroiliac Belt
Speech Therapist
Splints
Medicare
Surgeon
Vaccines
Wheelchairs
X-rays

You can also claim transportation for medical expenses at .20 per mile plus parking and tolls or actual fares for taxis or buses, etc. This is just a partial list. Claim anything you believe is a medical expense.

Does the VA Need My Medical Receipts?

You do not have to send in receipts to prove you paid for the medical expenses listed on your VA Form 21-8416 unless the VA asks for them. If they do ask for them and you don't have them, they can readjust your pension and make you pay back any monies you were paid on a reimbursement. So, keep all your receipts for about 2 or 3 years just in case.

Annual Income Report

Every year your pension income status is reevaluated by mailing you an income form for update. The VA calls the form an Eligibility Verification Report (EVR). Send in your VA Form 21-8416 (Request for Medical Expenses) with your EVR to receive reimbursement.

How to Apply

Send in a FAX claim immediately. Call the VA at 1-800-827-1000 and obtaining the FAX number. Send your FAX stating your filing for NSC Pension (with housebound or aid and attendance benefits if applicable).

You will be sent an application, VA Form 21-526 and possibly supplemental forms depending on your circumstances. Fill them all out and get them back to VA ASAP! Tell the VA representative on the phone to send you a copy of the receipt of the FAX claim.

Reapply at Anytime

If a veteran is not eligible for VA pension for any reason, he or she can reapply over and over again if personal circumstances change (i.e. disability level, income, medical costs, move to nursing home, etc).

CHAPTER 21

▼

SURVIVORS' BENEFITS

Widows • Children • Parents • Compensation
• Pension • Education

There are benefits awarded to eligible survivors of deceased veterans of the armed services regardless of whether the veterans served in peacetime or wartime. Survivors of Reservists and National Guard members who died while on active duty may also be eligible. Benefits vary based upon whether or not the death was service-connected.

Surviving Spouse

The VA has certain rules regarding spouses of veterans. To be considered an eligible surviving spouse, here's what you need to know:

- Widow has to have been married to the veteran (and lived with him/her) for at least one year prior to the veterans death, or for any period of time if a child was born of the marriage or was born to them before the marriage.

- Remarriage constitutes a bar to survivors' benefits.

• Termination of a remarriage means possible reinstatement of survivors' benefits. Reapply as soon as possible after a remarriage ends by death or divorce.

Filing a Claim for Death Benefits

When a veteran dies, the surviving spouse can file for three benefits at the same time. Accrued benefits, Dependency and Indemnity Compensation (DIC), and Death Pension. All benefits are claimed on VA Form 21-534. Depending on what benefit(s) a widow is eligible for depends on what other benefits are available.

Accrued Benefits

Accrued benefits are those, which were due and unpaid at the time of the death of the veteran. Accrued benefits can also be based on claims filed prior to death that were already decided on prior to death but where payment had not been made. By filing VA Form 21-534 you'll be asking for payment of any accrued benefits.

Dependency and Indemnity Compensation (DIC)

DIC monthly payments are paid to widows of veterans whose death was due to a disease or injury incurred or aggravated on active duty or active duty for training; or a disability compensable under laws administered by the VA. Death cannot be due to a veteran's own "willful misconduct", i.e. drunk driving, while committing a crime, etc.

Other dependents possibly eligible include any unmarried children under 18, or between the ages of 18 and 23 if attending a VA-approved school including children at any age who became incapable of self-support before age 18 by reason of physical or mental impairment (medical documentation required); and dependent parent(s). Entitlement to DIC opens up doors to many benefits, we've listed them here.

Entitlement Loss & Resoration

Entitlement to DIC terminates with remarriage. Termination of the remarriage will restore entitlement to DIC. A widow or widower who regains eligibility for DIC upon the termination of remarriage does not regain eligibility for medical care under CHAMPVA.

Application

Apply using VA Form 21-534. Call the VA at 1-800-827-1000 and have the form sent to you. When returning the application to the VA, attach the veteran's death certificate and the hospital summary regarding the veteran's stay at the hospital if the veteran died in a private hospital not under VA contract. If the veteran died in a VA hospital, it will be noted on the death certificate and if records are needed, the VA regional office will obtain them for you. If the veteran did not die in a hospital, then it is not necessary to supply medical records regarding the veteran unless the VA regional office asks for them.

Your application, death certificate, and any necessary medical records will be sent to the VA regional office rating board for a formal decision on whether the death of the veteran was service related. Depending on the evidence, some cases are very quick, while others may take months and months if outside records are needed from the military or some other source.

In general, the VA "quickly" processes claims for widows and dependent children of deceased veterans. Don't be afraid to ask questions or ask to have your claim expedited.

Special Law DIC

There's a special law that allows DIC payments to eligible dependents if the veteran's death was not caused or aggravated by military service but the veteran was collecting other service-connected disability benefits.

Payments are authorized for eligible dependents (as noted above) if the veteran was continuously rated permanently and totally disabled by VA for 10 or more years prior to death; or if rated for less than 10 years, was rated for at least 5 years from date of discharge.

To qualify for this provision, a spouse must have been married to the veteran for at least 1 year prior to death.

Payment of DIC

If a veteran's death occurred on January 1, 1993, or later, qualified spouses receive a fixed monthly amount of $948. The monthly amount increases to $1,185 if the surviving spouse has one dependent child, $1,422 for two children, $1,659 for three, and $1,896 for four children. Annual Congressional increases take place on December 1 of every year and are received in the January 1 payment. The nominal increase is supposed to help keep pace with inflation.

Additional DIC—8 Year Rule

The above figure(s) are increased by $204 monthly if the veteran was rated totally disabled 8 continuous years prior to death and surviving spouse was married to the veteran those same 8 years.

Additional DIC—Housebound Benefit

For a surviving spouse who is permanently confined to their home, but other wise capable of taking care of himself or herself, this housebound benefit adds $113 to monthly DIC payments. This benefit applies to surviving spouses only.

Additional DIC—Aid & Attendance Benefit

For a surviving spouse or parent(s) who are in a nursing home or in the regular need of aid and assistance of another person for active daily functions, this benefit adds $237 monthly to DIC payments. This benefit is received in place of the housebound benefit, not in addition to it.

Survivors Benefit Plan (SBP)

DIC isn't affected by income of surviving spouses except if the surviving spouse is receiving Survivors Benefit Plan (SBP) payments from the military. A surviving spouse will lose one dollar in DIC for every dollar received under the SBP. It is advised that an eligible surviving spouse take DIC over SBP as the VA DIC benefit is not taxable and SBP is taxable.

Month of Death Payment

If you are not entitled to death benefits and the veteran was receiving service-connected disability compensation at the time of his/her death; the surviving spouse is entitled to the veteran's rate for the month of death. You must file a claim for widow's pension in order to receive the month of death payment. Once again, VA Form 21-534 is used.

DIC Payments to Parents and Children

The monthly payment for parents of deceased veterans depends upon their income. There are additional payments for dependent children. To apply for death compensation, parents should use VA Form 21-509.

SURVIVORS' AND DEPENDENTS EDUCATIONAL ASSISTANCE PROGRAM • CHAP 35

This program provides education and training opportunities to eligible dependents of certain veterans. There is a full range of educational programs; this information will help you understand how the program works and basic eligibility rules. If you're eligible for DIC than you'll be eligible for Chapter 35 education benefits.

Eligibility

Commonly referred to as Chapter 35 benefits, the Survivors' and Dependents Educational Assistance Program provides financial aid for the education of dependent sons, daughters, and spouses of:

- Veterans who die of, or are permanently and totally disabled as the result of a service-connected disability. The disability must arise out of active service in the Armed Forces.

- Veterans who died from any cause while such service-connected disability were in existence.

- Service persons missing in action or captured in line of duty by a hostile force.

- Service persons forcibly detained or interned in line of duty by a foreign government or power.

Entitlement

Eligible spouses and dependent children may be entitled to receive up to 45 months of education benefits. You may receive a maximum of 48 months of benefits under more than one VA education program. For example, if you used 36 months of your own benefits as a veteran, and are eligible as a dependent, you could have 12 more months to use.

Time Limits on Eligibility

Spouses: Benefits end 10 years from the date VA finds you eligible or from the date of death of the veteran. In certain instances, VA can grant an extension of this period. This is possible if a physical or mental disability prevented you from using some portion of your education benefits. The physical or mental disability must occur during your 10-year period of eligibility.

Children: To receive benefits for attending school or job training under the program, you must be between the ages of 18 and 26. In certain instances, it is possible to begin before 18 and to continue after age 26. Marriage of a child is not a bar to this benefit. It's possible to receive an extension to your 31st birthday for extenuating circumstances (i.e. joining the military, religious mission, etc.).

Approved Training and Education Programs

You may receive benefits for a wide variety of training. A State agency or VA must approve each program offered by a school or a company. If you want to know if you can receive benefits for a particular program, contact the VA regional office in the State where you will train or attend school. Here are some types of training that are approved through the VA.

- Degree programs (associate, bachelor, master, and doctorate) through an approved college or university.

- Courses leading to a certificate or diploma from business, technical, or vocational schools.

- Apprenticeship or job training programs offered by a company or a union.

- Spouses can take correspondence courses.

- Farm cooperative courses.

- Foreign education programs only if leading to a college degree.

- Secondary school programs if you are not a high school graduate.

- Secondary school deficiency or remedial courses to qualify for admission to an educational institution.

Education Payments

Education payments vary depending on what type of training you're taking. The most common is college or university schooling. You receive payments on the first of every month. All payments are tax-free.

Training Time	Monthly Rate
Full-Time	$680
Three-Quarter	$511
One-Half	$340

If you are training less than half-time, you receive the lessor of:

• The monthly rate based on the tuition and fees for course(s); or

• $340 for less than one-half time or $170 for one-quarter time.

Call the VA at 1-800-827-1000 for information of payments for apprenticeship and job training, cooperative training, and correspondence training under Chapter 35 Educational Assistance.

Tutorial Assistance

You may receive a special allowance up to $1200 for individual tutoring if you're training at the half-time rate or more. To apply, complete VA Form 22-1990t and give it to the certifying official in the office handling VA paperwork at your school.

VA Work Study Program

The work-study program allows you to perform work for the VA in return for an hourly wage. You are paid tax-free. You may perform outreach services under the supervision of a VA employee, prepare and process VA paperwork, work at a VA medical facility, or other approved activities. You must train at the three-quarter or full-time rate. Contact the Work Study Office at your closest VA regional office at 1-800-827-1000 for an application and more information on the program.

Counseling Services

An eligible dependent can receive counseling services from the VA for the purpose of assisting the dependent in selecting an educational or vocational objective, developing a plan to achieve that objective, and overcoming any obstacles standing in the way of successful completion of educational or vocational objective(s). Contact the Vocational Rehabilitation Office at 1-800-827-1000.

Education Loans for Surviving Spouses

Loans are available to spouses who qualify for educational assistance. Spouses who have passed their 10-year period of eligibility may be eligible for an educational loan. During the first two years after the end of their eligibility period, they may borrow up to $2,500 per academic year to continue a full-time course leading to a college degree or to a professional or vocational objective, which requires at least 6 months to complete. The VA may waive the six-month requirement. Loans are based on financial need. Contact the Vocational Rehabilitation Office at your nearest VA regional office.

RESTORED ENTITLEMENT PROGRAM FOR SURVIVORS (REPS)—VERY IMPORTANT PROGRAM!

This program is administered and paid by the VA, using entitlement criteria from the Social Security Administration, and funded by the Department of Defense.

In 1981, certain Social Security benefits for survivors were terminated through Public Law (PL) 97-35. At the time, Senator Dan Quayle helped pass an amendment that replaced most of the lost or reduced benefits. This concerned surviving spouses and children of members and former members of the armed forces who died on active duty before August 13, 1981, or died as a result of a service-connected disability that was incurred or aggravated prior to August 13, 1981.

This is a little confusing but it is an important benefit. Any veteran, who currently has a service-connected condition that began prior to August 13, 1981, and has dependents, needs to be aware of this benefit. A surviving spouse and any dependent children (between 18-22 yrs old) will be eligible for REPS benefits if they meet program criteria, and if the veteran dies from his service-connected condition that was acknowledged by VA prior to August 13, 1981.

This is important because it could mean a lot of extra money for eligible survivors. The monthly benefits are paid on the first of the month. Benefit amounts range anywhere from $175 to $950 per month depending on the circumstances.

Eligible surviving spouses can receive REPS payments for dependent children in their care. The youngest child in their care must be between the ages of sixteen and eighteen. A surviving spouse becomes potentially eligible for REPS for their child when their child reaches age 16.

Eligible surviving school children of deceased veterans need to be at least 18 years old, unmarried and enrolled in an approved post secondary school full-time.

You can receive Chapter 35 and REPS at the same time! Apply through your closest VA regional office using VA Form 21-8924. Don't be surprised if there is some confusion when you ask about REPS benefits. Most VA representatives don't know about it and/or don't understand it. Make them find someone who knows about REPS. If you have to, insist that they call the St. Louis, MO Regional Office for instruction on how to handle a REPS, all applications are processed at the St. Louis VA Regional Office.

CHAMPVA Medical Care

Civilian Health and Medical Program through Veterans Affairs (CHAMPVA) is a health care program for eligible surviving spouses and dependent children of a veteran who died as the result of a service-connected disability or who, at the time of death had a total disability, permanent in nature, resulting from a service-connected disability. Eligible spouses and children may be entitled to medical care coverage under this program provided they are not entitled to care under CHAMPUS or Medicare.

NOTE: A widow or widower who regains eligibility for DIC upon the termination of remarriage does not regain eligibility for medical care under CHAMPVA.

Contact the closest VA Medical Center for application. See the section of VA Facilities on page 111.

Commissary and Exchange Store Privileges

Unremarried surviving spouses of veterans who die from service connected causes are entitled to unlimited exchange and commissary store privileges through U.S. military installations. The VA provides you a statement of eligibility that you provide to the military or a military retired affairs office.

Home Loan Program

If a veteran's death is service-connected, the VA will help a surviving spouse purchase a home under the VA Home Loan Program. The unmarried surviving spouse of a veteran who died in service, or as the result of a service-connected disability, may be eligible to a guaranteed loan made by a private lender. If eligible, the surviving spouse may use the guaranteed loan to purchase, construct or improve a home; to purchase a manufactured home and/or lot; or to refinance existing mortgages or other liens of record on a dwelling owned and occupied by the surviving spouse as his or her home.

Contact the VA at 1-800-827-1000 and complete VA Form 26-1817 to establish eligibility for a home loan as a surviving spouse.

Also, any widow of a veteran who had a VA loan in force at the time of his or her death, is eligible for an Interest Rate Reduction Refinancing Loan (IRRRL) through the VA. Contact the VA about an IRRRL with questions about refinancing your home.

POW/MIA Wives

Effective December 24, 1970, the wives of American servicemen who are missing-in-action or are prisoners of war are eligible for GI loans to buy a home. To qualify, the active duty serviceman must be listed by his branch of service for more than 90 days as missing-in-action, captured in the line of duty by a hostile force, or forcibly detained or interned in the line of duty by a foreign government or power.

Only one loan may be granted under this provision. If not used, entitlement terminates automatically when the serviceman is no longer officially listed in one of the above categories. Use of the wive's entitlement won't reduce the veteran's entitlement.

Burial Benefits

A valid dependent of a deceased veteran is authorized burial at any National Cemetery in any State as long as there is documentation that confirms the status of the dependent spouse or minor child.

WIDOW'S DEATH PENSION

This is one of the three benefits claimed on VA Form 21-534. Widow's Death Pension is a benefit based on financial need and is designed as supplemental income to whatever income a widow already currently receives from other sources. Income and net worth are determining factors. The program is based on surviving spouses and unmarried children of deceased veterans with <u>wartime service</u>. The program rules are basically identical to that of veterans nonservice-connected disability pension.

Read through this whole section then make an application to the VA. You may be eligible for thousands of dollars, medical care, nursing home care, burial benefits, state benefits, etc. Regardless of your current financial situation, you may need this program in the future. This could be an option if an unforeseen illness or accident changes your life.

Pay close attention to medical costs and how the VA Pension Program can be manipulated by your medical costs either on a regular basis or just once a year. If you pay close attention to detail regarding your medical costs, you could really be helping yourself to possibly receive big reimbursements.

Eligibility

There is no age requirement, only the following. You may be eligible (*all must apply*) if:

- The deceased veteran was discharged from service under other than dishonorable conditions,

- The veteran served 90 days or more active duty with at least 1 day during a war period,

- Your countable family income is below a yearly limit set by Federal law

NOTE: Your income can be lowered by your medical expenses to make you eligible.

War Periods

The veteran must have served at least 90 days on active duty and at least 1 day of duty must have been during one of the wartime periods listed below. It is not a requirement that a veteran served in combat or participated in combat missions, any service during a war period qualifies.

PERIOD	FROM	TO
Mexican Border War	05-09-1916	04-05-1917
World War	04-06-1917	11-11-1918
Russian Service (WWI)	04-06-1917	04-01-1920
World War II	12-07-1941	12-31-1946
Korean Conflict	06-27-1950	01-31-1955
Vietnam—In Country Service	02-28-1961	05-07-1975
Vietnam War	08-05-1964	05-07-1975
Persian Gulf War	08-02-1990	Present

Disability Requirements

The VA has no disability requirements for surviving spouses applying for basic pension. However, there are disability requirements to meet the housebound or aid and attendance level pension.

Basic Pension

The basic level pension is paid based on low or no income. Out-of-pocket medical expenses reduce income dollar for dollar.

Housebound (HB)

The housebound level requires medical documentation showing the widow is unable to leave her home without the assistance of another person.
Example: A widow has chronic arthritis and needs a walker to get around safely. Usually cannot drive.

Aid & Attendance (A&A)

The aid and attendance level requires medical documentation showing the services of another person are required to help the widow with the daily chores of living (feeding, dressing, bathing, etc.).
Example: Widow moves into foster or nursing home; or hires an in-home care provider for daily needs.

Individual circumstances will vary widely and you won't know if you're eligible for any level of pension unless you apply. *You must apply; you've got nothing to lose.* It's not for you to judge if you're eligible, the VA rating board will make that decision. This information helps you to understand how the VA views these situations.

Income Limits

Listed below are pension income limits for all levels of pension. The VA sets annual income limits depending on how many dependents a widow has. The chart below shows the pension annual limits broken down to <u>monthly amounts</u>.

MONTHLY WIDOW'S PENSION INCOME LIMITS

STATUS	BASIC	HB	A & A
Widow—No Dependents	$541	$662	$866
Widow with One Dependent	$709	$829	$1032

Add $138 for each additional child.

The VA counts total family income for pension purposes to include Social Security for widows and children.

Family Income

All available income less immediate family medical expenses paid out of pocket. The VA counts almost all sources of income to include earned income, wages, other pensions, insurance, Social Security, interest from stocks, bonds, CD's, investment properties, and net worth (not including your primary place of residence). The VA does not count SSI or AFDC as income but it still must be reported on the application.

Final Expenses and Debts

Expenses paid but not reimbursed regarding the veteran's illness prior to death can be used to lower a widow's income for pension purposes. This also includes burial expenses paid by the surviving spouse that have not been reimbursed.

Debts of the veteran or the veteran and his spouse that are paid by the surviving spouse are considered a final expense and can lower a widow's income also. These expenses are asked for on VA Form 21-534.

Medical Expenses

Income can be reduced dollar for dollar by acceptable medical expenses. This may bring your income below the listed limits and the VA can then pay you the difference. This is generally paid in 12 equal monthly payments rounded down to the nearest dollar. If your medical expenses are higher than the limit(s) listed, your income could be considered to be zero and you would be paid the maximum amount listed. The VA is only concerned that you paid your medical costs yourself and you were not reimbursed by any other source.

Example: A widow lives alone on her Social Security of $1000 monthly. She has a stroke and must move into a foster home because she can no longer live alone safely. She can feed herself but cannot bath or dress herself without assistance. The cost of the foster home is $1,800 monthly. The widow is approved for Death Pension with aid and attendance (A&A). Because the foster home expense is more than her $1000 Social Security, her income is considered zero and she is paid $866 monthly (the maximum available—the difference between her income $0 and the max rate for A&A $866) to help cover the cost of her foster home care.

Other issues like receipt of Medicaid, or state veterans foster or nursing care can play a part in whether or not a veteran will receive pension and if so, how much.

Medical expenses are broken down into two groups: 1) Ongoing monthly medical expenses (i.e. Medicare, health insurance, foster home care, nursing home care, in-home care costs, etc.). 2) Annual medical expenses; i.e., prescriptions, outpatient costs (doctor visits, etc.), ambulance bills, medical equipment bills, lab tests, etc.

Annual Reimbursement Check

Any annual medical costs that cannot be considered ongoing can be claimed at the end of each year for a reimbursement check. The only requirement is that you have to have already paid the medical bill yourself. All you do is list all your *paid* medical expenses on VA Form 21-8416 during the year as you pay them. At the end of the year you mail in the form and the VA will reimburse you in about 1-4 months. A small deductible is used in calculating your reimbursement check. Widows with no dependents have an annual deductible of about $324 and with one dependent it raises to about $425. Any amount above the deductible will be reimbursed back to you.

Note: You are not eligible for any reimbursement if the VA is paying you the maximum amount payable under your circumstances.

Money for You Even When You Appear Ineligible

You could be ineligible for monthly pension because your income is over the limit. Keep track of all your annual medical expenses over the year on VA Form 21-8416 and mail it in at the end of the year to see if it reduces your income enough to receive an annual pension check in the form of a reimbursement. Many people receive thousands of dollars in reimbursement once every year. See the examples below and keep track of all your PAID medical expenses.

Examples of Medical Expenses

The following are examples of medical expenses to claim for reimbursement on VA Form 21-8416. LIST ANYTHING YOU BELIEVE

IS A MEDICAL EXPENSE. The VA will determine if it falls under the rules or not.

Abdominal Supports
Acupuncture
Ambulance Hire
Anesthetist
Arch Supports
Artificial Limbs and Teeth
Back Supports
Braces
Cardiographs
Chiropodist
Chiropractor
Convalescent Home
Crutches
Dental Service
Dentures
Dermatologist
Eyeglasses
Food Prescription
Gynecologist
Hearing Aids & Batteries
Home Health Services
Hospital Expenses
Insulin Treatment
Medical Insurance
Invalid Chair
Lab Tests
Lip Reading Lessons
Neurologist
Nursing Services
Occupational Therapist

Ophthalmologist
Optician
Optometrist
Oral Surgery
Osteopath
Pediatrician
Physical Examinations
Physical Therapy
Podiatrist
Prescriptions and Drugs
Psychiatrist
Psychoanalyst
Psychologist
Psychotherapy
Radium Therapy
Sacroiliac Belt
Speech Therapist
Splints
Medicare
Surgeon
Vaccines
Wheelchairs
X-rays

You can also claim transportation for medical expenses at .20 per mile plus parking and tolls or actual fares for taxis or buses, etc. This is just a partial list to help you know what is possible. Claim anything you believe is a medical expense.

Does the VA Need My Medical Receipts?

You do not have to send in receipts to prove you paid for the medical expenses listed on your VA Form 21-8416 unless the VA asks for them. If they do ask for them and you don't have them, they can readjust your pension and make you pay back any monies you were paid on a reimbursement. So, keep all your receipts for about 2 or 3 years just in case.

Annual Income Report

Every year your pension income status is reevaluated by mailing you an income form for update. The VA calls the form an Eligibility Verification Report (EVR). Send in your VA Form 21-8416 (Request for Medial Expenses) with your EVR to receive reimbursement.

Net Worth & Insurance

Eligibility for widows' pension requires that your net worth be less than $50,000. You'll be asked to furnish net worth information on VA Form 21-534. A reason a widow's net worth increases quickly is due to the receipt of life insurance upon the death of the veteran. When you file your claim for widow's pension, you must list life insurance proceeds if you have received them.

IMPORTANT! 45 Day Rule

The best way to obtain maximum benefits for widow's pension is to file a claim *after* you've received life insurance and *after 45 days* from the date of death of the veteran.

Reapply at Anytime

If a veteran is not eligible for VA pension for any reason, he or she can reapply over and over again if personal circumstances change (i.e. disability level, income, medical costs, move to nursing home, etc).

How to Apply

File a phone claim immediately by calling the VA at 1-800-827-1000 and stating you request to file a phone claim for widow's death pension, housebound pension, or pension with aid and attendance.

You will also be sent an application, VA Form 21-534 and possibly supplemental forms depending on your circumstances. Complete them and get them back to VA ASAP! Tell the VA representative on the phone to send you a copy of the FAX claim. Ask a lot of questions if you don't understand.

Spina Bifida Allowance

Spina bifida patients are children of Vietnam veterans. They are eligible for vocational training, health care, and a monthly allowance. The monthly allowance is set at three levels, depending upon the degree of disability suffered by the child. The three levels are based on neurological manifestations that define the severity of disability: impairment of the functioning of the extremities, impairment of bowel or bladder function, and impairment of intellectual functioning. Level 1 monthly rate is $208, level 2 monthly rate is $725, and level 3 monthly rate is $1,242.

Spina bifida assistance: A child with spina bifida, who is parented by a Vietnam veteran, can receive vocational training to guide the child, parent or guardian in choosing a vocational training program. The VA also will provide up to 24 months of training to achieve a vocational goal.

Federal Employment Preference

Widows of veterans can apply for a 10 point hiring preference when applying for federal employment. To apply, contact the personnel or human resources office of any federal government agency for Standard Form 15.

State and Local Benefits

State and local benefits vary widely from state to state and depending on the particulars of the veterans death. Review the State and Local Benefits Section to get an idea of what your state may offer. After you review the State benefit section, we suggest you call the State Veterans

Affairs office and talk with them about your individual circumstances. Phone numbers and addresses are listed for your convenience.

CHAPTER 22

▼

BURIAL BENEFITS

Reimbursements • National Cemeteries • Presidential Certificates

Veterans and their families very often misunderstand VA burial benefits. Like many VA benefits, the right answer is "it depends on the situation". In this case, it depends on the veteran's situation at the time of his or her death. There are some "basic" burial benefits for any veteran, and there are some additional benefits including reimbursements for other more qualified veterans, under the law. Contact the VA at 1-800-827-1000 for information on how to proceed at the time of death of a veteran. Funeral homes routinely handle veteran's death preparations for family members, also.

BE PREPARED—A Message for All Veterans

Make preparations before your death on what you want and how you want it done. Let your spouse or someone in your family know where your discharge papers are and what kind of funeral you want. Make sure it's known whether you want to be buried or cremated. If cremated, what do you want done with your ashes? By not planning ahead, you may find that your surviving spouse decides you need the best burial even if she/he can't afford it. *Funeral homes routinely charge unreasonable costs to grieving widows and family members.* People often make poor choices when a loved one dies simply because they're grieving and depressed.

Inexpensive Cremations and Burials

If your budget is limited or you're not interested in an expensive burial, then think about being cremated. Cremations can be done for as little as $350 or even less in some areas of the United States. Don't hesitate to call attention to funeral homes charging anywhere from $800 to $2000 for a cremation, they're unreasonable. Contact a cremation society in your area. Look in your local yellow pages under "Cremation or Cremation Services". Make some calls and you'll be surprised at the difference in costs from crematories to funeral homes. They'll explain how to proceed at the time of death, make sure your family knows what to do.

Reimbursement of Burial Expenses
Service Connected Death
$1500—$2000 Reimbursement

The VA will pay a burial allowance reimbursement up to $1500 if the veteran's death is a direct result of a service-connected condition *or a contributing cause of the death prior to September 10, 2001*. For deaths on or after September 11, 2001, VA will pay $2,000. If the veteran is buried in a VA national cemetery, some or all of the cost of moving the deceased may be reimbursed.

Remember that service connection must be awarded through the VA for reimbursement purposes. There is no time limit in filing a reimbursement claim on a service-connected death.

Non-Service Connected Death
$300 Reimbursement

VA will pay up to $300 reimbursement toward burial and funeral expenses for those who qualify.

To establish entitlement to reimbursement, ONE of the following conditions must be met:

- The veteran was receiving VA pension or compensation on the date of death (or was in receipt of military retired pay in lieu of pension or compensation).

- The veteran had a claim pending on the date of death, which would have resulted in entitlement to compensation or pension.

- The veteran died while hospitalized by VA or died while traveling under VA authorization and expense for the purpose of examination, treatment or care.

- The veteran served during a period of war or was discharged from service for disability incurred in line of duty, the body is unclaimed and sufficient resources do not exist to cover the funeral expenses.

TIME LIMIT

There is a 2-year time limit from the date of death to file for non-service connected burial expenses.

Transportation Costs Reimbursed In Full

The VA will pay full transportation costs of transporting a deceased veteran from place of death to the nearest national cemetery or place of burial under the following circumstances:

a.   If the veteran's death was in a VA medical facility or under VA contract care.

b. If the veteran was rated at least 10% service connected disabled <u>and</u> is buried in a national cemetery.

c. If service connected death is paid, transportation can only be paid also if the veteran died in a VA medical facility <u>and</u> is buried in a national cemetery.

$150—$300 Burial Plot Reimbursement

The VA will pay a $150 or $300 plot allowance reimbursement when a veteran is <u>not</u> buried in a national cemetery and:

• Veteran was receiving VA compensation or pension on the date of death.

• The veteran died while hospitalized in a VA medical facility, VA nursing home, or under VA contract medical care or died while traveling under VA authorization and expense for the purpose of examination, treatment or care. This is regardless if any benefits are being paid for disabilities. File claim within 2 years of death.

The plot-interment allowance is $300 for deaths on or after December 1, 2001

$600 Reimbursement

If the deceased veteran is buried somewhere other than a National Cemetery, the total reimbursement can be up to $600 for a nonservice related death depending on the date of the death. On a nonservice related death and buried in a National Cemetery, only $300 would be reimbursed. Always claim reimbursement for transportation costs and let the VA explain if they're not reimbursable.

Filing A Burial Claim for Reimbursement

Call the VA at 1-800-827-1000 and give them the information regarding the veteran's death. You will be sent the proper form(s); usually just

VA Form 21-530 is all that is needed. Return the form with a certified copy of the death certificate, a copy of the receipted funeral bill showing the bill was paid, and who paid the bill. Whoever paid the funeral bill should be the one signing the VA Form 21-530.

Basic Burial Benefits

All veterans who have a discharge under conditions other than dishonorable are eligible for "basic" VA burial benefits regardless of place of burial or cremation. That includes:

• U.S. Flag

• Grave Marker (anywhere in the world) or Memorial Marker

Eligibility for burial in a national cemetery has minimum qualifications that must be met in order for veterans or dependents to be buried in that facility. When qualified, burial benefits in a VA national cemetery include the gravesite, a headstone or marker, opening and closing of the grave, and perpetual care. Many national cemeteries have columbaria or gravesites for cremated remains.

VA NATIONAL CEMETERIES
Verifying Eligibility

In order to establish eligibility without delay, it is critical that funeral homes be provided appropriate proof of military service. The veteran's discharge is the normal means of verification. Veterans should make every effort to see that copies of their discharge(s) are conveniently available at any time. Those who have burial plans through funeral homes should ensure that copies of discharges are made a part of these arrangement records. These steps eliminate the requirements for hurried or difficult searches for discharges at the time of death. When a family is unable to locate a discharge, it often may be found filed in the clerk's office of the county in which the veteran resided at the time of release from active duty.

When discharges are unavailable, those acting on behalf of the decedent should provide the funeral home with as much military information as possible. This includes: Military service number, branch of service, Social Security number, duty dates or their estimates, etc. This information may be drawn from old letters, training certificates, "dog tags", newspaper articles or other memorabilia that may be in the family's possession. Discharge may be available from local government offices in the county where the veteran resided at the time of his/her release from active duty. VA medical cards or information on past VA hospitalization or other benefits are especially useful. Loan numbers under state veterans home loan programs may also be helpful.

It is important to realize that the government <u>does not</u> maintain computerized records for most former military service members.

Eligibility

Eligibility for burial in a national cemetery is extended to those currently serving on active duty, veterans who served on active duty, and their spouses and dependent children. Veterans must have been discharged under conditions other than dishonorable.

Required Time Served

There is no required minimum period of active duty for veterans whose first date of entry was <u>prior</u> to September 7, 1980. Those entering the military after that date must have at least 24 months consecutive months of active duty unless they were discharged for a service-connected disability, hardship or other special circumstance.

Reservists, National Guard and ROTC Personnel

Members of reserve and National Guard units who were called to active duty for national emergencies and other major conflicts are eligible if they honorably completed the particular period for which they were activated.

Also eligible are career reservists who are entitled to retired pay under Chapter 67 of Title 10. This provision also applies to those who would have received retired pay at the age of 60, but for their death prior to that date. Appropriate documentation of this status is necessary for verification purposes.

Except as noted above, reservists, National Guard and ROTC personnel are eligible only where death occurs while on training duty or as a result of a condition or injury incurred during such training. Those who were never called to active duty or were called to active duty for training purposes only ARE NOT ELIGIBLE for burial benefits.

Other Personnel

Eligibility is granted to members of the US Merchant Marine and civil service members of the Army and Naval Transportation Services who served on ocean-going duty between December 7, 1941 and August 15, 1945. Merchant Mariners from this period are encouraged to secure an updated discharge from the US Coast Guard by filing DD Form 2168 through your local VA office. You can call VA at 1-800-827-1000 and ask that a form be sent to you.

United States citizens who served during wartime in the armed forces of allied nations are eligible. Certain civilian or contractual groups serving the US government during World War II have also been granted burial benefits. The cemetery should be contacted for particulars. See the VA Facilities Directory at the end of the book for address and phone information.

Commissioned officers of the US Public Health Service and those of the NOAA (formerly the Coast and Geodetic Survey) are eligible if the duty occurred within specific periods.

In all of these or other proposed cases, interested parties should contact the national cemetery to verify their authorization for burial rights.

Spouses and Dependent Children

Spouses of eligible veterans referred to above are also approved for burial in national cemeteries. Divorced spouses lose their entitlement to interment, as do those widows or widowers who remarry non-veterans. Widowed spouses who have remarried non-veterans automatically reacquire their eligibility if death, divorce or annulment ended the subsequent marriage.

Dependent children retain their eligibility for burial until they reach the age of 21. This age limit is extended to their 23rd birthday if they are attending an approved educational institution on a full time basis. Adult children may be buried only if they are unmarried and are incapable of self-support due to a physical or mental condition incurred before their 21st birthday. In these cases, appropriate medical documentation must be provided to verify eligibility. Non-veteran parents and siblings are not authorized for burial in national cemeteries.

It is not required that a veteran already be interred before burial of a dependent is authorized. Casketed remains are placed at a sufficient depth to allow for the later burial of eligible survivors in the same gravesite. Eligible survivors retain the option to be buried in another cemetery if they wish.

Arranging for Burial in a National Cemetery

No pre-arrangements or reservations are available in national cemeteries. Space is assigned only on an as-need basis. At the time of need, funeral homes or cremation societies normally act on behalf of families in arranging for burial. Where families are already in possession of cremated remains, they may find it more convenient to make application directly with the cemetery office. Three major areas will be addressed in any cemetery arrangements: Verification of eligibility, scheduling of the committal service or delivery of remains and the securing of accurate information for inscription of the marker. A burial flag for a veteran is normally provided by the funeral home or cremation society.

Where one has not been provided, it may be secured from the cemetery office.

Gravesite Assignment

Those applying for burial should inform the funeral home of any spouse or children already interred in the cemetery. Burial locations for new gravesites are normally assigned the day prior to interment. Placement of a cremation may be made in either an in-ground plot or a Columbarium niche.

Marker Inscriptions and Ordering (National Cemetery)

It is the responsibility of the next-of-kin to submit accurate marker inscription data. If requested, an approved religious emblem will be inscribed at no cost to the family. National Cemetery System regulations allow for the inscription of the highest rank achieved in a particular branch of service. Higher ranks received in reserve units are authorized where the reserve component is associated with the same branch as the veteran's active service. It is important that proof of a higher rank is provided prior to burial. Where space permits, additional inscriptions may be requested at no extra charge. These inscriptions may take the form of professional titles, terms of endearment or other phrases in good taste. Nicknames are not authorized on the name line but may be coupled with a term of endearment as an added inscription at the bottom of the marker. Regulations also do not authorize any special emblems as added inscriptions, and do not permit the permanent attachment of medallions, photographs or other items to grave markers. Further details regarding inscription regulations are available from the cemetery office.

No Cost

There are no charges for any gravesite, interment activity, grave marker or burial flag by the national cemetery. Use of committal shelters for services is also without cost.

Memorial Markers

To memorialize an eligible veteran whose remains are not available for burial, VA will provide a memorial headstone or marker. The headstone or marker is the same as that used to identify a grave except the mandatory phrase "In Memory of" precedes the inscription. The headstone or marker is available to memorialize eligible veterans or deceased service members whose remains were not recovered or identified, were buried at sea, donated to science, or cremated and scattered. The memorial marker may be provided for placement in a cemetery other than a national cemetery. In such a case, VA supplies the marker and pays the cost of shipping, but does not pay for the plot or the placement of the marker. Only a relative recognized as the next of kin may apply for headstones and markers.

Military Honors

The national cemetery provides for the playing of "Taps" and the folding and presentation of a burial flag to the next of kin at the conclusion of each service for a veteran. The cemetery can provide names of organizations, military units or volunteer groups that can provide an Honor Guard. Securing them remains the responsibility of the family. Where a veteran was a career retiree or received high valor awards, certain military installations in the region may be able to assign uniformed personnel to carry out full military honors. Full military honors are available as a matter of course for those whose death occurred while on active duty or during military training.

Burial Flags

A United States flag is provided, at not cost, to drape the casket of a deceased veteran who served honorably in the U.S. Armed Forces. It is furnished to honor the memory of a veteran's military service to his or her country. The VA also will issue a flag on behalf of a service member who was missing in action and later presumed dead, or for a Reservist who was entitled to retired military pay at the time of death.

Generally, the flag is given to the next-of-kin, as a keepsake, after its use during the funeral service. When there is no next-of-kin, the VA will furnish the flag to a friend making request for it.

Flags are usually provided by funeral homes but can be easily obtained from any VA Regional Office, national cemetery or U.S. post office using VA Form 2008.

Presidential Memorial Certificates

Presidential Memorial Certificates express the country's grateful recognition of the veteran's service in the United States Armed Forces. Certificates bearing the signature of the President are issued honoring deceased veterans with *honorable* discharges.

Eligibility

Eligible recipients include next-of-kin, other relatives or friends. There is no limit regarding how many certificates can be issued on a veteran. If everyone in the family wants one they can have one.

Application

Application for a *PMC* can be made over the phone or through the mail with any VA Regional Office. It is suggested you call the VA at 1-800-827-1000 to see if the veteran's record is established on the VA computer system. If it is, you probably won't need to send in any documentation to show an honorable discharge or date of death. Just tell the representative on the phone you want a *PMC* and give them your full name, address and relationship to the veteran (spouse, brother, son, friend, etc.). The veteran may have died at any time in the past.

Requests for additional, replacement, or corrected certificates may be made through the local VA Regional Office, or by writing to the Director, Office of Memorial Programs (403D), National Cemetery System, U.S. Department of Veterans Affairs, 810 Vermont Avenue NW Washington, DC 20420.

For veterans whose service was prior to July 16, 1903, requests should be sent to the VA Regional Office, 941 North Capitol Street, NE, Washington, DC 20420.

ARLINGTON NATIONAL CEMETERY

Arlington National Cemetery is under the jurisdiction of the Army. Eligibility for burials is stricter than at other national cemeteries. Eligibility for cremated remains in Arlington's Columbarium is the same as eligibility for burial in VA national cemeteries. For information on Arlington burials, write to Superintendent, Arlington National Cemetery, Arlington, VA 22211, or call (703) 695-3250.

STATE VETERANS CEMETERIES

For burial in state-run veterans cemeteries contact the State Department of Veterans Affairs for information. See the state listing in Section 24, page 98.

HEADSTONES AND MARKERS FOR PRIVATE GRAVES

The VA provides headstones and markers for the unmarked graves of veterans anywhere in the world and of eligible dependents of veterans buried in national, state veteran or military post cemeteries.

Flat bronze, flat granite, flat marble, upright granite and upright marble types are available to mark the grave in a style consistent with the cemetery. Niche markers are also available for identifying cremated remains.

When burial is in a national, state or military post cemetery, the headstone or marker is ordered through the cemetery. They will place it on the grave. Information on style, inscription and shipping can be obtained from the cemetery.

When burial occurs in a cemetery other than a national, military post or state veteran's cemetery, the headstone or marker must be applied for from the VA. It is shipped at government expense. The VA, however, does not pay the cost of placing the headstone or marker.

Twenty-year reservists are eligible for a headstone or grave marker if they are entitled to military retired pay at the time of death.

Application

To apply, obtain VA Form 40-1330 from the VA Regional Office nearest you by calling 1-800-827-1000. The form provides pictures and descriptions of headstones and markers for your choice.

CHAPTER 23

▼

VETERANS SERVICE ORGANIZATIONS

Veterans Service Organizations (VSO) are designed to do nothing else but help veterans. They are groups that have special authority under federal law to represent veterans in cases before the VA or any VA body. VSOs have service officers who are trained to represent veterans in all facets of VA claims, paperwork, and appeals. Most service officers understand the VA system fairly well, and like anything else, some understand a lot better than others. In any case, if you choose, they will act as your advocate and assist you with processing a claim.

VSOs must offer their services free of charge, to any veteran or survivor, and you don't have to be a member of their organization. Keep in mind that some service officers are more effective than others, or have more experience and training. You can contact different VSOs and find out for yourself. Don't be afraid to ask questions of their training and experience, you'll probably find that some if not many service officers are disabled veterans and are very familiar with the VA system and can help you. Check your phone book for local VSO numbers, or call the VA at 1-800-827-1000 and ask for the number of the local VSO office you seek. Below are the organizations chartered by Congress and/or recognized by VA for claim representation:

Air Force Sergeants Association
American Defenders of Bataan and Corregidor
American Ex-Prisoners of War
American G.I. Forum
American Gold Star Mothers, Inc.
American Legion
American Red Cross
American Veterans Committee
American War Mothers
AMVETS
Army and Navy Union, USA, Inc.
Blinded Veterans Association
Blue Star Mothers of America, Inc.
Catholic War Veterans, USA, Inc.
Congressional Medal of Honor Society of the United States of America
Disabled American Veterans
Fleet Reserve Association
Gold Star Wives of America, Inc.
Italian American War Veterans of the USA
Jewish War Veterans of the USA
Legion of Valor of the USA, Inc.
Marine Corps League
Military Chaplains Association of the United States of America
Military Order of the Purple Heart of the U.S.A., Inc.
Military Order of the World Wars
National Amputation Foundation, Inc.
National Association for Black Veterans, Inc.
National Association of County Veterans Service Officers, Inc.

National Association of State Directors of Veterans Affairs (NASDVA)
National Veterans Legal Services Program, Inc.
Navy Club of the United States of America
Navy Mutual Aid Association
Non Commissioned Officers Association
Paralyzed Veterans of America
Pearl Harbor Survivors Association, Inc.
Polish Legion of American Veterans, USA
Swords to Plowshares: Veterans Rights Organization
The Retired Enlisted Association
US Submarine Veterans of World War II
Veterans of Foreign Wars of the United States
Veterans of the Vietnam War, Inc.
Veterans of World War I of the USA, Inc.
Vietnam Veterans of America, Inc.
Women Air Force Service Pilots of World War II
Women's Army Corps Veterans Association

CHAPTER 24

▼

CLAIM TIME

Take Action Now!

You now have the information necessary to get your claim started. You are your own best asset, don't waste any time, be proactive, and call the VA to begin the process!

No matter if you're a veteran of WWII, Korea, Vietnam, the Gulf War, or a peacetime veteran, you're entitled to your benefits. Whether you're disabled or not, you're entitled to your benefits. Don't be intimidated by the process.

You've been provided detailed benefit information and outlets for assistance, use this information to your advantage when dealing with the VA. And although dealing with the VA can be extremely frustrating, it's worth the fight. And believe me, it will seem like a fight at times. However, the end product may very well prove to change your life for the better and in ways you never imagined.

Apply for your benefits and be persistent, it literally could be worth tens of thousands of dollars to you.

Email Your Story

Please send your comments and VA benefit success stories to: myvastory@yahoo.com

▼

STATE AND LOCAL BENEFITS

State and local benefits for veterans, survivors and dependents vary greatly from state to state. There are many benefits to take advantage of. Each benefit will have it's own eligibility criteria. The easiest way to learn about all of your state and local benefits (and the inside information that goes with each one) is to review the information we have on your state and then contact the State Department of Veterans Affairs to make a claim for benefits. You may need to ask some clarifying questions depending on your circumstances.

Some basic benefits included are education assistance, vocational rehabilitation, hunting and fishing license, property tax exemptions, transportation assistance, nursing homes, disabled veterans job finding assistance, disabled license plates, etc. This information can change at any time depending on your state legislature and what veteran's benefits they feel are important enough to provide and maintain. Please contact your state office with specific questions and to confirm the benefits listed.

ALABAMA DEPARTMENT OF VETERANS AFFAIRS

MAILING ADDRESS:
  POST OFFICE BOX 1509
  MONTGOMERY, AL 36102-1502
LOCATION:
  RSA Plaza
  770 Washington Avenue
  Suite 530
TELEPHONE: (334) 242-5077
FAX: (334) 242-5102
E-MAIL: fwilkes@va.state.al.us

1. SERVICES PERFORMED.

A. This Department furnishes representation to veterans, dependents and survivors by virtue of Power of Attorney made to one of the following organizations:
  Alabama Dept. of Veterans' Affairs
  The American Legion
  Military Order of the Purple Heart
  American Ex-POWs Inc.
  Non-Commissioned Officers Assoc.
  Veterans of WWI of the USA, Inc.
  Vietnam Veterans of America
  Fleet Reserve Association
  Blinded Veterans Association
  (All county veterans service officers are employees of this
  Department)
B. Scholarships: This Alabama GI Dependents Scholarship Program is administered by the Alabama Department of Veterans Affairs and is governed by the Code of Alabama 1975, Section 31-6-1. The veteran must meet the following qualifications to establish eligibility of his/her dependents (child, stepchild, spouse or un-remarried widow(er): Military Service: The veteran must have honorably served at least 90 or

more days of continuous active federal military service or honorably discharged by reason of service-connected disability after serving less than 90 days. Disability Requirements: The veteran must be rated 20% or more due to service-connected disabilities or have held the qualifying rating at the time of death or; be a former prisoner of war (POW) or; declared missing in action (MIA) or; died as the result of a service-connected disability or; died while on active military service in the line of duty.

Residency Requirements: The veteran must have been a permanent civilian resident of the State of Alabama for at least one year immediately prior to (a) the initial entry into active military service or (b) any subsequent period of military service in which a break in service occurred and the Alabama civilian residency was established. Permanently service-connected veterans rated at 100% may qualify after establishing at least five years of permanent residency in Alabama prior to filing of an application or immediately prior to death, if deceased. Entitlement: Four standard academic years or part-time equivalent at any Alabama state-supported institution of higher learning or a prescribed course of study at any Alabama state-supported technical school without payment of any tuition, required textbooks or laboratory fees. Exception: A spouse or un-remarried widow (er) of a veteran who is rated 20—90% due to service-connected disabilities are only entitled to two standard academic years without payment of tuition, required textbooks and laboratory fees or a prescribed technical course not to exceed 18 months of training. Widow (er) forfeits benefits upon remarriage. Spouse forfeits benefits upon divorce from veteran in which the spouse derived their eligibility. Age Deadline: The child or stepchild must initiate training prior to their 26th birthday. Age 30 deadline may apply in certain situations. There is no age deadline for submission of the application by the spouse or un-remarried widow(er).

These entitlements may be applied at the undergraduate or graduate level.

C. Service organizations not associated with the State Department of Veterans Affairs but are co-located with the U.S. Department of Veterans Affairs (USDVA) Regional Office, 345 Perry Hill Road, Montgomery 36109 are:

Veterans of Foreign Wars
Disabled American Veterans
AMVETS
Paralyzed Veterans of America

2. STATE BENEFITS:

A. Tax Exemption: Income tax exemption on all Armed-Forces retirement benefits.

B. Veterans' Nursing Home: Alabama currently has three state veterans nursing homes: The Bill Nichols Home located in Alexander City, the Floyd E. "Tut" Fann Home located in Huntsville, and the William F. Green Home is located in Bay Minette. Each Home provides 150 beds of skilled-nursing care. The Homes are operated by contract with USA Healthcare, Inc., Cullman, Alabama. A one-year in state residency is required for admission. Presently, only wartime veterans qualify. Comprehensive nursing care and medical services, medications, laundry, physical therapy and rehab services are provided to residents with a cost of less than $19.76 per day to the veteran.

C. State Bonus: A $500 bonus is paid to any Alabama veteran who was a P.O.W. in North/South Vietnam or Cambodia. If P.O.W. died in captivity, the bonus is paid to the surviving spouse or next of kin.

D. Loan Program: None

E. License Plates: Ex-POWs, Purple Heart Recipients and MOH recipients are furnished one (1) License Plate without payment of taxes or fees. Tags are for life and do not need to re-register each year. The surviving spouse may retain the tag without taxes or fees until death or remarriage.

Disabled Veterans Plate: Any veteran resident requiring special mechanical control devices because of a service-connected disability or a veteran whose service-connected disabilities exceed 50 percent may be entitled to a license plate for all vehicles owned by the veteran (solely or jointly) after paying a tag fee and ad valorem taxes. Service-connected disabled veterans rated 10%-40% are entitled to one (1) license plate for a vehicle owned by the veteran (solely or jointly) after paying a tag fee and ad-valorem taxes.

Active or retired member of the Alabama National Guard or any resident of Alabama at the time of entering the United States Armed Forces Reserves who are still residents of Alabama at the time the exemption is claimed, shall be exempt from the operation of the privilege or license tax and registration fee now and hereinafter to be levied on automobiles and motor vehicles by the State of Alabama.

Tags are not transferable. Additionally, an extensive commemorative tag program is available for all eligible honorably discharged war era veteran from World War II to the Persian Gulf War after payment of all fees, taxes and a tag fee.

3. VITAL STATISTICS:

State Registrar/Bureau of Vital Statistics
P.O. Box 5625
Montgomery, AL 36103

4. USDVA REGIONAL OFFICE:

345 Perry Hill Road
Montgomery, AL 36109

5. GENERAL INFORMATION:

Alabama recognized its obligation to render services to veterans in 1927 when, by legislative act, the State Service Commission was established. This act charged the state service commissioner "to aid all residents of the State of Alabama who served in any war in which the United States has been engaged, to receive any and all compensation, hospitalization, insurance or other aid or benefit to which Alabama veterans may be entitled."

In 1943, the legislature, recognizing the workload of required services, which was expected at the conclusion of World War II, passed permissive legislation authorizing all counties in Alabama to employ county service commissioners. However, these commissioners were to be hired and paid by each county and, therefore, were not under the direct supervision of the state service commissioner.

In 1945, the Legislature again recognized the inadequacies of existing agencies handling the affairs of veterans, thus passed legislation creating the State Department of Veterans Affairs to Junction under a State Board of Veterans Affairs. Operation of the Department began officially on October 1, 1945. It was created with one general aim "All rights and benefits provided by law for the veteran and his wife, widow, or children shall be translated into reality."

The State Board of Veterans Affairs consists of the Governor as chairman and representatives from veterans organizations in Alabama, namely: The American Legion, Veterans of Foreign Wars, Disabled American Veterans, AMVETS, Vietnam Veterans of America, Military Order of the Purple Heart, and American Ex-Prisoners of War, Inc— the number of representatives being determined on the basis of membership of each veterans organization.

The personnel of the Department consists of a state service commissioner or director, administrative assistants, chief of claims, district managers, county veterans service officers in all 67 counties, claims' personnel; plus clerical employees as the State Board deems necessary. All personnel are under the supervision and control of the director subject to the approval of the State Board of Veterans Affairs. The county offices are also under the supervision of a district manager. It is the responsibility of the Department to maintain a comprehensive state-wide veterans assistance program; to represent the state and its veterans before the U.S. Department of Veterans Affairs or any other matters dealing with the interest of the veteran. The Department is also charged with the administration of the "Alabama GI and Dependents Educational Benefits Act."

The Department, by contract, pays the Veterans of Foreign Wars and Disabled American Veterans for claims service. Veterans service offices of this Department complete and transmit claims and other support data to those organizations for processing when Power of Attorney is in their favor.

ALASKA DEPARTMENT OF MILITARY AND VETERANS' AFFAIRS

MAILING ADDRESS:
  POST OFFICE BOX 5800
  FORT RICHARDSON, AK 99505-5800
LOCATION:
  Bldg. 49000
  Camp Denali
  Suite C-209
  Ft. Richardson AK
TELEPHONE: (907) 428-6016
FAX: (907) 428-6019
E-MAIL: Laddie_Shaw@ak-prepared.com

1. SERVICES PERFORMED.

The Alaska Division of Veterans Affairs is dedicated to providing service to the veteran. Advocacy and assistance is provided to veterans, their dependents and survivors. The Division also contracts with various veterans service organizations to assist veterans and their dependents and survivors throughout the state in filing claims for U.S. Department of Veterans Affairs (USDVA) entitlements and benefits, and to provide general assistance and advocacy.

2. STATE BENEFITS:

A. Property Tax Exemption: Property tax exemption on the first 150,000 of assessed valuation for veterans who are 50% or more disabled.

B. Property Tax Equivalency:

C. State Soldiers Home: None.

D. Loan Programs: Interest rate subsidy on home loans for qualifying veterans through Alaska Housing Finance Corporation. Lower interest rate for veterans for small business loans.

E. State Bonus: None.

F. Free License Plate: For Ex-POWs and Pearl Harbor survivors.

G. License Plate for Disabled Veterans: Furnished without payment of fee to veterans with a 70% or greater disability.

H. Burial Allowance: None.

I. Educational Assistance: Free tuition for dependents of POWs and those MIA in Southeast Asia.

J. Motor Vehicle Fee Registration Waiver: For veterans 70% or greater disabled.

K Hunting and Sport Fishing License: Free to veterans 50% or greater disabled.

L. State Camping Pass: Free to veterans 50% or greater disabled.

M. Purchase of Public Land: One time discount for veterans. Veterans purchase preference of unoccupied residential land.

3. VITAL STATISTICS:

Dept. of Health & Social Services/Bureau of Vital Statistics
Post Office Box H
Juneau, AK 99811

4. USDVA REGIONAL OFFICE:

2925 Debarr Road
Anchorage, AK 99508

5. GENERAL INFORMATION:

What was in past years known as the Territorial Veterans Commission, the Alaska World War II Veterans Board and Veterans Affairs Office, Department of Commerce and Economic Development became the Division of Veterans Affairs in March, 1984. A direct result of concerns expressed by Alaskan veterans prompted Executive Order #58 to be issued by Governor Bill Sheffield in early 1984, which created the Division of Veterans Affairs under the Adjutant General, who is also the Commissioner, Department of Military and Veterans Affairs. The Division of Veterans Affairs was staffed and became operational in July, 1984. This reorganization significantly elevated the status and visibility of Alaska's veterans within a central point of contact within the state to coordinate veterans issues and programs, acts as a liaison with federal and state agencies, veterans organizations and the executive branch of state government. The goal of the Division is to improve the efficiency and effectiveness of state programs available to Alaska's veterans.

AMERICAN SAMOA VETERANS' AFFAIRS

MAILING ADDRESS:
  POST OFFICE BOX 8586
  PAGO PAGO
  AMERICAN SAMOA 96799
  TELEPHONE: (001) 684-633-4206
  FAX: (001) 684-633-2269
  E-MAIL: Not Available

ARIZONA DEPARTMENT OF VETERANS' SERVICES

MAILING ADDRESS & LOCATION:
  3225 N. CENTRAL AVENUE
  SUITE 910
  PHOENIX AZ 85012
  TELEPHONE: (602) 255-3373

FAX: (602) 255-1038
E-MAIL: director@azvets.com

MISSION: The AZ Department of Veterans' Services
*Delivers a series of seamless services to eligible veterans and their families; and
*Unifies the veteran community by building alliances to enhance financial resources available to the community. Vision: The Voice for Veterans

1. SERVICES PERFORMED.

A. Assist veterans, dependents and survivors in establishing and presenting claims for federal and state benefits to which they are entitled.

B. Act as guardian or conservator of incapacitated veterans, minor children and surviving spouses.

C. Assist in obtaining employment preferences authorized by law.

D. Approve and disapprove courses of study offered by the educational institutions or business establishments in accordance with Title 38, U.S. Code and state regulations.

E. Conduct monthly outreach services to approximately forty communities and state prisons/hospitals.

F. Determine eligibility for special vehicle license plates.

G. Inform veterans about federal, state and local laws enacted to benefit them.

H. Provide long-term care services and skilled nursing care to veterans and their spouses in a State Veteran Home.

I. Register individuals, organizations, fund raising groups, and businesses that intend to solicit donations in the name of American veterans.

2. STATE BENEFITS:

A. Property Tax Exemption:

(1) Persons who are on active duty in military service and are absent from the state, or those confined in any licensed hospital, may submit an eligibility affidavit certified by any authorized official. Any person applying for exemption from taxation by reason of military service shall, before application is made, record their discharge papers with the county recorder in the county where the application is made. The exemption applies first to real estate, then to a mobile home or automobile.

(2) Widows/Widowers—An exemption from property taxation is available for each widow/widower who resides in Arizona. To qualify for this exemption the applicant must have lived with their spouse in Arizona in the year immediately preceeding the year for which claimant applies and the applicants family income, including children residing with the applicant, shall not exceed: $13,200 if there are no children under the age of 18 living with the applicant or; $18,840 if one or more of the applicant's children under the age of 18 resides with them, or one or more children over the age of 18 is/are certified as being totally and permanently disabled, either physically or mentally.

(3) Disabled Persons—An exemption from property taxation is available to any person who, after age 17, has been medically certified as totally and permanently disabled in the year immediately preceeding the year for which claimant applies. The income from all sources of a disabled person and their spouse, together with the income from all sources of any children residing with the disabled person shall not exceed: $13,200 if there are not children under the age of 18 residing with the applicant or; $18,840 if one or more of the applicant's children under the age of 18 is certified as being totally and permanently disabled, either physically or mentally.

B. Vehicle Exemption: No license tax or registration fee shall be collected fro 'any veteran for a personally-owned vehicle if such veteran is certified by the U.S. Department of Veterans Affairs (VA) to be one hundred percent service-connected disabled and drawing compensa-tion on that basis. A veteran claiming an exemption prescribed by this section shall present satisfactory proof of U.S. Department of Veterans Affairs financial aid or government compensation and certificate on determination of one hundred percent disability, as applicable. Such exemption may be claimed and granted during each 12 month period for only one vehicle or any replacement of such vehicle owned by the veteran.

C. Soldiers Home: A domiciliary run by the VA Medical Center in Prescott, AZ. For more information, call (520) 776-6117 or (800) 949-1065, ext. 611.

D. State Bonus: None

E. State Loan Program: None

F. Conservatorship/Guardianship: Fiduciary service to incapacitated veterans, minor children of deceased veterans and surviving spouses. Call (602) 248-1554 for further information.

G. Arizona State Veteran Home: Arizona State Veteran Home located in Phoenix, Arizona, is a 200 bed, state of the art, skilled nurs-ing facility for veterans and their spouses operated and maintained by the Arizona Department of Veterans' Services. Contact (602) 248-1555 for further information and/or an application for admis-sions.

H. Employment Preference: A veteran who passes an examination for employment by the state, county or city will have 5 points added to their certification score. The veteran must have served for more than six (6) months and be separated under honorable conditions. Veterans entitled to compensation for a service-connected disability will have 10 points added to the certification score. Certain spouses or surviving spouses shall be given a 5 point preference if the veteran died of a ser-vice-connected disability; or as a member of the Armed Forces serving on active duty is (a) missing in action, (b) captured, or (c) forcibly detained or interned by a foreign power; or has a total and permanent service-connected disability, or who died while such disability was in force.

I. Educational: A veteran or eligible dependent that has applied for educational benefits at state-supported community colleges, colleges and universities may defer payment of tuition fees for a period of 120 days.

J. Resident Hunting and Fishing License: For members of the Armed Forces on active duty, stationed in-state is available upon application. Complimentary licenses may be granted to veterans 70 years or older who have been residents of this state for 25 years. Complimentary licenses will be issued to veterans verified by the U.S. Department of Veterans Affairs to be one hundred percent service-connected disabled.

K. State Veterans Cemetery: Scheduled to be opened no later than March, 2002. Eligibility requirements to be determined. Call (602) 255-3373 for further information.

L. Special License Plate: Eligible veterans may purchase special veteran license plates. A fee is charged for the special plates in addition to the normal vehicle registration costs.

A Veteran special plate consists of a red, white and blue design, has an American flag in the center of the plate, and the designation "veteran" at the bottom of the plate. A $25 fee is required for the original veteran special plate and for the annual renewal of such plate. Of the $25 annual fee, $17 is deposited in the state home for veterans trust fund.

A Former P.O.W. license plate has an initial fee of $15 with an annual renewal charge of $5. Of the $15 initial fee, $5 is deposited in the state home for veterans trust fund.

A Purple Heart medal recipient license plate has an initial fee of $25 with an annual renewal charge of $5. Of the $25 initial fee, $5 is deposited in the state home for veterans trust fund.

A Pearl Harbor survivor license plate has an initial fee of $25 with an annual renewal charge of $5. Of the $25 initial fee, $5 is deposited in the state home for veterans trust fund.

A Medal of Honor license plate is free of charge to all verified recipients of the Medal of Honor.

M. Public Records: Public officials shall, without charge, certify copies of public records for use in making a claim for pension, compensation, allotment allowance, insurance, or other benefits from the United States.

N. Military, Discharge Papers: Shall be recorded by any county recorder, free of charge. Location of each County Recorder's Office may be found in the blue pages of local area telephone directories.

3. VITAL STATISTICS:
Birth and Death:

Library, Archives & Public Records
1700 W. Washington, Suite 442
Phoenix, AZ 85007
(602) 542-4159
Fax (602) 542-4402

Marriage and Divorce:

Courthouse in County concerned.

4. USDVA FACILITIES:
Regional Office:

3225 N. Central Avenue
Phoenix, AZ 85012
1-800-827-1000

VA Medical Centers:

Carl T. Hayden VA Medical Center
650 E. Indian School Rd.

Phoenix, AZ 85012
Prescott VA Medical Center
500 Highway 89 North
Prescott, AZ 86313
Tucson VA Medical Center
3601 S. 6th Ave.
Tucson, AZ 85713

Phone:

(602) 277-5551
1-800-359-8262
(520) 445-4860
1-800-949-1005
(520) 792-1450
1-800-470-8262

USDVA Vet Centers:

141 E. Palm Lane, Suite 100, Phoenix, AZ 85004 (602) 379-4769
3055 N. 1st Avenue, Tucson, AZ 85713 (520) 332-0333
161 S. Granite St., Suite B, Prescott, AZ 86303 (520) 778-3469
P.O. Box 267, Keams Canyon, AZ 86034 (520) 738-5166
P.O. Box 1934, Chinle, AZ 86503 (520) 674-3682

Veterans Integrated Service Network 18

60001 S. Power Road, Bldg 237
VISN 18: Southwest Network
Mesa, AZ 85206-0910
480-222-2681

5. NATIONAL CEMETERIES:

National Memorial Cemetery of Arizona
23029 N. Cave Creek Rd.
Phoenix, AZ 85024

VA Medical Center
500 Hwy. 89 North
Prescott, AZ 86301

Phone:

(602) 379-4615
(520) 776-6028

ARKANSAS DEPARTMENT OF VETERANS' AFFAIRS

DIRECTOR: NICK D. BACON (Medal of Honor Recipient)
MAILING ADDRESS:
    POST OFFICE BOX 1280
    NORTH LITTLE ROCK, AR 72115
LOCATION:
    FORT ROOTS—ROOM 119, BLDG. 65
    NORTH LITTLE ROCK
TELEPHONE: (501) 370-3820
FAX: (501) 370-3829
E-MAIL: nick.smith@mail.state.ar.us

1. SERVICES PERFORMED.

A. Assist veterans, their dependents and survivors in their claims with the U.S. Department of Veterans Affairs (USDVA) for benefits they are entitled to under Title 38, United States Code. All claims officers assigned are accredited representatives of the following service organizations:
    The American Legion
    Marine Corps League
    AMVETS
    Military Order of the Purple Heart
    AR Dept. of Veterans' Affairs
    American Ex-Prisoners of War, Inc.
    Catholic War Veterans

Veterans of Foreign Wars
Fleet Reserve Association
Veterans of World War I of USA, Inc.
Jewish War Veterans
Blinded Veterans Association
Non-Commissioned Officers Assoc.
B. Supervise a network of county veterans service officers.
C. Maintain a 61-bed intermediate care nursing and 55-bed Veterans Domiciliary at 4701 West 20th Street, Little Rock, AR.

2. STATE BENEFITS:

A. Tax Relief

Totally and permanently disabled service-connected veterans are exempt from payment of state taxes on homestead and personal property. Service-connected disabled veterans who have been, or might hereafter be, awarded special monthly compensation by the USDVA for the loss, and/or loss of or use of, one or more limbs, or total blindness in one or both eyes are also exempted.

Exemption is also provided for unmarried surviving spouses and dependent children of members who were killed in action, or who died in service in line of duty, or died of service-connected disabilities and unmarried surviving spouses and dependent children of service-connected veterans who had the tax exemption.

Provides an exemption from the Arkansas Gross Receipts Tax for the sale of a new car to veterans who have been blinded by service-connected injury. Limited to one car every two years. Provides an exemption of the first $6,000 of service pay or allowance to members of the Armed Forces of the United States, and of retirement pay and disability benefits of retired service members.

B. Veterans Domiciliary and Intermediate Care Nursing Home: A state institution that became operational in 1980. The facility serves honorably discharged veterans who have become disabled and are unemployable. It is under the supervision of the Director, Arkansas Department of Veterans' Affairs.

C. Bonus: None

D. Loan Program: None

E. Educational Benefits: Provides for free tuition at state-supported institutions of higher learning and vocational-technical schools for dependents or Arkansas citizens who are prisoners of war or missing in action or killed in action, after January 1, 1960.

F. Burial Assistance: None

G. License Plates: Congressional Medal of Honor recipients, Purple Heart recipients, Ex—Prisoners of War, Disabled Veterans, Pearl Harbor Survivors, Armed Forces Retired, and Military Reserve.

3. USDVA REGIONAL OFFICE:

The main office of the agency is located in the Little Rock USDVA Regional Office, with Hospital representatives in the USDVA Medical Centers at Little Rock and Fayetteville. The Veterans Home is located at 4701 West 20th, Little Rock.

4. GENERAL INFORMATION:

Our mission is to ensure that the veterans, their dependents and survivors receive the maximum benefits to which they are entitled to under federal and state laws.

We have 75 counties with county veterans service officers who are trained and supervised by ADVA to serve the veterans, their dependents and survivors.

The last available count of veterans residing in Arkansas is 262,300 as of July 1, 1993. ADVA Service Officers are accredited to the following nationally recognized active veterans organizations:

The American Legion

Marine Corps League

AMVETS

Military Order of the Purple Heart

AR Dept. of Veterans' Affairs
American Ex-Prisoners of War, Inc.
Catholic War Veterans
Veterans of Foreign Wars
Fleet Reserve Association
Veterans of World War I of USA, Inc.
Jewish War Veterans
Blinded Veterans Association
Non-Commissioned Officers Assoc.

The personnel of the Arkansas Department of Veterans Affairs endeavor to provide a quality of service to veterans, their widows, orphans and dependents commensurate with the sacrifices made by these individuals in the time of this Nation's peril.

CALIFORNIA DEPARTMENT OF VETERANS AFFAIRS

MAILING ADDRESS & LOCATION:
1227 O STREET, SUITE 300
SACRAMENTO, CALIFORNIA 95814
TELEPHONE:
(916) 653-2158
1-800-952-5626 (CA only)
1-800-221-8998 (US only)
FAX: (916) 653-2611
E-MAIL: maurice.johannessen@cdva.ca.gov

1. SERVICES PERFORMED.

A. The Department represents veterans, widows and dependents through Power of Attorney. We act as exclusive representative for:
Blinded Veterans Association
National Association of County Veterans Service Officers
Catholic War Veterans
Ex-POWs Association
Regular Veterans Association

Jewish War Veterans

Veterans of World War I of the USA, Inc.

B. While not a part of the California Department of Veterans Affairs (CDVA), county veterans service officers qualify for state funding totaling $1 million in fiscal year 1993-94 for 56 of 58 counties. In addition, $770,835 in Medi-Cal funds were allocated to the counties for cost avoidance activities.

C. Service organizations not associated with CDVA are the:

AMVETS

Paralyzed Veterans of Association

Disabled American Veterans

The American Legion

Fleet Reserve Association

Veterans of Foreign Wars

Military Order of the Purple Heart

2. STATE BENEFITS:

A. The Veterans Home of California, Yountville, provides five levels of care: acute, skilled nursing, intermediate nursing licensed residential and residential. The fully accredited and licensed medical-surgical hospital and skilled nursing Facility contains 483 beds. The bed capacity of the entire home is 1,421.

B. The Cal-Vet Home Loan Program provides long-term, low interest financing (7. 75% as of August 1, 1994), to war time veterans for the purchase of farms and homes, including townhouses, condominiums and mobile homes on land owned by the veteran. The current maximum loan on these types of properties ranges from $170,000 to $242,100, based upon the median purchase price in the area. The maximum loan on working farms range from $200,000 to 160% of the maximum home loan in higher cost areas. The maximum loan on a mobile home in an approved park is $90,000.

C. The Dependent's College Fee Waiver Program provides college tuition and fee waiver at state-owned colleges and universities for dependents of service-connected deceased and disabled California veterans when the dependents' income and support from their parents is less than $7,000 per year.

D. The Southern California Veterans Homes: Under a law effective October 1991, the Department may establish and construct a second state veterans home which may be located on one or more sites in a 7-county area of Southern California. As recommended by a Governor's Commission, four sites are planned, each serving 400 veterans in Domiciliary, Intermediate and Skilled Nursing levels of care. The first, located in Barstow, is now open and operational.

3. VETERANS ORGANIZATIONS, STATE HEADQUARTERS:

The American Legion
117 Veterans War Memorial Bldg.
San Francisco, CA 94102-4587
Disabled American Veterans
13733 E. Roscrans Ave.
Santa Fe Springs, CA 90670

Veterans of Foreign Wars
7111 Governors Circle
Sacramento. CA 95827-2500

4. GENERAL INFORMATION:

The Department was established in May of 1946, under an act of the Legislature, consolidating the administration of the principal veterans' benefits in California. The Governor appoints the Department director who serves at his pleasure. The director administers the Department in accordance with policy adopted by the California Veterans Board, composed of seven veteran members, appointed by the Governor and subject to Senate confirmation. Of the seven board members, one member shall also be retired from the active or reserved forces of the

U.S. Military service. The Department reports to the Governor via the Secretary of the State and Consumer Services Agency.

The Department administers three major programs. The Division of Farm and Home Purchases administers the Cal-Vet home loan program, established in 1921. Qualified veterans of any war period may acquire homes or farms at low interest rates. Cal-vet offers low cost life, disability, and property insurance. The program is entirely self-supporting, is funded through the sale of state general obligation bonds and revenue bonds repaid by the veteran purchasers.

The Division of Veterans Services coordinates all veterans' programs in the state, offers informational and advisory services to agencies counseling veterans, and assists veterans and dependents in presenting claims against the United States to which they are legally entitled under federal or state laws. The Division also administers the county veterans service officers program, partially funded by the state. Veterans' claims proceed from the counties to the division s district offices in Los Angeles, San Diego, or San Francisco, and then to regional offices of the United States Department of Veterans Affairs (USDVA). The Division also administers the Veterans Dependents' College Fee Waiver Program and the new Veterans License Plate Program.

The Veterans Home of California is located in Yountville in Napa County. The Home first opened in April 1884. It was operated by and for veterans of the Mexican and Civil Wars until 1897. In January of that year, it was deeded, 'fee simple, " to the State of California which has since operated the Home. The Home offers total medical care including residential and hospital care for aged and disabled veteran residents. Facilities include an acute hospital, nursing care, including skilled and intermediate care, and residential facilities. Couples may reside at the Home as long as one is a veteran. The Home offers extensive recreational and therapeutic rehabilitation facilities.

Presently, 3.0 million veterans reside in California.

All nationally recognized veterans organizations are active in the state. Approximately 250,000 of the state's veterans are members of at least one of these organizations:

AMVETS
Paralyzed Veterans of Association
Blinded Veterans Association
Regular Veterans Association
Catholic War Veterans of the USA
The American Legion
Coast Guard League
The Chosin Few
Disabled American Veterans
The Retired Officers Association
Fleet Reserve Association
United Spanish War Veterans
Jewish War Veterans of USA, Inc.
Veterans of Foreign Wars
Legion of Valor of the USA, Inc.
Veterans of World War I of USA, Inc.
Marine Corps League
Vietnam Veterans of America, Inc.
Military Order of the Purple Heart
WAVES National
Non-Commissioned Officers Assoc.
Women Marines Association

COLORADO DIVISION OF VETERANS AFFAIRS DEPARTMENT OF HUMAN SERVICES

DIRECTOR: E. William Belz
MAILING ADDRESS & LOCATION:
  789 SHERMAN STREET
  SUITE 260
  DENVER, COLORADO 80203-1714

TELEPHONE: (303) 894-7474
FAX: (303) 894-7442
E-MAIL: eugene.belz@state.co.us

1. SERVICES PERFORMED.

A. This Department furnishes representation to veterans, and by virtue of Power of Attorney executed in favor of one of the following organizations:
American Red Cross
Regular Veterans Association
Colorado Div. of Veterans Affairs
The Retired Enlisted Association
Military Order of the Purple Heart
Vietnam Veterans of America
Non-Commissioned Officers Assoc.
Veterans of WWI of the USA, Inc.

Responsible for County Veterans Service Officers. Conducts a continuous training program for 63 County Veteran Service Officers. Under certain conditions partially reimburses counties for the salaries and expenses of their County Veterans Service Office. The counties supplement the amount not paid by the State.
B. Service Organizations Not Affiliated With The Division
The American Legion
Paralyzed Veterans of America
Disabled American Veterans
Veterans of Foreign Wars
C. Information Service: Conducts a current and factual information service throughout the State for all veterans, their dependents and survivors.
D. Personal service made available through representation in the name of the Division to veterans, their dependents, widow, orphans and others, before certain agencies of the State and Federal government.

2. STATE BENEFITS:

A. Tax Exemption: There is excluded from gross income, retirement pay' received by members of the Armed Forces, to the extent it is excluded from Federal income tax and not to exceed $20,000 in any one taxable year.

B. State Veterans' Home: Admission preference is given to veterans, spouses, widows and mothers at State Veterans Center, Homelake, Colorado. With 40 operating beds in the domiciliary unit and 60 beds in nursing care service.

C. State Veterans Nursing Home: The Colorado State Veterans Nursing Home at Florence, Colorado with a bed capacity of 120 beds. Colorado State Veterans Nursing Home at Rifle, Colorado with a capacity of 100 beds. Colorado State Veterans Nursing Home at Walsenburg with a capacity of 120 beds.

D. State Loan Program: None

E. State Bonus: None

F. Burial Allowance: County allowance of up to $50 for burial and up to $50 for setting markers for pauper veterans.

G. License Plates: The State provides, without cost, to certain disabled wartime veterans, special disabled veterans license plates, and special license plates for former POWs. Plates for honorably discharged veterans may be purchased for nominal fee.

H. Motor Vehicles: No fee shall be charged to certain disabled veterans or Ex-Pows who have established their right to benefits under public laws. Applies to subsequent vehicles, but only one at a time.

I. Fishing license: No fee to a member of the Armed Forces stationed as a resident patient at a military hospital or convalescent station, or any resident patient at a USDVA hospital located within the State, nor for any veteran who is permanently and totally disabled.

J. Small Game Hunting and Fishing License: Resident veteran with a service-connected disability of 60% or more is eligible for a free lifetime combination small-game hunting and fishing license.

K. Civil Service Rights: Disabled veterans shall have 10 points added to their grades and non-disabled veterans shall be credited with an additional 5 points.

3. VITAL STATISTICS:

Section of Records & Statistics
Department of Public Health
4300 Cherry Creek Drive South
Denver, Colorado 80222-1530

4. USDVA REGIONAL OFFICE:

155 Van Gordon Street
Box25126
Denver, Colorado 80225

5. VETERANS ORGANIZATIONS, STATE HEADQUARTERS:

The American Legion
3003 Tejon
Denver, CO 80211
Disabled American Veterans
1400 South Federal Boulevard
Denver, CO 80219

Paralyzed Veterans of America
44 Union Boulevard
Denver, CO 80225
Veterans of Foreign Wars
1280 Kalamath
Denver, CO 80204

6. GENERAL INFORMATION:

The Colorado Department of Veterans' Affairs was created by an Act of the 1947 Colorado General Assembly to provide assistance and service to veterans, their dependents and survivors. The Reorganization Act of State Government of 1968 placed the Department of Veterans Affairs under the Department of Human Services. In July 1994, the Division became a part of the new Department of Human Services.

The Board of Veterans Affairs is an advisory body to the Division of Veterans Affairs and is composed of seven members, appointed by the Governor and confirmed by the State Senate.

The Colorado State Veterans Center at Homelake, the State Nursing Home at Florence and the State Veterans Nursing Home at Rifle, and the State Veterans Nursing Home at Walsenburg, provide care and treatment to Colorado veterans, their wives, widows and mothers.

The Director of Veterans Affairs is authorized and directed to establish uniform procedures for the performance of service work among the County Service Officers; to maintain contact and close cooperation with them; to provide assistance, advice and instructions with respect to changes in law, regulations and administrative procedures; and he is authorized to require reports from such County Service Officers, reflecting the character and progress of their duties.

The Director also supervises, trains and directs the operation of the County Service Officers, who are county employees. The County Commissioners fix their compensation, set their work hours, and furnish their office space. Counties, in complying with the statutes, are reimbursed from funds of the Division in accordance with the law. The County Veterans Service Officers provide assistance and service to veterans, their dependents and survivors at county level.

The Division conducts a continuous training program for all Division personnel involved in claims work or releasing information. The Division conducts an annual training conference in the Spring and district conferences in the Fall for all County Veterans Service Officers.

CONNECTICUT DEPARTMENT OF VETERANS' AFFAIRS

COMMISSIONER: EUGENE A. MIGLIARO, JR.
MAILING ADDRESS & LOCATION:
   287 WEST STREET
   ROCKY HILL, CT 06067
TELEPHONE: (860) 721-5891
FAX: (860) 721-5904
E-MAIL: eugene.migliaro@po.state.ct.us

1. SERVICES PERFORMED.

A. Provides general medical care for wartime veterans honorable discharged from the Armed Forces.

B. Provides a Home for eligible veterans. The Home provides its residents with a continuum of rehabilitation called the "Veterans Improvement Program (VIP)". Through this program, veterans receive substance abuse treatment, educational and vocational rehabilitation, job skills development, self-enhancement workshops, employment assistance and transitional living opportunities.

C. Administers aid and services to qualifying veterans and their dependents.

2. STATE BENEFITS:

A. Real Property Tax Exemptions: There are many kinds of tax exemptions for eligible veterans in the state.

B. Motor Vehicles: State law grants free motor vehicle registrations and special plates to disabled wartime veterans with service-connected disabilities, former POWs, and recipients of the Congressional Medal of Honor. A disabled wartime veteran is also exempt from overtime parking fees, provided his vehicle does not remain in one location for more than 24 hours (CGS Secs. 14-21d and 14-254). Veterans who were state residents at the time of induction and who apply within two years of receiving an honorable discharge are exempt from paying for an operator's license and examination fees for one licensing period (CGS Sec. 14-50(c)).

C. Medical: Wartime veterans who need medical care and treatment as a result of disease, wounds or accident are entitled to admission to the Veterans' Home and Hospital or any other veterans' hospital (CGS Sec. 27-108).

D. Financial and General Aid: Veterans who are state citizens and who need temporary financial assistance due to disability or other causes related to military service, may receive that assistance from the Department of Veterans Affairs. The amount and duration of the assistance is discretionary with the department (CGS Sec. 27-125).

E. Soldiers, Sailors and Marines Fund: The Soldiers, Sailors and Marines Fund provides benefits, such as food, clothing, medical and surgical aid, and general care and relief, to veterans who served in any branch of the military during specific period conditions.

F. Occupational Licenses: State law authorizes a variety of benefits occupational licensing, fees, examinations and renewals.

3. MAJOR VETERANS ORGANIZATIONS:

The American Legion
Italian-American War Veterans
Veterans of Foreign Wars
The Catholic War Veterans
Disabled American Veterans of U.S.
The Polish Legion of American Veterans
Jewish War Veterans
The Marine Corps League
AMVETS
Franco-American War Veterans
Military Order of the Purple Heart
The Retired Officers Association

4. GENERAL INFORMATION:

The Veterans Home and Hospital was established in 1864. Control is vested in a Board of Trustees of nine citizens appointed by the Governor. The Hospital is licensed by the state to operate 300 chronic and 50 acute beds. The Joint Commission on Accreditation of Hospitals accredits it. The average daily census in 1998 was 200. There are eight medical wards and twelve specialty clinics. The staff includes 8 permanent physicians, one dentist, and a consulting staff of 80. The veterans home for domiciliary care has a capacity of 650. There are 44 buildings on 250 acres. There are 343 classified positions and 180 patient help. There are federal reimbursements from the U. S. Department of Veterans Affairs (USDVA) and Medicare.

The Veterans Home and Hospital Commission is responsible for administering aid and services to qualified veterans and their dependents.

Eligibility for admission to Home and Hospital and veterans benefits is determined by state statutes and Commission policies. A veteran must have been honorably discharged and have entered service from the State of Connecticut irrespective of his present residence, or must have resided in Connecticut for two years immediately prior to admission. He must have 90 days wartime service to be eligible.

Admission of a veteran not acutely ill will be deferred until proper arrangements can be made and a bed is available. Applicants who require nursing home care are not eligible for admission. As a general medical hospital, the limited bed capacity must be reserved for eligible veterans who are actually ill. There are not facilities at the Veterans Home and Hospital for the care of mentally ill patients. . Domiciliary care in the Veterans Home is for ambulatory veterans who require no nursing or attendant care; are able to take their own medication; are able to go some distance to the dining room without help; can dress themselves; can make their own beds; and can participate in an assigned therapeutic activity.

A veteran may be charged for care if he is able to pay. Following the death of a veteran who has been furnished care, the State may file a claim against his estate.

Copies of laws effecting veterans and their dependents are available and fact sheets for admission to the home and hospital are available upon request from the Veterans Home and Hospital.

DELAWARE COMMISSION OF VETERANS' AFFAIRS

EXECUTIVE DIRECTOR: ANTONIO DAVILA
MAILING ADDRESS & LOCATION:
Robbins Bldg
802 Silverlake Blvd, Suite 100
DOVER, DE 19904
TELEPHONE: (302) 739-2792
1-800-344-9900 (In state only)
FAX: (302) 739-2794
E-MAIL: adavila@state.de.us

1. SERVICES PERFORMED.

A. The Commission provides representation to veterans, dependents and survivors in conjunction with services offered by one of the following organizations:
American Legion
Veterans of Foreign Wars
Disabled American Veterans
Vietnam Veterans of America
Paralyzed Veterans of America
American Veterans (AMVETS)
B. Provides a quarterly Newsletter to veterans.
C. Provides information through World Wide Web at: Delaware Commission of Veterans Affairs
D. Provides State Veterans Service Officer assistance to veterans in claims processing.

2. STATE BENEFITS:

A. Employment Preference: A veteran who passes an examination for employment by the state, will have 5 points added to their certification score. Veterans entitled to compensation for a service-connected disability will have 10 points added to their certification score. Any preference points for which a veteran would qualify after complying with the provisions above, may be claimed by his or her unmarried widow or widower providing he or she achieves a passing examination grade.

B. State Veterans Cemetery: Established in 1989, no charge to any veteran who received an honorable discharge from the Armed Forces of the United States and was a legal resident of the State of Delaware at the time of entry in active military service, or at death (as defined by law) shall be eligible for burial in the state veterans cemetery. The spouse and dependent children may also qualify for interment under certain circumstances for a fee of $300.00.

C. Indigent Veteran Burial: Fees and services are provided for eligible indigent veterans through the Office of the State Adjutant General and the State Veterans Cemetery.

D. Free Registration and Inspection of Motor Vehicles of Disabled Veterans: For any motor vehicle owned by a disabled veteran who shall ever have been eligible for certain benefits under 38 U.S.C., subsection 1901 et seq, or Public Law 539, 93rd Congress shall be registered, but shall be exempted from the payment of registration fees; provided that such exemption shall be limited to one automobile per eligible veteran at any one time.

E. Special License Plates: The owner of any private passenger vehicle or a truck with a 3/4 ton or less manufacturer's rated capacity may apply for the assignment to that vehicle of a special Prisoners of War; Missing in Action, Purple Heart, Disabled Veterans, Retired Military, Korean War Veterans, Valor, and National Guard and Reserve registration number. Eligibility information available through the Division of Motor Vehicles.

F. Free Death Certificates for Veterans: The State Registrar shall furnish free of charge to the relative of a veteran, one time, a certified copy of the veteran's certificate of death providing that said certified copy is essential to the settlement of a claim involving the veteran's affairs. All other copies shall be issued at the statutory fee.

G. Discharge Certificates: The DCVA is the Repository for all DD Forms 214. Veterans can obtain a certified copy at no charge.

H. Notary Services: Delaware Commission of Veterans Affairs and Service organizations appointed notaries public may notarize documents and papers for the benefit of veterans, their families, or dependents. These notaries public shall make no charge for any service rendered in connection with filing claims on behalf of the veteran or their dependents.

I. Hunting, Trapping and Fishing Licenses for Armed Forces Stationed in Delaware: Any member of the armed forces of the U.S. of America while actually stationed within this State shall be deemed a resident of this State for the purpose of obtaining a license to hunt, trap and fish in this State.

J. Veterans' Preference—Admission to Governor Bacon Health Center: The Department of Health and Social Services shall give veterans of World War I, World War II, the Korean Conflict and the Vietnam Era who are eligible for admission to the Health Center a preference over other persons with respect to admission thereto.

K. Pension Benefits for Paraplegic Veterans: Each paraplegic veteran (as defined by law) eligible for benefits hereunder shall receive a pension from the State of $1,200 per year payable in equal monthly installments at the end of each month in which such veteran is eligible.

L. Educational Benefits for Children of Deceased Veterans: Specific information can be obtained by contacting the Delaware Post Secondary Education Commission.

M. Income Tax Exemption: $2,000 Income Tax exemption on Federal and State retirements (under age 60); $3,000 for age 60 and older. (Deduct from gross income on state income tax return).

N. Veterans Outreach Center: Listening Post-Lower Delaware (LP Lo-DEL) provides outreach services to the lower counties of Kent and Sussex.

FLORIDA DEPARTMENT OF VETERANS' AFFAIRS

EXECUTIVE DIRECTOR:
Warren R. (Rocky) McPherson. Col. USMC Ret.
MAILING ADDRESS:
　PO Box 31003
　St. Petersburg, FL 33731
LOCATION: 2540 Executive Center Circle West, Douglas Building, Suite 100,Tallahassee, FL 32301
TELEPHONE: (727) 319-7400
FAX: (727) 319-7780
E-MAIL: mcphersonr@fdva.state.fl.us

1. SERVICES PERFORMED.

A. The FDVA is the advocate for all 1.7 million Florida veterans and provides representation for veterans, and their beneficiaries by virtue of an "Appointment of a Veteran Service Organization" (VA 21-22) made to one of the following veterans' organizations:
　The American Legion
　American Red Cross
　Fleet Reserve Association
　American Ex-Prisoners of War, Inc.
　FL Dept. of Veterans ' Affairs
　Non-Commissioned Officers Assoc.
　The Retired Enlisted Assoc.
　Marine Corps League
　Jewish War Veterans of USA
　Veterans of WWI, USA, Inc.
　Vietnam Veterans of America
　Blinded Veterans' Assoc.

National County Veteran Service Officer Association (CVSOA) County Veteran Service Officers are employed by County governments.

B. Service organizations not associated with this Department, but collocated in the VA Regional Office in St. Petersburg FL:

USDVA (Veterans Service Div.)

AMVETS

Military Order of the Purple Heart

Disabled American Veterans

Veterans of Foreign Wars

Paralyzed Veterans of America

2. STATE BENEFITS:

The Clerk of the Circuit Court shall record, without cost to the veteran, certificates of discharge or separation form the Armed Forces of the United States.

The Department of Veterans' Affairs may issue an identification card to any veteran who is a permanent resident of the state and who has been adjudged by the United States Department of Veterans Affairs or its predecessor to have a100-percent, service-connected permanent and total disability rating for compensation, this could also be a rating of Individual Unemployability from the VA, or who has been determined to have a service-connected total and permanent disability rating of 100 percent and is in receipt of disability retirement pay from any branch of the United States Armed Services, upon the written request of such veteran. Such card may be used by the veteran as proof of eligibility for any benefit provided by state law for 100-percent, service-connected permanently and totally disabled veterans except this card may not be used as proof of eligibility for Exemption of Homesteads. The identification card shall bear a statement that it is unlawful for any person other than the veteran to whom it was issued to use the card.

To obtain a card:

Contact the Florida Department of Veterans' Affairs' at 1-800-827-1000, extension 7400 or commercial at (727) 319-7440 and request an application or contact the local County Veteran Service Office.

A. Education for Children of Deceased or Disabled Florida Veterans:

The State of Florida provides scholarships for dependent children of Florida veterans or servicemen who died in action or died from service-connected diseases or disabilities, have been verified by the Florida Department of Veterans' Affairs as having service-connected 100% total and permanent disabilities, have been determined to have service-connected total and permanent disability ratings of 100% and are in receipt of disability retirement from any branch of the United States Armed Services, or are classified as prisoners of war or missing in action. Specific residency requirements apply and the veteran must have served during specific wars, conflicts or events.

Applications may be obtained from the financial aid offices at most Florida colleges and universities, by calling C. Renee Day at the Florida Department of Veterans' Affairs (727-219-7414), or downloaded from the Florida Department of Education Web Site.

B. Tuition Deferment:

Any veteran or other eligible student who receives benefits under Chapters 30, 31, 32, or 35 of Title 38, U.S.C. or Chapter 1606 of Title 10, U.S.C., and is attending one of Florida's public universities, community colleges or vocational schools is entitled to one tuition deferment each academic year and an additional deferment each time there is a delay in the receipt of benefits.

C. Reduced Tuition For National Guard:

Active Florida Guard members in good standing as of June 30, 1997 are exempt from payment of one-half of tuition and fees. Individuals who enlist in the Guard after June 30, 1997 are eligible for full exemption of tuition and fees. Contact your National Guard Unit for details.

D. World War II Veterans High School Diploma

The State Legislature has approved and the Governor has signed a bill sponsored State Senator George Kirkpatrick and State Representative Howard Futch, together with the Florida Department of Education and the Florida Department of Veterans' Affairs that will grant a high school diploma to any World War II veteran who was not able to complete their high school curriculum due to their military service.

Veterans who meet the following criteria will be eligible:
- inducted into military service between Sept. 16, 1940, and Dec. 31, 1946;
- received an honorable discharge;
- started high school between 1937-1946; and,
- scheduled to graduate from high school between 1941-1950.

These diplomas are for any veteran who currently resides in Florida, regardless of whether they were living in Florida at the time they went to high school. Also, family members who would like to apply for a diploma posthumously for a veteran who has died may do so.

The Department of Education will send a standard Florida high school diploma upon receiving a completed and notarized application. They will also notify the local school superintendent of the new graduate and encourage appropriate ceremonies and recognition.

Applications are available at the following places:
- Call the Department of Veterans' Affairs (727-319-7400)
- Call the Department of Education (850-488-7591)
- Contact your County Veterans' Service Officer

E. Korean War Veterans High School Diploma

A new act, effective July 1, 2002, will allow some Florida veterans an opportunity to receive a high school diploma. Senate Bill 292 provides for the award of a high school diploma to certain Korean War veterans who started high school between 1946 and 1950. Veterans who were inducted into the armed forces between June 1950 and January 1954 and scheduled to graduate between 1950 and 1954 are eligible recipients. The revised law amends s. 232.246, F. S., which originally awarded high school diplomas to World War II veterans.

Veterans who meet the following criteria will be eligible:

- must be a Florida resident;

- inducted into military service between June 1950 and January 1954;

- received an honorable discharge;

- started high school between 1946 and 1950; and

- scheduled to graduate from high school between 1950 and 1954.

The Departments of Education and Veterans Affairs will work together to assist veterans with the application process for their diplomas. Interested veterans should contact the Department of Veterans Affairs at 1-800-827-1000 X7400. Additional information may also be obtained by contacting Debra Rackley, Division of Workforce Development, Florida Department of Education, 325 W. Gaines Street, Room 744, Tallahassee, Florida 32399-0400 or by dialing (850) 922-5961.

F. Hunting and Fishing License

Upon request a state hunting and fishing license shall be issued for a five year period, by the Florida Game and Fresh Water Fish Commission, to any person who is a resident of the state, and who is permanently and totally disabled and currently certified by a licensed physician of this state or the VA, or who holds a valid identification card issued by the FDVA.

No license shall be required for military service personnel who are Florida residents while they are home on leave for periods of 30 days or less.

A saltwater fishing license is issued without fees, from the Department of Environmental Protection's Division of Marine Resources, to members of any branch of the U.S. Armed Services or any person who is a resident of the state and who is permanently and totally disabled as certified by the VA or the DOD, or who holds a valid identification card issued by the FDVA.

G. Driver's License

Any veteran honorable discharged from the Armed Forces who has been issued a valid identification card by the FDVA in accordance with the provisions of FS 295.17 or has been determined by the VA or DOD to have a 100% total and permanent service-connected disability and who is qualified to obtain a Drivers' License, from the Department of Highway Safety and Motor Vehicles, under this chapter is exempt from all fees required by this section. Other fees may apply.

H. DMV License Plates

Call or visit your local auto tag agency or call the Florida Department of Veterans' Affairs at (727) 518-3202 ext 508 for information on how you can purchase your "FLORIDA SALUTES VETERANS" license plate!

Your purchase of the "Florida Salutes Veterans" license plate helps people who need it most, when they need it most. The entire $15 surcharge goes into a Trust Fund for the Operation and Maintenance of critically needed Veterans' Homes in Florida.

Many Floridians will require nursing home care at some point during their lives. For the average person, even a short stay in a nursing home can devastate savings and leave a family destitute. Medicaid costs for nursing home care in Florida are already one of the State's largest expenses.

State Veterans' Nursing Homes offer a unique opportunity for Florida. Operation of our current Veterans' Homes have substantially reduced the State's share of the costs for care to a small fraction of what it must otherwise pay for this critical service.

I. DISABLED VETERAN PLATES

A motor vehicle license plate will be issued for use on any motor vehicle owned or leased by an disabled veteran who has been a continuous resident of Florida for the last five years or has established a domicile as provided by FS 222.17(1) or (2) and (3), upon application accompanied by proof that:

The vehicle was acquired through financial assistance from the VA, or the veteran has been determined by the VA to have a service-connected disability of100% rating for compensation, or,

the veteran has been determined to have a service-connected disability of 100% and is in receipt of disability retirement pay from any branch of the uniformed Armed Forces. A plate fee is charged.

J. Homestead Exemptions

Any real estate used and owned as a homestead by a veteran who was honorably discharged with a service-connected permanent and total disability and for whom a letter from the United States Government or VA or its predecessor has been issued certifying that the veteran is totally and permanently disabled is exempt from taxation, provided the veteran is a permanent resident of the state on January 1 of the tax year for which exemption is being claimed or on January 1 of the year the veteran died.

The production by a veteran or the spouse or surviving spouse of a letter of total and permanent disability from the United States Government or VA or its predecessor before the property appraiser of the county in which property of the veteran lies shall be prima facie evidence of the fact that the veteran or the surviving spouse is entitled to such exemption.

In the event the totally and permanently disabled veteran pre-deceases his or her spouse and upon the death of the veteran, the spouse holds the legal or beneficial title to the homestead and permanently resides thereon as specified in FS 196.031, the exemption from taxation shall carry over to the benefit of the veteran's spouse until such time as he or she remarries or sells or otherwise disposes of the property. If the spouse sells the property, an exemption not to exceed the amount granted from the most recent ad valorem tax roll may be transferred to his or her new residence as long as it is used as his or her primary residence and he or she does not remarry. FS 196.081

Veterans who are paraplegic, hemiplegic, are permanently and totally disabled, must use a wheelchair for mobility, or are legally blind are exempt from real estate taxation if gross annual household income does not exceed the adjusted maximum allowed. The veteran must be a resident of the State of Florida to qualify. Certificate of such disability from two licensed doctors of this state or from the VA or an award letter from the Social Security Administration to the property appraiser is prima facie evidence of entitlement to such exemption.

Homestead Exemption (10% to 100% BUT not Permanent in nature)

Eligible veterans with service-connected disabilities of 10% or more shall be entitled to a $5000 property tax exemption. To qualify for homestead exemption a veteran must be a resident of the state.

Every person who is entitled to homestead exemption in this state and who is serving in any branch of the Armed Forces of the United States may file a claim for homestead exemption. Servicemen unable to file in person may file through next of kin or duly authorized representatives.

K. PERMITS AND FEES

Disabled Veterans Exempt from Certain License or Permit Fees

No totally and permanently disabled veteran who is a resident of Florida shall be required to pay license or permit fees to any county or municipality in order to make certain improvements to assist with his or her disability on any mobile home owned by the veteran and used as his/her residence. Improvements are limited to ramps, widening of doors, and similar improvements for the purpose of making the mobile home habitable for veterans confined to wheelchairs. FS 295.16

L. Handicapped Toll Permit

Any handicapped person who has a valid driver's license, who operates a vehicle specially equipped for use by the handicapped, and who is certified by a licensed physician or by the VA Adjudication Officer as being physically disabled and having permanent impairments which impair the person's ability to deposit coins in toll baskets shall be allowed to pass free through all tollgates. A vehicle window sticker will be issued.

M. Exemption Parking Permit: Persons With Permanent Mobility Problems

A disabled veteran who is a resident of this state and honorably discharged, and has been determined by the VA or the Federal Government to have a service-connected disability rating for compensation of 50% or greater and has a signed physician's statement of qualification is eligible for the permit. The fees are $1.50 for the initial parking permit, $1 for each additional parking permit, $1.50 for renewal parking permit and $1 for each additional renewal parking permit. The fee must be paid to the tax collector of the county in which the fee was generated. The department shall not issue to any one eligible applicant more than two exemption parking permits upon request of the applicant.

N. SCHOOL TUITION DEFERMENT

Available to any veteran or other eligible student covered under Title 38, U.S.C. Allows one tuition deferment each academic year and an additional deferment when a delay in benefits occurs.

O. REDUCED TUITION FOR NATIONAL GUARD

Active Florida Guard members in good standing are exempt from payment of one-half of tuition and fees.

For additional assistance check with the Financial Aid office in the school you will be attending.

P. VETERANS PREFERANCE

(1) GENERAL

Chapter 295, Florida Statutes, sets forth certain requirements for public employers to accord preferences, in appointment, retention and promotion, to certain veterans and spouses of veterans who are Florida residents. The relevant portions of the law apply to "the state and its political subdivisions". Public utilities, state universities, school districts and special taxing districts are subject to the requirements of Chapter 295

(2) CATEGORIES OF PROTECTED INDIVIDUALS

Section 295.07, Florida Statutes, extends veterans' preference to:

- A veteran with a service-connected disability who is eligible for or receiving compensation, disability retirement, or pension under public laws administered by the U.S. Department of Veterans Affairs and the Department of Defense.
- The spouse of a veteran who cannot qualify for employment because of a total and permanent service-connected disability, or the spouse of a veteran missing in action, captured, or forcibly detained by a foreign power
- A veteran of any war who has served on active duty for one day or more during a wartime period, excluding active duty for training, and who was discharged under honorable conditions from the Armed Forces of the United States of America.
- The unremarried widow or widower of a veteran who died of a service-connected disability.

(3) REQUIRED NOTICE BY EMPLOYERS

Public employers must give notice in all announcements and advertisements of vacancies, that preference in appointment will be given to eligible veterans and spouses, and application forms must inquire whether the applicant is claiming veterans' preference, and whether the applicant has claimed such a preference. The regulations provide that an applicant claiming preference is responsible for providing required documentation at the time of making application, but also state that the covered employer must inform applicants of the requirements for documentation

(4) PREFERENCE REQUIRED AT EACH STEP

An eligible veteran is entitled to preference at each stage of the hiring process; however, the preference is not absolute.

(5) EMPLOYMENT PREFERENCE WHEN A NUMERI-CALLY BASED SELECTION PROCESS IS USED

• Employment preferences, where numerically based examinations are used as a device for selections, consists of adding ten points to the score of the first category of applicants (disabled veterans and spouses of disabled or missing veterans) and five points to the score of other preference-eligible applicants.

• The rules provide that where the requisite points (ten points to individuals in the first category, and five points to other applicants) have been adjusted to test scores, the names of all the preference-eligible applicants shall be placed on a register or employment list, beginning with those disabled veterans with disability ratings of 30 percent or more, and followed by all other preference-eligible applicants in the order of their augmented ratings.

• The regulations state "appointments to positions will be made from the appropriate register or employment list in the rank order of their augmented ratings."

(6) PREFERENCE WHEN A NUMERICALLY BASED SELECTION PROCESS IS NOT USED

Preference must be given to protected individuals provided such persons possess the minimum qualifications necessary to the discharge of the duties involved. The rule defines "minimum qualifications" to mean a "specification" of the kinds of experience, training, education and/or licensure or certification that provides "appropriate job-related evidence that an applicant possesses the minimum required knowledge, skills, and abilities necessary to the discharge of the duties involved."

(7) OTHER PROVISIONS REGARDING PREFERENCE

• Single claim to preference
The rules incorporate the concept that an eligible veteran or spouse has a single claim to preference, exercisable only once. A veteran's employment preference expires once the veteran has applied and

been employed by the agency or any political subdivision of the state.

• Preference in layoffs

Where a layoff is necessitated in a covered position, similar preferences must be given to the covered employee in the retention process.

• Preference in reinstatement or reemployment

When an employee in a covered position leaves employment for the purpose of serving in the armed forces, he or she is entitled to reinstatement or reemployment upon release or discharge from active military service.

• Promotion preference

Promotion preference applies only to a veteran's first promotion after reinstatement or reemployment, without exception.

(8) EXEMPT POSITIONS

Chapter 295, Florida Statutes, provides for a preference in employment for certain classes of covered positions. However, section 295.07(2)(a), exempts from the law positions that are exempt from the state career service system under Section 110.205 (2), Florida Statutes.

The 2001 session of the Florida Legislature enacted a significant change to the law concerning exempt positions for veteran's preference at the political subdivision level. Governor Bush signed the bill and the change became effective July 1, 2001. Senate Bill 1344 eliminates the exemption for some of the previously exempted positions. As of the effective date of the law, city managers, county managers, and management and policymaking positions of political subdivisions of the state are now eligible for preference in appointment and retention as provided in s. 295.07(1).

(9) ENFORCEMENT

If an applicant claiming veterans' preference for a vacant position is not selected, he/she may file a complaint with the Florida Department of Veterans' Affairs (FDVA)

Mary Grizzle Building, Suite 332-A
11351 Ulmerton Road
Largo, Fl 33778-1630

A complaint must be filed within twenty-one days of the applicant receiving notice of the hiring decision made by the employing agency or within three months of the date the application is filed with the employer if no notice is given. The enforcement mechanism established by the regulations provide for an initial investigation by the Florida Department of Veterans' Affairs, followed by an evidentiary proceeding before the Public Employees Relations Commission if the matter cannot be earlier resolved.

For additional information concerning veterans' preference, please contact the Florida Department of Veterans' Affairs
By phone at: (727) 518-3202, ex. 548
By email: burnsj@fdva.state.fl.us

Or write:
Florida Department of Veterans' Affairs (FDVA)
Mary Grizzle Building, Suite 332-A
11351 Ulmerton Road
Largo, Fl 33778-1630

Please visit the FDVA website for more information and/or changes to Florida state benefits.

3. VITAL STATISTICS:

Department of Health and Rehabilitative Services
Office of Vital Statistics
P.O. Box 210
Jacksonville, FL 32201-0042

4. USDVA REGIONAL OFFICE:

Post Office Box 1437
144 1st Ave S., Room 418, St.
Petersburg, FL 33731
Phone: Toll-free (FL) 1-800-827-1000

5. VETERANS ORGANIZATIONS, STATE HEADQUARTERS:

The Florida Department of Veterans' Affairs proudly provides representation for the following accredited veteran service organizations. These are not all the veterans' organizations in Florida, but those that offer national service representation and are Congressionally chartered.

AMER. EX-PRISONERS OF WAR
VIETNAM VETERANS OF AMERICA
THE AMERICAN LEGION
VIETNAM VETERANS OF FLORIDA COALITION
AMVETS
NONCOMMISSIONED OFFICERS ASSOCIATION
DISABLED AMERICAN VETERANS
THE RETIRED OFFICERS ASSOCIATION
JEWISH WAR VETERANS
COUNTY VETERANS SERVICE OFFICER ASSN.
MARINE CORPS LEAGUE
FLEET RESERVE ASSOCIATION
MILITARY ORDER OF THE PURPLE HEART
WAVES NATIONAL

PARALYZED VETERANS OF AMERICA
AIR FORCE ASSOCIATION
RESERVE OFFICERS ASSOCIATION
AIR FORCE SERGEANTS ASSOCIATION
POLISH LEGION OF AMERICAN VETERANS
THE RETIRED ENLISTED ASSOCIATION
VETERANS OF FOREIGN WARS

6. GENERAL INFORMATION:

The Florida Division of Veterans' Affairs was established in 1921. In 1988, Florida's voters decided to establish it as a separate Department, effective January 1989. The Department's mission is to assist former members of the U.S. Armed Forces and their beneficiaries in securing benefits or privileges to which they are, or may become entitled under any federal or state law or regulation.

The Department's Veterans Claims Examiners are charged with the responsibility of pursuing claims for veterans, their widows and dependents with the VA, or any other governmental agency from which a veteran, widow or dependent may be entitled to receive a benefit. This is accomplished through use of an Appointment of Veteran Service Organization (VA Form 21-22) given this Department, with the Agency's Veterans Claims Examiners acting as representatives for the veteran/and or beneficiaries to present claims to the VA and other governmental agencies.

We maintain representatives throughout the entire state, with locations at the VA Regional Office, St. Petersburg, FL, as well as representatives at each of Florida's six VA hospitals, located in Lake City, Bay Pines, Miami, Gainesville, West Palm Beach and Tampa. We also have state Veterans Claims Examiners in nine of the state's ten satellite outpatient clinics operated by the VA Medical Centers.

The Department routinely sends information directly or indirectly to all the veterans' organizations in the state to educate veterans and their survivors about veterans' benefits to which they are, or may become, entitled. Our information services cover a much broader scope than the veterans' organizations alone could provide. The Department disseminates information to veterans through mail outs, TV programs, radio spots, newspapers, training seminars, etc. The county veteran service officers (CVSOs) in the state are employees of the various counties; however, this agency is required to initially certify and annually recertify each CVSO as being sufficiently knowledgeable about veteran entitlements.

There is excellent and ongoing coordination between the Department and the various CVSOs throughout the State. All work processed by the CVSO in connection with veterans or their claims with the VA, where the veteran gives Power of Attorney to an organization represented by this Department, is forwarded to us for completion and/or forwarding to the VA. This Department works closely with the veterans' organizations' post and chapter service officers throughout Florida to ensure that the veteran is given proper representation on his/her claim.

The Department is aggressively pursuing the expansion of its state homes for veterans' program. The first state home for veterans, located in Lake City (Columbia County), opened in May 1989 as a 150-bed Domiciliary Home. The first nursing home, a 120-bed skilled care facility, located in Daytona Beach (Volusia County), opened in December 1993. Our second 120-bed skilled nursing home, in Land O'Lakes (Pasco County) opened in April 1999. Unlike the first Nursing Home, this facility is capable of housing residents with mental impairments such as dementia, including Alzheimer's disease. Our newest nursing home, located in Pembroke Pines (Broward County) opened its doors to its first residents in June 2001. It is also a 120-bed facility capable of accommodating 60 residents with Alzheimer's disease. Construction of nursing homes four and five, to be located in Bay and Charlotte counties, is scheduled for early 2003.

GEORGIA DEPARTMENT OF VETERANS' AFFAIRS

COMMISSIONER:
PETE WHEELER
MAILING ADDRESS & LOCATION:
FLOYD VETERANS MEMORIAL BLDG
SUITE E-970
ATLANTA, GA 30334
TELEPHONE: (404) 656-2300
FAX: (404) 656-7006
E-MAIL: ga.vet.svc@mindspring.com

1. SERVICES PERFORMED.

A. Represents veterans and their dependents under Power of Attorney made to the following organizations:
Georgia Department of Veterans Service
The American Legion
Veterans of World War I, USA, Inc.
Jewish War Veterans
Fleet Reserve Association
Veterans of Foreign Wars
American Red Cross
American Ex-Prisoners of War
Non-Commissioned Officers Association
The Retired Enlisted Association
B. State Approval Agency administers Veterans Educational Assistance Programs for U.S. Department of Veterans Affairs (USDVA).
C. Veterans in every county served by 48 field offices and Claims Division.

2. STATE BENEFITS:

A. Tax Exemptions:

(1) Sales Tax on Vehicles: A disabled veteran who receives a VA grant for the purchase and special adapting of a vehicle is exempt from paying the state sales tax on the vehicle (only on the original grant).

(2) Homestead Tax: Certain disabled veterans and certain widows/ widowers, or minor children are allowed the maximum amount which may be granted under Section 2102 of Title 38 of the United States Code.

(3) Ad Valorem Tax on Vehicles: Exempt are veterans who are verified by VA to be 100 percent totally and permanently service-connected disabled, and veterans who are receiving or who are entitled to receive statutory awards from VA for:

(1) loss or permanent loss of use of one or both feet;

(2) loss or permanent loss of use of one or both hands;

(3) loss of sight in one or both eyes; or

(4) permanent impairment of vision of both eyes to a prescribed degree. Exemption is granted on the vehicle the veteran owns and upon which the free Handicapped Veterans (HV) Motor Vehicle license plate are attached.

(4) Certificate of Exemption: Disabled veterans are exempt from payment of occupational taxes, administration fees, and regulatory fees imposed by local governments for peddling, conducting a business, or practicing a profession or semi-profession upon meeting the following eligibility requirements:

(1) be discharged under honorable conditions from the armed forces of the United States;

(2) have ten percent disability for certain wartime veterans or a twenty-five percent service-connected disability for peacetime-only veterans; and

(3) have an income that is not liable for state income taxes.

(5) State Income Tax: The period of time military personnel served on active duty as members of the armed forces of the United States in

combat activities during a period designated by the President, plus the
next 180 days thereafter, are disregarded in determining whether any
filing requirement has been performed within the time limit prescribed
for filing. For individuals who are hospitalized as a result of an injury
or confined as a prisoner of war the period of service in the combat
zone, plus the period of confinement and the next 180 days thereafter,
shall be disregarded in determining whether any filing requirement has
been performed within the time prescribed for filing.

B. State War Veterans Homes

Skilled Nursing Home in Augusta, GA has 132 beds. Vinson Building in Milledgeville, GA is also a skilled home and has 120 beds. Wood
Building in Milledgeville, GA is also a skilled nursing home and has
150 beds. Wheeler Building in Milledgeville, GA is a Domiciliary and
has 288 beds.

C. Licenses:

(1) HV Automobile License Tags are issued free of charge to certain
disabled service connected veterans.

(2) DV Automobile License Tags are issued to veterans severely disabled from nonservice connected disabilities, but tags must be purchased at cost of regular license plates. The veteran must meet the same
degree of disability requirements as the veteran eligible for the free HV
Tags.

(3) POW Automobile License Tag will be issued free to veterans
who are former Prisoners-of-War, who were subsequently honorably
separated from military service, and who are a legal resident of Georgia.

(4) Medal of Honor Tag is issued free to a veteran who is a legal resident of Georgia and who has been awarded the Medal of Honor.

(5) Purple Heart Tag is issued free to veterans who have been
awarded the Purple Heart.

(6) Retired personnel of the United States Armed Forces or individuals who served during WWI, WWII, Korean War, Vietnam War or
Operation Desert Storm are eligible to purchase special and distinctive

vehicle license plates. All requests must be accompanied by payment of the appropriate taxes, registration fees and manufacturing fees.

(7) Pearl Harbor Tags Veterans of the armed forces of the United States who survived the attack on Pearl Harbor are eligible to receive a special and distinctive vehicle license plate upon application and payment of an additional fee.

(8) Veterans Drivers' Licenses are issued free to veterans honorably discharged with wartime or conflict service from Georgia or have resided in Georgia for five years immediately preceding the date of applying for the license. Also applies to all members or former members of the National Guard or Reserve Forces who have twenty or more years creditable service.

(9) Personal identification cards are available to veterans who do not have a motor vehicle driver's license and who would otherwise be entitled to issuance of a free veterans driver's license.

(10) Honorary Driver's Licenses are extended to:

(a) A resident of Georgia who is a surviving spouse of a veteran who was eligible for veteran's drivers license so long as that person remains unremarried.

(b) To be a resident of Georgia who is the spouse of a veteran who would be qualified for a veterans driver's license, but who is permanently disabled to the extent that he cannot operate a motor vehicle.

(11) Hunting and Fishing Licenses: Any veteran who is a legal resident of Georgia who files with the Game and Fish Division, Department of Natural Resources, a letter from VA or a certificate from the Social Security Administration, Medicaid, Medicare, Railroad Retirement System or a unit of federal, state or local government recognized by the Board of Natural Resources by rule or regulation, stating that he/she is a totally and permanently disabled veteran, is entitled to a lifetime honorary hunting and fishing license allowing the veteran to fish and hunt within the state without the payment of any fee. Persons who are at least 65 years old or who are rated totally blind also qualify.

D. Handicapped Parking

Disabled veterans who are holders of HV or DV tags do not have to purchase handicap parking permits. These distinctive tags will serve as sufficient evidence that they are eligible to park in special designated areas for the handicapped.

E. Guardianship

Provides for appointment of guardian for incompetent veterans or for children when U.S. Department of Veterans Affairs is involved.

F. Employment Preference: To war veterans under State Merit System.

G. Vital Statistics, Documents

If vital statistics, documents, records (birth, death, marriage, divorce) are needed for a veteran or dependent's claim, the request should be directed to the Commissioner, Department of Veterans Affairs, Floyd Veterans Memorial Building, Suite E0970, Atlanta, GA 30334. Otherwise a fee will be charged to those going directly to the Department of Human Resources.

H. DD 214 and Discharges: Discharges are recorded free by the County Clerk of the Superior Court.

I. Reduced Fees for Disabled Veterans for Use or Occupancy of State Parks, Historic Sites, and Recreational Areas Available to service-connected veterans who were discharged under honorable conditions and are residents of the State. Must apply to the Department of Veterans' Service.

3. VITAL STATISTICS:

INFORMATION NOT AVAILABLE

4. USDVA REGIONAL OFFICE:

730 Peachtree Street, NE.
Atlanta. GA 30365

5. VETERANS ORGANIZATIONS, STATE HEADQUARTERS:

The American Legion
3035 Mt. Zion Road
Stockbridge, GA 30281
Disabled American Veterans
4462 Houston Avenue
P.O. Box 3C87
Macon, GA 31205

AMVETS
730 Peachtree Street, N.E.
Atlanta, GA 30365
Veterans of Foreign Wars
4952 Columbus Road
P.O. Box 11526
Macon, GA 31212-1526

6. GENERAL INFORMATION:

INFORMATION NOT AVAILABLE

GUAM VETERANS AFFAIRS OFFICE
OFFICE OF THE GOVERNOR

ADMINISTRATOR: JOHN O. BLAZ
MAILING ADDRESS:
   VETERANS AFFAIRS OFFICE
   P.O. BOX 3279
   AGANA, GUAM 96932
LOCATION:
   "M" STREET
   HSE #105
   TIYAN, GUAM

TELEPHONE: (671) 475-4222 or 475-4225
E-MAIL: NOT AVAILABLE

UPDATED INFORMATION NOT AVAILABLE

HAWAII DEPARTMENT OF DEFENSE
OFFICE OF VETERANS SERVICES

DIRECTOR: BG IRWIN K. COCKETT, JR., USA, RETIRED
MAILING ADDRESS:
  459 PATTERSON RD.
  E-WING, RM 1-A103
  HONOLULU, HI 96819
LOCATION:
  TRIPLER ARMY MEDICAL CENTER
  WARD ROAD
  VAMROC, E-WING, RM 1-A103
  HONOLULU, HI 96819
TELEPHONE: (808) 433-0420
FAX: (808) 433-0385
E-MAIL: ovs@dod.hawaii.gov OR hicocki@vba.va.gov

1. SERVICES PERFORMED.

Provides information, counsel and aid to veterans, dependents and their families.

2. STATE BENEFITS:

A. Tax Exemption: Tax exemption on real property owned and occupied as a home by a totally disabled veteran or his widow.
B. Employment and Reemployment: Preference is given veterans for civil service positions. Reemployment rights for veterans who left state, county, or other political subdivisions on the same basis as provided by federal law.

C. Relief and Assistance: Payment by the State of $5,000 in addition to the amount provided by the U.S. Department of Veterans Affairs (USDVA) specially adapted housing program to provide disabled veterans with specially equipped homes.

D. Burial Benefits: Hawaii State Veterans Cemetery on Oahu, veterans cemeteries on five other islands.

3. VITAL STATISTICS:

Free certified copies of vital statistics when needed in connection with veteran's claims, and free recording of discharge certification. For veterans, send request to the Office of Veterans Services.

Office of Health Status Monitoring
State Department of Health
P.O. Box 3378
Honolulu, HI 96801

Birth or Death:

$10.00 State Office has had records since 1853. Check or money order should be made payable to State Department of Health. Personal checks are accepted for the correct amount only. To verify current fees, call (808) 548-5819 (recorded message).

Marriage:

$10.00 same as birth/death.

Divorce:

$2.00 same as birth/death. If state does not have record, write to Circuit Court in County where divorce was granted. Fee varies.

4. VETERANS SERVICES COUNSELORS:

OAHU
919 Ala Moana Blvd.
Suite 100

Honolulu, HI 96814
Telephone: (808) 433-0427
HAWAII
101 Aupuni St., Room 212
Hilo, Hl 96720
Telephone: (808) 933-0315

MAUI, MOLOKAI AND LANAI
333 Dairy Road
Suite 106
Kahului, HI 96732
Telephone: (808) 243-5818
KAUAI
3215 Kapule Highway, #2
Lihue, HI 96766
Telephone: (808) 241-3346

5. MEDICAL AND REGIONAL OFFICE:

300 Ala Moana Blvd.
Rm. 1004
P.O. Box 50188
Honolulu, HI 96850-0001

Medical Office:
(808) 566-1000

Regional Office:
(from Oahu) (808) 566-1000
(from Hawiian neighbor islands) 800-827-1000
(from Guam) 475-8387
(from American Samoa) 1-1-800-844-7928

6. VET CENTERS:

120 Keawe St.
Suite 201
Hilo, HI 96720
(808) 969-3833
1680 Kapiolani Blvd.
Suite F-3
Honolulu, HI 96814
(808) 566-1764

Pottery Terrace, Fern Bldg.
75-5995 Kuakini Hwy.
Kailua-Kona, HI 96740
(808) 329-0574
3367 Kuhlo Hwy.
Suite 101
Lihue, HI 96766
(808) 246-1163

35 Lunalilo
Suite 101
Wailuku, HI 96793
(808) 242-8557

7. NATIONAL CEMETERY:

National Memorial Cemetery of the Pacific
2177 Puowaina Dr.
Honolulu, HI 96813
(808) 566-1430

8. STATE DIRECTOR OF ADULT EDUCATION (For GED Test Results):

Administrator Community Education Section
595 Pepeekeo Street, H-2
Honolulu, HI 96825
(808) 395-9451
FAX: (808) 395-1826

IDAHO DIVISION OF VETERANS' AFFAIRS

ADMINISTRATOR: RICHARD W. JONES
MAILING ADDRESS & LOCATION:
320 COLLINS ROAD
BOISE, ID 83702
TELEPHONE: (208) 334-3513
FAX: (208) 334-2627
E-MAIL: jonesr@idvs.state.id.us

1. SERVICES PERFORMED.

A. Represents veterans, dependents and survivors—Office of Veterans Advocacy located at USDVA Regional Office, 805 W. Franklin Street, Boise, ID 83702-5560. Telephone (208) 334-1245.

This unit furnishes representation to veterans, widows, children, and parents of deceased veterans, and to organizations before the USDVA by virtue of Power of Attorney executed in favor of the following organizations:

Veterans of World War I, USA, Inc.
The American Legion
Veterans of Foreign Wars
AMVETS
Division of Veterans Services
Fleet Reserve Association
Military Order of the Purple Heart

Blinded Veterans of America

Vietnam Veterans of America, Inc.

American Ex-Prisoners of War

The Retired Enlisted Association

B. County service officers are NOT under this Division, but full cooperation is offered and requested.

C. Temporary Emergency Relief: Division dispenses grants to honorably discharged Idaho veterans meeting basic eligibility criteria and their dependents.

D. Idaho service organization not represented by this Division, but located in the USDVA Regional Office in Boise:

Disabled American Veterans

2. STATE BENEFITS:

A. Tax Exemptions: For veterans of certain wars and qualified disabled veterans.

B. Veterans Homes: Bernard Bufford III, Administrator, P.O. Box 7765, 320 Collins Road, Boise, ID 83707; telephone (208) 334-5000. Division has full power and authority to operate and manage this 10-bed domiciliary care, 136-bed skilled nursing care, and 36-bed residential care facility.

Paul "Jeff" Piper, Administrator, 1957 Alvin Ricken Dr., Pocatello, ID 83201; telephone (208) 236-6340. Division has full power and authority to operate and manage this 66-bed skilled nursing care facility.

Ronald W. Barnes, Administrator, 821 21st Avenue, Lewiston, ID 83501; telephone (208) 799-3422. Division has full power and authority to operate and manage this 66-bed skilled nursing care facility.

C. State Loan Program: None

D. State Bonus: None

E. Emergency Relief: For honorably discharged Idaho veterans meeting basic eligibility criteria and their dependents.

F. Education: Scholarship for children of MIA/POW.

G. License: Free vehicle license plates for eligible disabled Idaho veterans. License plates for Purple Heart recipients also are available to eligible veterans, as well as a veterans license plate for any Idaho veteran. There is a license plate fee for the Purple Heart and veteran plates.

> **Fish & Game License:** All eligible Idaho residents over age 70 may take fish and game with a free fishing license obtained through the Department of Fish and Game. Those under age 70 may obtain hunting and fishing licenses at a reduced cost. All Idaho residents in military service may receive free fish and game permits while on furlough or leave.

H. Veterans Preference: Public employment preference.

3. VITAL STATISTICS:

State Registrar
Center for Vital Statistics and Health Policy
450 West State, 1st Floor—or—P.O. Box 83720
Boise, ID 83720-0036

4. USDVA REGIONAL OFFICE:

805 West Franklin Street
Boise, ID 83702-5560

5. VETERANS ORGANIZATIONS, STATE HEADQUARTERS:

The American Legion
901 Warren Street
Boise, ID 83706

Disabled American Veterans
VA Regional Office

805 W. Franklin Street
Boise, ID 83702-5560

Veterans of Foreign Wars
1425 South Roosevelt
Boise, ID 83705

6. GENERAL INFORMATION:

A pioneer in the Veterans Affairs field, the Idaho Veterans Affairs Commission was created in 1921, and consists of five members, appointed to serve at the pleasure of the Governor. The Office of Veterans Advocacy (OVA) was added to the Commission's jurisdiction in 1925. Prior to that date, service work was carried on through volunteer agencies.

The Idaho Veterans Home was transferred to the jurisdiction of the Commission in March 1955, where it remained until it was placed under the Department of Health and Welfare in 1974. The "Old Soldiers Home", formally opened in May, 1895, was replaced by a new Home, which was constructed at a different location in Boise and dedicated in November, 1966. On July 1, 2000, the Idaho Division of Veterans Services became a Self-Governing Agency.

During the latter part of the 1960s and early 1970s, the veterans of Idaho recognized the need for a veterans nursing facility and "The Idaho United Veterans Council to Build a Nursing Home" was formed. In the spring of 1978, the Idaho Legislature appropriated funds for the construction of an 80 bed skilled-care facility and a 10-bed female domiciliary. The facility was built adjoining the Idaho State Veterans Home in Boise and dedicated on November 11, 1980. The facility is currently home to 172 veterans—136 in skilled nursing care and 36 in residential and domiciliary care.

In 1984, an effort was started to locate regional State Veterans Homes in Idaho. The culmination of that effort came in 1989 when the State Legislature appropriated state matching funds for a Home in

Pocatello. In 1990, the Legislature again appropriated state matching funds for a Home in Lewiston. The Pocatello Home opened in the summer of 1992 and the Lewiston Home followed in the spring of 1994.

The Office of Veterans Advocacy (OVA) works closely with county service officers, post and barracks service officers, and coordinates all veterans training programs in the state. Veterans' claims usually proceed from these service officers to the OVA and then to the USDVA Regional Office.

Rather than granting a general bonus to Idaho veterans, the Legislature established a program, which is designed to assist veterans discharged under honorable conditions at a time when the veteran or his/her dependents are actually in need of assistance. Emergency Relief is administered by the Division of Veterans Services through the OVA. This program provides assistance to disabled and destitute Idaho wartime veterans and their dependents. Grants are issued for necessities such as food, shelter, heat, utilities, and in some cases, medicine and clothing.

The Idaho Division of Veterans Services Office of Veterans Advocacy (OVA) publishes a bimonthly bulletin that contains information of interest to all veterans, technical information to service officers, and current rules and regulations affecting veterans' benefits. The Division also supports and participates in an ongoing "outreach" program designed to inform veterans of their benefits.

Idaho is in the design phase of constructing its first State Veterans Cemetery, which will be operated and maintained by the State of Idaho. Groundbreaking is anticipated in the fall of 2002, construction will begin in 2003, and burials will begin summer of 2004. Today, there are approximately 124,630 veterans residing in Idaho.

ILLINOIS DEPARTMENT OF VETERANS' AFFAIRS

DIRECTOR: JOHN W. JOHNSTON
ASSISTANT DIRECTOR: GEORGE CRAMER

DEPUTY DIRECTOR, OPERATIONS: DAN BOATRIGHT
DEPUTY DIRECTOR, PROGRAMS & SERVICES: HAROLD
FRITZ
MAILING ADDRESS & LOCATION:
  833 SOUTH SPRING STREET
  POST OFFICE BOX 19432
  SPRINGFIELD, IL 62794-9432
TELEPHONE: (217) 782-6641
FAX: (217) 524-0344
E-MAIL: webmail@dva.state.il.us

1. SERVICES PERFORMED.

A. Assists veterans, their families and survivors to receive all federal and state benefits to which they are entitled.
B. Maintains 43 full time field offices and 56 itinerant offices.
C. Operates Illinois Veterans Homes at Quincy, Manteno, LaSalle and Anna.

2. STATE BENEFITS:

A. Tax Exemption: An exemption of up to $58,000 on assessed value of specially adapted housing resided in by the veteran, or his unmarried surviving spouse for which federal funds were used.
B. Veterans Homes: Quincy Home provides hospital, skilled nursing and domiciliary care. Manteno Home provides skilled nursing care and is scheduled to open a 40 bed Alzheimer's unit this spring. LaSalle Home provides skilled nursing care. Anna Veterans Home provides skilled nursing and domiciliary care.
C. Education: Veterans, POW/MIA dependents, and totally disabled veterans' dependents eligible for scholarship of full payment of tuition and fees at any state-supported institution of higher learning. There is a four year equivalent limitation. Annual grants to children in secondary and elementary public schools.

D. Bonus: Desert Storm, Vietnam, World War II, Korean Conflict, Vietnam POWs and survivors compensation.

E. Burial Allowance: Up to $100 per claim for cartage and erection of federally provided headstones.

F. Adapted Housing: Contribute up to 25 percent of housing cost, not to exceed $15,000 to aid veterans receiving a federal grant to construct or remodel their homes, or $3,000 to make certain adaptations to an existing home.

G. Maintenance and Travel for Aided Persons: Transportation of veterans home residents to service outside the home.

H. Auto License Plate: Totally disabled service-connected veterans or those entitled to an automobile from the federal government may receive a special license plate without charge for a motor vehicle of the first division. Former POWs, Congressional Medal of Honor recipients, Purple Heart recipients, Gold Star Mothers, Armed Forces Reserves, National Guard, U.S. Armed Forces Retired, and Korean War Veterans may receive a distinctive plate for a motor vehicle of the first division. A Universal License Plate is now available through the Secretary of State's office with the decals (applicable to the veteran's service record) being made available through veterans organizations and may be affixed to the license plate. This license plate will have an outline of the State of Illinois with the words Illinois Veteran encircling it with a stacked "US" suffix. There is a Vietnam Veteran and World War II plate that is in the design stage and will be available later this year. There are also Bronze Star and Pearl Harbor Survivor plates available to eligible veterans.

I. State Approving Agency: Approves and supervises veterans on-the-job training apprenticeship and educational programs.

J. Hunting and Fishing Licenses: Issued free to minimum 10 percent service-connected disabled veterans.

K. Free Camping Privilege: To certain disabled veterans and former POWs.

L. Public Records: Certified copies of public records furnished without charge when needed in connection with claims for veterans benefits. Honorable discharges recorded for free.

M. Notary Service: Free to Illinois veterans.

3. ILLINOIS VETERANS' HOMES:

Illinois Veterans Home at Quincy
1707 N. 12th
Quincy, IL 62301
Illinois Veterans Home at Manteno
One Veterans Drive
Manteno, IL 60950

Illinois Veterans Home at LaSalle
1015 O'Conor Avenue
LaSalle, IL 61301
Illinois Veterans Home At Anna
792 N. Main Street
Anna, IL 62902

4. VITAL STATISTICS:

Department of Public Health Div. of Vital Records
605 W. Jefferson
Springfield, IL 62761

5. USDVA REGIONAL OFFICE:

536 S. Clark Street
P.O. Box 8136
Chicago, IL 60611

6. USDVA MEDICAL CENTERS:

333 E. Huron St. (Lakeside)
Chicago, IL 60611

820 S. Damen (Westside)
P. O. Box 8195
Chicago, IL 60680

1900 E. Main St.
Danville, IL 61832
3001 Green Bay Rd.
N. Chicago, IL 60064

Roosevelt R. & 5th Ave.
Hines, IL 60141
2401 W. Main St.
Marion, IL 62959

7. STATE APPROVING AGENCY:

Department of Veterans' Affairs
833 S. Spring Street
P.O. Box 19432
Springfield, IL 62794-9432

8. FEDERAL CEMETERIES:

Camp Butler National Cemetery
5063 Camp Butler Rd.—RRI
Springfield, IL 62707
Mound City National Cemetery
P.O. Box 128—Jct. 37 & 51
Mound City, IL 62963

Rock Island National Cemetery
Rock Island Arsenal
Rock Island, IL 61265
Danville National Cemetery

1900 E. Main St.
Danville, IL 68132

Quincy National Cemetery
36th & Maine St.
Quincy, IL 62301
Alton National Cemetery
600 Pearl St.
Alton, IL 62003

Abraham Lincoln National Cemetery
27034 South Diagonal Road
Elwood, Illinois 60421

9. VETERANS EMPLOYMENT REPRESENTATIVE:

Veteran Employment Representative
Office of Illinois Employment Security
1300 S. 9th Street
Springfield, IL 62705

10. VET CENTERS:

Chicago Heights Vet Center
1600 Halsted Street
Chicago Heights, IL 60411
Chicago Vet Center
1514 E. 63rd St.
Chicago, IL 60637

Oak Park Vet Center
155 S. Oak Park Avenue
Oak Park, IL 60302
Peoria Vet Center

3310 N. Prospect St.
Peoria, IL 61603

Evanston Vet Center
565 Howard Street
Evanston, IL 60202
Springfield Vet Center
624 S. Fourth Street
Springfield, IL 62702

East St. Louis Center
1269 N. 89th Street
Suite 1
East St. Louis, IL 62203
Moline Vet Center
1529 46th Avenue, #6
Moline, IL 61265

INDIANA DEPARTMENT OF VETERANS' AFFAIRS

DIRECTOR: WILLIAM D. JACKSON
MAILING ADDRESS & LOCATION:
    302 W. WASHINGTON
    RM. E120
    INDIANAPOLIS, IN 46204-2738
TELEPHONE: (317) 232-3910
FAX: (317) 232-7721
E-MAIL: idva@source.isd.state.in.us

1. SERVICES PERFORMED.

A. Assist veterans and their dependents in applying for any benefits to which they are entitled.
B. Supervise and instruct a network of county veterans service offices.

C. Maintain state approving agency for G.I. Bill educational programs.
D. Implementation of state statutes regarding benefits.

2. STATE BENEFITS:

A. Tax Exemption: Personal property and excise tax exemptions for veterans and/or widows. Unused portion may be applied to motor vehicle excise tax.
B. Indiana State Veterans Home: West Lafayette, Indiana 47906.
C. Indiana State Veterans Nursing Care Unit: West Lafayette, Indiana 47906.
D. Indiana Soldiers & Sailors Children's Home: Knightstown, Indiana 46148.
E. Education: Remission of tuition to state universities for children of disabled wartime veterans or Purple Heart veterans with one year residency in Indiana. Free tuition for children of POW/MIAs after January 1, 1960.
F. Burial: County benefit for burial of veterans or spouse.
G. License Plates: For former POWs, certain disabled veterans, and Purple Heart recipients.
H. Point Preference: For selected merit positions in state government.
I. Indiana Veterans Cemetery, Madison, Indiana: Under construction, estimated completion in 1999.

3. VITAL STATISTICS:

Indiana State Department of Health
2 North Meridian Street
Indianapolis, IN 46024

4. STATE SOLDIERS' HOME:

Indiana Veterans' Home
3851 North River Road
West Lafayette, IN 47906

5. U.S. DEPARTMENT OF VETERANS AFFAIRS (USDVA) REGIONAL OFFICE:

575 North Pennsylvania Street
Indianapolis, IN 46204

6. USDVA MEDICAL CENTERS:

2121 Lake Avenue
Fort Wayne, IN 46805
1481 W. 10th Street
Indianapolis, IN 46202

1700 East 38th Street
Marion, IN 46953
500 E. Walnut Street
Evansville, IN 47713-2499

7. SMALL BUSINESS ADMINISTRATION:

575 N. Pennsylvania Street
Indianapolis, IN 46204

8. STATE APPROVING AGENCY (SAA):

Department of Veterans Affairs
302 W. Washington Street
Rm. E120
Indianapolis, IN 46204-2738

9. VETERANS CHILDREN'S HOME:

Indiana Soldiers' and Sailors' Children's Home
Knightstown, IN 46148

10. FEDERAL CEMETERY:

East 38th Street
Marion, IN 46952

11. VETERANS' EMPLOYMENT REPRESENTATIVE:

10 North Senate Avenue
Room 203
Indianapolis, IN 46204

12. VETERANS ORGANIZATIONS, NATIONAL HEADQUARTERS:

The American Legion
National Headquarters
700 N. Pennsylvania
Indianapolis, IN 46204
-or-
P.O. Box 1055
Indianapolis, IN 46206

13. VETERANS ORGANIZATIONS, STATE HEADQUARTERS:

The American Legion
Department of Indiana
777 North Meridian Street
Indianapolis, IN 46204
The American Legion
Department Service Office
575 N. Pennsylvania Street
Indianapolis, IN 46204

Disabled American Veterans
Department of Indiana

2439 W. 16th Street
Indianapolis, IN 46222
Disabled American Veterans
National Service Office
575 North Pennsylvania Street
Indianapolis, IN 46204

AMVETS
Department of Indiana
829 Earl Drive
Connersville, IN 47331-1728
AMVETS
Department of Indiana Service Office
575 North Pennsylvania Street
Indianapolis, IN 46204

Veterans of Foreign Wars
Department of Indiana
1402 N. Shadeland Ave.
Indianapolis, IN 46219
Veterans of Foreign Wars
Department of Service Office
575 North Pennsylvania Street
Indianapolis, IN 46204
Paralyzed Veterans of America
575 North Pennsylvania Street
Rm. 154
Indianapolis, IN 46204
The American Legion Auxiliary
Department of Indiana
777 North Meridian Street
Indianapolis, IN 46204

IOWA COMMISSION OF VETERAN'S AFFAIRS

EXECUTIVE DIRECTOR: PATRICK J. PALMERSHEIM
MAILING ADDRESS:
  7700 N.W. BEAVER DRIVE
  CAMP DODGE, BUILDING A6A
  JOHNSTON, IOWA 50131-1902
LOCATION: CAMP DODGE, IOWA
TELEPHONE: (515) 242-5331
FAX: (515) 242-5659
E-MAIL: patrick.palmersheim@icva.state.ia.us

1. SERVICES PERFORMED

A. Payments of State Bonus to World War I veterans. Deadline date for filing was December 31,1944.
B. Payment of Additional Bonus and Disability Fund to eligible World War I eligible dependents Fund expired in 1979.
C. Payment of State Bonus to World War II veterans. Deadline date for filing was June 30, 1957.
D. Payment of State Bonus to Korean Conflict veterans. Deadline date for filing was July 4, 1963.
E. Payment of State Bonus to Vietnam Conflict veterans. Deadline date for filing was June 30, 1977.
F. Administration of Graves Registration Records received from County Commissions of Veterans Affairs.
G. Payment of War Orphans Educational Aid to eligible War Orphans of World War I, World War II, Korean Conflict, Vietnam Conflict, and Reserve Components.
H. Permanently maintain the 570,000 records of Iowa personnel who served in World War I, World War II, Korean Conflict, and Vietnam Conflict.
I. Assist U.S. Department of Veterans affairs (USDVA) and Federally chartered service organizations concerning veterans' service records of Iowa wartime veterans.

J. Annually visit and evaluate the Iowa Veterans' Home at Marshall-town, Iowa.

K. Assist county commissioners and directors of Veterans Affairs, as per statute, in guidelines and administrative operations.

2. STATE BENEFITS:

A. Tax Exemption: The following exemptions from property shall be allowed:

(1) Mexican War or War of the Rebellion: The property not to exceed $11,111 in taxable value.

(2) War with Spain, Tyler Rangers, Colorado Volunteers in the War of the Rebellion (1861-1865), Indian Wars, Chinese Relief Expedition or Philippine Insurrection: The property not to exceed $56,667 in taxable value.

(3) World War I: (April 6, 1917 to November 11, 1918): The property not to exceed $2,768 in taxable value.

(4) World War II: (December 7, 1941 to December 31, 1946): The property not to exceed $1,852 in taxable value.

(5) Korean Conflict: (June 25, 1950 to January 31, 1955): The property not to exceed $1,852 in taxable value.

(6) Vietnam Conflict: (December 22, 1961 to May 7, 1975): The property not to exceed $1,852 in taxable value.

B. State Veterans Home: Iowa Veterans Home, Marshalltown, Iowa 50158

C. Education: War Orphans Educational Aid, Iowa Department of Veterans Affairs.

3. USDVA REGIONAL OFFICE:

210 Walnut Street
Federal Building
Des Moines, Iowa 50309

4. USDVA MEDICAL CENTERS:

30th & Euclid Avenue
Des Moines, Iowa 50310
Iowa City, Iowa 52240
Knoxville, Iowa 50138

5. CHARTERED SERVICE ORGANIZATIONS, STATE HEADQUARTERS:

The American Legion
720 Lyon Street
Des Moines, Iowa 50316
Disabled American Veterans
210 Walnut Street
Room 1033B
Des Moines, Iowa 50309

AMVETS
210 Walnut Street
Room 1029
Des Moines, Iowa 50309
Veterans of Foreign Wars
3601 Beaver Avenue
Des Moines, Iowa 50310

6. GENERAL INFORMATION

An Iowa Bonus Board was established by legislation in 1921, with four members; namely, the Auditor of the State, Treasurer of State, the Adjutant General of the American Legion. Other appointments were granted by legislation in payment of World War II, Korean and Vietnam Service Compensation (bonus).

In July 1978, the Iowa Legislature repealed the Bonus Board. The Iowa Legislature established an Iowa Department of Veterans Affairs, with five commissioners appointed by the Governor of Iowa; one of each from the American Legion, Veterans of Foreign Wars, Disabled American Veterans, American Veterans (AMVETS) and one appointment at large. The Commission appoints their director and administrative staff. The state government reorganized in 1986 and placed the renamed Veterans Affairs Division under the Department of Public Defense. The Commission is an advisory body with no change in appointment criteria. The Director was given the title "Administrator" and is appointed by the Governor.

Each of our 99 counties within Iowa has a County Commission of Veterans Affairs. Their respective County Board of Supervisors appoints three members to the Commission, each being a wartime veteran. This totals 297 commissioners. In 66 counties there are paid directors, appointed by their commission. It is our pleasure to work closely with these county officials annually.

We maintain some 570,000 military records of wartime veterans from Iowa, coupled with a growing graves registration record system that has some 289, 000 deceased burial records on file, and 59, 000 copy VI of DD Form 214's for Iowa. These will grow annually.

KANSAS COMMISSION ON VETERANS' AFFAIRS

EXECUTIVE DIRECTOR: GENE "STONEY" WAGES
MAILING ADDRESS & LOCATION:
    JAYHAWK TOWERS
    SUITE 701
    700 S.W. JACKSON STREET
    TOPEKA, KS 66603-3714
TELEPHONE: (785) 296-3976
FAX: (785) 296-1462
E-MAIL: KCVA001@Ink.Org

1. SERVICES PERFORMED.

A. Represents veterans, dependents and survivors by virtue of Power of Attorney made to one of the following veterans' organizations:
The American Legion
Veterans of Foreign Wars
B. Maintains organizations designated offices in USDVA facilities in the state.
C. Maintains 14 field offices, providing regularly scheduled itinerant service to the entire state.

2. STATE BENEFITS:

A. Tax Exemption: None
B. Kansas Veterans Home: Located in Winfield, KS: 347 Bed Capacity, 227 Intermediate or Skilled Nursing Beds, 120 Assisted Living Beds
C. Kansas Soldiers Home: Located at Fort Dodge, KS 86 Nursing Beds 98, Assisted Living Beds
D. State Hospital: Not USDVA approved.
E. Education: Education Benefit for dependent children of a deceased S/C Vietnam veteran, who was a resident of the State of KS at the time he entered service, while serving in said U.S. Armed Forces, declared to be a POW/MIA/KIA.
F. Guardianship: None
G. Loan Program: None
H. Bonus: World War I, only.
I. Burial Allowance: None
J. Persian Gulf War Veterans: Health Initiative Program.

3. VITAL STATISTICS, DOCUMENTS:

Kansas Department of Health
Division of Vital Statistics

First Floor, Landon State Office Building, Rm. 151
Topeka, KS 66612

4. USDVA REGIONAL OFFICE:

5500 E Kellogg
Wichita, KS 67218

5. VETERANS ORGANIZATIONS, STATE HEADQUARTERS:

The American Legion
1314 Topeka Blvd.
Topeka, KS 66612
Disabled American Veterans
PO Box 16261
Wichita, KS 67216

Veterans of Foreign Wars
P.O. Box 1008
Topeka, KS 66601

6. GENERAL INFORMATION:

The Kansas Commission on Veteran's Affairs has been in existence in some form since 1937. The present agency consolidated all veterans service programs with the State and was created by the Legislature as of July 1, 1951. This agency now administers all State Veterans Benefits.

The agency consists of a Commission of five members, all of whom must be veterans, appointed by the Governor for four-year-terms. The Commission appoints the Executive Director and the Superintendents of the Kansas Soldiers home and Kansas Veterans' Home, who in turn appoint necessary staff to operate the programs.

The Agency is involved in four basic functions: The Veterans Service Program, all State Approval functions under the G.I. Bills, the operation of the Kansas soldiers Home and Kansas Veterans Home, and the operation of the State Veteran Cemetery System.

The Veterans Service Division consists of 14 Field Officers operating throughout the State and furnishing regular itinerant services to the entire State. There are also 6 offices within VA Facilities in this State with State employees in designated veterans organizations. Powers of Attorney for claims are taken in the names of the American Legion, Disabled American Veterans and the Veterans of Foreign Wars.

It also includes the Persian Gulf War Veterans Health Initiative. This was authorized by Governor Graves in FY 1997. It tasked the KCVA to determine if Persian Gulf War Syndrome was having an impact on the health or economic well being of Kansans who served in the Gulf War or their dependents. The KCVA was also to determine if Social Services were being impacted. An advisory Board to the Commission was created, and one FTE was authorized to manage the program. A survey has been compiled of 2000 Kansas Veterans, the Data analyzed, and final reports will be produced and submitted for scientific peer review by the Summer of 1999. Significant results are indicated in the preliminary findings.

The State approval Agency Division is operated through the staff members of the Field Offices, plus one full-time position in Central Office. This involves the inspection, approval and supervisor of over 100 separate schools in the State and other training establishments.

The Kansas Soldiers' Home, located at Fort Dodge, Kansas, consists of 3 dormitories, one 88 bed nursing facility and 54 cottages presently housing 230 members. Facilities are available to handle veterans in almost any condition, from the ambulatory domiciliary members to the terminal nursing home cases. Cottage facilities are available for families who have the capability of maintaining themselves independently.

The Kansas Veterans' Home is located at Winfield, Kansas. The Campus covers over 200 acres, will have over 340 veterans and spouses, and is planned to be the site of a State Veterans cemetery. No cottages, except for 3 staff cottages, are available. The campus is shared with the Winfield Correctional Facility, which provides some logistic support to include grounds maintenance and labor.

The veterans population within the State is 262,000 approximately 115,000 of these at this time are members of veterans organizations.

KENTUCKY DEPARTMENT OF VETERANS AFFAIRS

DIRECTOR: BG (Ret.) LESLIE "Les" BEAVERS
MAILING ADDRESS & LOCATION:
    1111 LOUISVILLE RD.
    NGAKY BLDG
    FRANKFORT, KY 40601
TELEPHONE: (502) 564-9203
FAX: (502) 564-9240
E-MAIL: John.Kramer@mail.state.ky.us OR
Marty.Pinkston@mail.state.ky.us

1. SERVICES PERFORMED

A. This agency furnishes representation for veterans, widows and dependents by virtue of Power of Attorney made to one of the following:
    Kentucky Department for Veterans Affairs
    Blinded Veterans Association
    Non-Commissioned Officers Association
    Marine Corps League
    American Ex-POW Inc.
    Fleet Reserve Association
    American Red Cross
    Retired Enlisted Association
    Catholic War Veterans
    Vietnam Veterans of America
    Jewish War Veterans of the USA
    Disabled American Veterans

AMVETS
Veterans of Foreign Wars
The American Legion
Military Order of the Purple Heart
Paralyzed Veterans of America

B. Service organizations not represented, but who have their own representatives within the same building:

2. STATE BENEFITS:

A. Tax Exemption:

1. All federal and state military or government service retirement annuities are excluded from gross income.

2. Homestead Exemption:

a) Every person filing an application for exemption under the homestead exemption provision must be 65 years of age or older during the year for which application is made or must have been classified as totally disabled under a program authorized or administered by an agency of the United States Government or by the railroad retirement system on January 1 of the year in which application is made.

b) Every person filing an application for exemption under the homestead exemption provision must own and maintain the property for which the exemption is sought as his personal residence.

c) Every person filing an application for exemption under the disability provision of the homestead exemption must have received disability payments pursuant to the disability and must maintain the disability classification through December 31 of the year in which application is made.

d) Every person filing for the homestead exemption that is totally disabled and is less than 65 years of age must apply for the homestead exemption on an annual basis.

B. State Veterans Nursing Home

The 1988 General Assembly funded a 300-bed Nursing Home (Thomson-Hood Veterans Center 1-800-928-4838) which opened on July 6, 1991, for all Kentucky veterans who have an other than dishonorable discharge and have been a resident of the state two years prior to application or initially entered service from Kentucky. Two additional Nursing Homes were opened in 2002. Eastern Kentucky Veterans Center 1-877-856-0004, Western Kentucky Veterans Center 1-877-662-0008.

State Veterans Nursing Homes Authorizes the establishment and operation of state nursing homes for veterans of the Commonwealth. Such veterans' nursing homes are to be under the administrative authority of the Department of Veterans Affairs.

C. Loan Program: None

D. State Bonus: All wars up to, and including Korean Conflict (expired 31 December 1962.) Vietnam Veterans Bonus enacted by Special Session in December 1988 (expired 31 October 1991.)

E. Education: Provides free tuition in state-supported universities, junior colleges, or vocational training institutions as follows:

F. Exemption from Tuition Fees for Survivors of Deceased Service Member or Guardsman

Provides for exemption from tuition fees for surviving family members of an active duty service member or member of the Kentucky National Guard who dies while in service or as a result of service connected wounds or conditions. Applies only to Kentucky's state-operated colleges, universities and vocational schools. State residency requirements apply.

G. Exemption from Tuition Fees for Family Members of Permanently and Totally Disabled Service Members or Guardsmen

Provides for exemption from tuition fees for family members of permanently and totally disabled veterans, National Guardsmen, prisoners of war and service members listed as missing in action. Applies only to

Kentucky's state-operated colleges, universities and vocational schools; state residency requirements.

H. War Veterans May Complete High School Without Tuition

Provides for veterans to complete high school without payment of tuition fees when service in the armed forces interrupts normal completion.

I. Exemption from Tuition Fees for Family Members of Deceased Veteran

Provides for exemption from tuition fees for family members of permanently and totally disabled veterans, National Guardsmen, prisoners of war and service members listed as missing in action. Applies only to Kentucky's state-operated colleges, universities and vocational schools; was a resident of the Commonwealth or was married to a resident at time of death.

J. Tuition Waiver for Child of Disabled Veteran

The child of a veteran who acquired a disability as a direct result of the veterans' service may be eligible for waiver of tuition.

K. Veterans' Preference: State Employment Preference Points for Veterans, Their Spouses, Widows, Widowers, And Parents

Provides 5 hiring preference points for honorably discharged veterans and for former members of the Kentucky National Guard; 10 points for veterans with service-connected disabilities and certain spouses of veterans with service-connected disabilities; surviving spouses of certain war veterans and parents who were dependent on a veteran who lost his life under honorable conditions while on active duty are entitled to 10 preference points. (Preference points are credited towards state employment when testing at the Personnel Cabinet in Frankfort.)

L. License Plates: Special military-related license plates—Administrative regulations

Sets forth conditions under which disabled veterans (70% disabled) may apply for and receive special license plates and conditions under which disabled veterans may legally exceed certain parking restrictions.

M. Special Registration Plates, Parking Privileges for Handicapped
Provides conditions under which veterans and other handicapped persons are eligible for special vehicle registration and parking fees.

N. Newsletter
Marty Pinkston Provides information concerning the Kentucky Department of Veterans Affairs activities as well as news of interest to Kentucky's veterans. Email the link above to be added to our mailing list.

This is a guideline to benefits for Kentucky veterans who served in the active or reserve component of the armed forces.

O. Credit For Service in the U.S. Armed Forces: Provides service credit for eligible State Police Officers who left the State Police to enter the armed services and were immediately re-employed by the State Police. Up to 6 years of service in the armed forces may be recognized.

P. Restoration of Public Employees to Position after Military Duty: Provides mandatory restoration of public employees to identical or similar positions held prior to leaving to perform military duty. The law is applicable regardless of whether the employee left voluntarily or involuntarily.

Q. Restored Employee Discharged for Cause: Requires employee who has been reinstated following military service, should not be discharged from his position without cause within one year after restoration.

R. Leave of Absence to Permit Induction in Military Service: Provides mandatory leave of absence for public employees for the purpose of being inducted in the armed forces.

S. Service Credit for Military Service: Provides for State employees to obtain service credit, seniority and benefits for time spent in the armed forces of the United States under certain conditions.

T. Examinations—Ratings—Eligibility Lists (For employment by cities, counties, and local units) Authorizes an increase of 5 percentage points on any local or County Civil Service Examination for employment for veterans who have served during a wartime period.

U. Service Credit—Computation: Defines the types of service, including military service, which are creditable for retirement under the police and fire fighters retirement fund and the method of computation of the amount of service credit to be awarded.

V. Examinations, Certifications Preference Points Eligibility Lists: Authorizes an increase of 5 percentage points on any City Civil Service Examination for employment for veterans who have served in the armed forces during a wartime period.

W. Credit Under Pension System for Time Spent in Armed Forces: Authorizes time spent in the armed forces to be credited to police or fire department personnel for retirement purposes under certain conditions.

X. Credit For Service—How Computed: Provides the method for computation of credit for service in the armed forces as it applies to State and local pension and employment benefits.

Y. Federal Annuities Excluded From Gross Income: Provides for computation of federal annuities excludable from state income tax. By amendment in 1997, excludes all federal refund tax retirement annuities from Kentucky State Income Tax.

Z. Hunting, Trapping or Fishing License Required—Exceptions: Authorizes Kentucky veterans with 50% or more service-connected disability to hunt or fish within the state with a special combination license. A small fee may apply.

AA. Prior Service Credit for Veterans: Establishes terms and conditions under which armed forces service may be credited toward Kentucky teacher's retirement.

BB. Uniform Veterans Guardianship Act: Provides for appointment and accountability requirements of persons who act as guardians for veterans.

CC. State Veterans Cemeteries: Expected to open in late 2003/2004, this cemetery located in Hopkinsville is in addition to the National

Cemeteries, and will serve eligible Kentucky veterans and their families.

DD. Homeless Veterans Program: Provides services to homeless veterans in the Commonwealth.

3. VITAL STATISTICS, DOCUMENTS:

Birth and Death Certificates:
Registrar of Vital Statistics
275 East Main Street
Frankfort, KY 40621
(502) 564-4212

DD-214:
Administration Services
Military Records & Research
1121 Louisville Road
Frankfort. KY 40601
(502) 564-4883

Certified Copies of Records—Fees (See: 213-141.PDF) Prevents State, County or City officials from charging any kind of fee for furnishing documents required to substantiate a claim for veteran's benefits.

4. USDVA REGIONAL OFFICE:

545 South 3rd Street
Louisville, KY 40202

5. VETERANS ORGANIZATIONS, STATE HEADQUARTERS:

The American Legion
P.O. Box 2123
Louisville, KY 40201

Disabled American Veterans
P O. Box 129
Shepherdsville, KY 41065

AMVETS
2041 Payne Street
Louisville, KY 40206
Veterans of Foreign Wars
P.O. Box 37050
Louisville, KY 40202

Paralyzed Veterans of America
1030 Goss Avenue
Louisville, KY 40217
American Red Cross
505 S. Third Street
Louisville, KY 40202

Vietnam Veterans of America
5206 Sprucewood Drive
Louisville, KY. 40291
Non-Commissioned Officers Assoc. of KY.
649 Pearman Avenue
Radcliff, KY. 40160

6. GENERAL INFORMATION

The duties of the Dept. of Veterans Affairs under is to collect all necessary data information regarding facilities and services available to veterans, their families and dependents. We cooperate with all service
agencies throughout the state in informing such persons regarding the
availability of educational training and retraining facilities, health,
medical, rehabilitation and housing services and facilities, employment
and re-employment services, federal, state and local laws affording

rights, privileges and benefits to said qualified veterans, their families and dependents, and all other matters of a related nature. The Center assists veterans and their families and dependents in the establishment of all claims and entitlements, which they have under federal, state or local laws, and cooperates with all national, state and local government and private agencies concerning these entitlements.

The agency provides counsel and guidance to veterans, their widows, orphans, and dependents concerning social security, unemployment, welfare, missing veterans, reemployment rights, and the full range of veterans benefits.

Presently, local counseling service and assistance is provided throughout the Commonwealth by a network of volunteer veterans assistance officers. Regional coordinators provide this service and assistance throughout the Commonwealth, in every county, at least once each month.

LOUISIANA DEPARTMENT OF VETERANS AFFAIRS

EXECUTIVE DIRECTOR: JOEY STRICKLAND
MAILING ADDRESS & LOCATION:
    1885 WOODDALE BLVD., 10th Floor
    P.O. BOX 94095, CAPITOL STATION
    BATON ROUGE, LA 70804-9095
TELEPHONE: (225) 922-0500
FAX: (225) 922-0511
E-MAIL: dperkins@vetaffairs.com

1. SERVICES PERFORMED.

A. Represents veterans, dependents, and survivors, contact service and claims representation through Powers of Attorney from the following:
    The American Legion
    Veterans of WWI, USA, Inc.
    Military Order of the Purple Heart
    Veterans of Foreign Wars

Blinded Veterans Association
Marine Corps League
Non-Commissioned Officers Association
American Prisoners of War, Inc.
AMVETS
Fleet Reserve Association
Regular Veterans Association

B. County (Parish) veterans assistance counselors are employees of Louisiana Department of Veterans Affairs.

C. Service organizations not affiliated with the LDVA:
American Red Cross
Disabled American Veterans
Paralyzed Veterans of America
Vietnam Veterans, Inc.

2. STATE BENEFITS:

A. Veterans' Home: Louisiana War Veterans' Home located in Jackson, capacity 245, and the Northeast LA War Veterans' Home located in Monroe, capacity 156.

B. Educational Benefits: Tuition exemption at state-supported colleges, universities, and technical institutes to dependents of Louisiana veterans who were killed in service or died as a result of a service-connected disability incurred in or aggravated by military service during a wartime period; and also children of service-connected veterans rated 90% and above, including Individual Unemployability, by the Schedule for Rating Disabilities.

C. Admissions to State Parks: Free admission to state parks and recreational areas for 50% or above service-connected disabled veterans or permanent and total as a result of nonservice-connected disabilities who are residents of the State of Louisiana.

D. Hunting and Fishing License: Free hunting and fishing license for 50% or above service-connected disabled veterans who are residents of the State of Louisiana.

E. License Plates: Free license plates for 50% or above service-connected disabled veterans and for those veterans who received an automobile grant from the U.S. Department of Veterans Affairs (USDVA); free license plates for former Prisoners of War and Purple Heart recipients.

F. Recording of Discharges: Free recording of discharges in the Register of Conveyance records.

G. Vietnam Agent Orange Directory: A directory of information concerning Agent Orange is maintained in the Administrative office and is available for public information.

3. VITAL STATISTICS, DOCUMENTS:

State Registrar
Bureau of Vital Statistics
State Board of Health
P.O. Box 60630
New Orleans, LA 70160

4. USDVA REGIONAL OFFICE:

Regional Office
701 Loyola Avenue
New Orleans, LA 70113

5. VETERANS ORGANIZATIONS, STATE HEADQUARTERS:

The American Legion
1885 Wooddale Blvd.
P. O. Box 1431
Baton Rouge, LA 70821-1431
Disabled American Veterans
1885 Wooddale Blvd.
Suite 113
Baton Rouge, LA 70806-5993

AMVETS
P. O. Box 50308
New Orleans, LA 70150-0308
Veterans of Foreign Wars
10185 Mammoth Avenue
Baton Rouge, LA 70814

Paralyzed Veterans of America
3650 18th Street
Metairie, LA 70002

6. OTHER STATE AGENCIES:

Department of Veterans Affairs
Veterans Education and Training
P.O. Box 94095
Baton Rouge, LA 70804-9095
Louisiana Department of Labor
Apprenticeship Division
P.O. Box 94094
Baton Rouge, LA 70804-9094

Louisiana National Guard
Office of the Adjutant General
Military Department
Jackson Barracks
New Orleans, LA 70146

7. GENERAL INFORMATION:

Service work was first established in Louisiana in 1924, with the creation of a State Service Commissioner who served until 1944, when the Department of Veterans Affairs was created. Within the Department is a Veterans Affairs Commission, appointed by the Governor and composed of nine (9) representatives from the various veterans' organizations. Duties are to make policies, rules, and regulations governing functions of the department. The executive director is appointed by and serves at the pleasure of the Commission. The Department is composed of Administrative, Claims, Field, State Approval Agency, Training and Information Divisions; and the Louisiana War Veterans' Home (Domiciliary and Nursing) and the Northeast LA War Veterans Home (Domiciliary and Nursing), which are supervised by the Deputy Assistant Secretary.

MISSION

To aid all residents of the State of Louisiana who served in the military forces of the United States during any war, combat, campaign, or any special periods of service during peacetime, along with the dependents and beneficiaries, to receive any and all benefits to which they may be entitled under the laws of the United States or the states thereof.

Administrative Division: Located in the State Office Building, 1885 Wooddale Towers; P.O. Box 94095, Capitol Station, Baton Rouge, LA 70804-9095. This division is under the direction of the Executive Director, Deputy Assistant Secretary of the Department and supervision of the Deputy Director. It is made up of the following sections: Administrative and Clerical, Human Resources, Accounting and Purchasing.

Claims Division: This office is maintained in the Regional Office of the U.S. Department of Veterans Affairs, New Orleans, LA. It is directed by a regional manager; provides liaison with USDVA on all cases on which any veterans organization participating in this Department holds Power of Attorney. This division is necessary to assure the veteran and/or his dependents that a just and proper decision has been made on his behalf Para-legal counselors review claims, advise veterans assistance counselors and claimants of development of claims, and represent claimants before various operating units of the USDVA. No

Powers of Attorney are accepted in the name of the Department of Veterans Affairs.

Contact Assistance Division: This division consists of Parish (county) veterans assistance counselors and regional managers. Veterans assistance counselors inform veterans and their dependents and the general public of federal and state veterans' benefits programs and assist applicants in applying for and securing all benefits to which they may be entitled. These offices are financed by joint contribution from local governing bodies and the State of Louisiana. State contributions may not exceed 75% of total cost of operations in any parish.

The Contact Assistance Division is under the supervision of this Department with employees being state classified service workers. These offices are under immediate supervision of regional managers who check detailed operation of each office.

Training and Information Division: Responsible for training of all veterans assistance counselors and for assembling, analyzing, distributing, and publicizing current information on laws, rules, regulations and procedures relating to veterans' benefits. This division conducts schools consisting of four weeks of classroom instruction for all newly-appointed veterans assistance counselors as well as periodic one-day schools in selected areas to apprise all veterans assistance counselors of new legislation, etc.

Louisiana War Veterans' Home (Domiciliary and Nursing): Administered by this Department, the War Veterans'' Home has 50 domiciliary beds and 195 nursing care beds. This massive facility', approximately two and a quarter acres of enclosed living and nursing space, sits on 81 acres two miles east of Jackson, Louisiana on LA Hwy. 10. Address: Louisiana War Veterans' Home, 4739 Highway 10, Jackson, LA 70748. Northeast Louisiana War Veterans' Home, also administered by this Department, has 156 nursing care beds. The facility sits on 20 acres on U.S. Highway 165 in Monroe. The mailing address is: P.O. Box 9270, Monroe, LA 71211.

MAINE BUREAU OF VETERANS SERVICES

DIRECTOR: COL ROLAND H. LAPOINTE
MAILING ADDRESS:
  STATE HOUSE STATION #117
  AUGUSTA, ME 04333
LOCATION: CP KEYES BLDG 7, Rm 100
TELEPHONE: (207) 626-4464
FAX: (207) 626-4471
E-MAIL: mvs@me-arng.ngb.army.mil

1. SERVICES PERFORMED.

A. To act upon request as the agent of any resident who has a claim against the United States, out of or by reason of, any war or any federal military or naval service and to prosecute such claims without charge.
B. Preserve records of all members of the Armed Forces from Maine who served in World War I to present.
C. Administer a program of temporary emergency financial aid for totally incapacitated or disabled war veterans and their dependents (pending funding).
D. Operate the Maine Veterans' Memorial Cemetery in Augusta and other locations determined by the legislature. Free burial plot and perpetual care of grave is available for Maine war veterans and their eligible dependent.
E. Determine eligibility of veterans for state Veterans Small Business Loan Program.
F. Administer the program to provide educational assistance to dependents of persons who die as a result of military service or who are totally and permanently disabled as a result of service.

2. STATE BENEFITS:

A. Tax Exemption: Property tax exemption for certain veterans and widows/widowers.

B. Veterans' Home: Five nursing home care facilities. Homes are located throughout the state in Caribou, Bangor, Augusta, S. Paris, and Scarborough.

C. State Loan Program: Provides 85% guaranty by state for small business loans up to $600,000 as wartime veteran and $500, 000 from Small Business Authority. 100% guaranty for $75,000 or less.

D. State Bonus: None

E. Educational Assistance: Free tuition at state-supported institutions of higher learning for eligible dependents of veterans who are permanently and totally disabled of a service-connected condition or who died as a result of service.

F. Emergency Financial Aid: Program for disabled veterans and dependents.

G. Burial: Free burial plot and perpetual care of grave is available for Maine war veterans and their eligible dependents.

H. Veterans' Preference: Includes reemployment rights in state government.

3. VITAL STATISTICS:

Division of Research and Vital Records/Department of Human Services
State House Station #11
Augusta, Maine 04333-0011
Telephone: 207-287-3181

4. USDVA REGIONAL OFFICE AND HOSPITAL:

Togus, Maine 04330
1-800-827-1000

5. FIELD OFFICES:

Bangor Field Office
44 Hogan Rd.
Bangor, Maine 04401

Telephone: 207-941-3005
Email: mvsb@mint.net

Portland Field Office
185 Lancaster Street, Rm 203
Portland, Maine 04101
Telephone: 207-822-0292
e-mail: mvsp@ime.net

Caribou Field Office
National Guard Armory
59 Bennett Drive
Caribou, Maine 04736
Telephone: 207-498-6077
e-mail: lizottemd@me-arng.ngb.army.mil

Springvale Field Office
23 Main Street
Springvale, Maine 04083
Telephone: 207-324-1839
e-mail: mvss@ime.net

Machias Field Office
14 E. Main Street
Machias. Maine 04654
Telephone: 207-255-3306
e-mail: mvsm@ime.net

Togus Claims Office
VAM & ROC
Bldg 248, Rm 117
Togus, Maine 04330

Telephone: 207-623-5732
e-mail: vsollett@vba.va.gov

Lewiston Field Office
Parkway Complex
29 Westminster Street
Lewiston, Maine 04240
Telephone: 207-783-5306
e-mail: mvslew@ime.net

Waterville Field Office
National Guard Armory
Drummond Avenue
Waterville, Maine 04901
Telephone: 207-872-7846
e-mail: mvsw@ime.net

6. VETERANS ORGANIZATIONS, STATE HEADQUARTERS:

The American Legion
Department of Maine
P. O. Box 900
Waterville, Maine 04901
Telephone: 207-873-3229

AMVETS
Department of Maine
P.O. Box 3416
Togus, Maine 04330
Telephone: 207-623-5724

Disabled American Veterans
P. O. Box 3151

Togus, Maine 04330
Telephone: 207-623-5725

Veterans of Foreign Wars
P. O. Box 3311
Togus, Maine 04330
Telephone: 207-623-5723

7. GENERAL INFORMATION

PURPOSE: The Bureau of Maine Veterans' Services provides support services to Maine veterans and their dependents seeking assistance through State and/or Federal programs. These programs include, but are not limited to, housing, medical and hospital care, educational aid and compensation, vocational rehabilitation, burials and nursing homes. The seven regional offices located throughout the State provide support to veterans statewide in addition to supplementing the USDVA claims office at Togas. The Bureau's regional offices also provide support to bedridden veterans. The State Claims Office, located at Togas, administers the claims support and appeals advocate program.

The Central Office, located at Camp Keyes in Augusta, administers the Financial Aid program for needy veterans, awards educational benefits to dependents of permanently and totally disabled veterans and their dependents at the Maine Veterans Cemetery, and issues certificates of eligibility for Veterans Small Business Loans.

Additionally, the Director sits on the Board of Trustees for the Maine Veterans Homes, serving as one of the advocates for Maine veterans. The Bureau acts as the veteran advocate throughout the state and nationally.

ORGANIZATION: After the Civil War, service to veterans was provided through specific acts or laws. The earliest coordinated service to veterans was the Soldiers Board of 1919. Council Order created Maine Veterans' Services in 1945 as the Division of Veterans Affairs. The agency received authorization in 1947 and was established with a state office and seven local offices. In 1950, a claims office was established at the Veterans Administration Center at Togas. The Division was renamed the Department of Veterans Services in 1963. In the spring of 1970, the Maine Veterans Memorial Cemetery became operational. Under reorganization legislation of 1972, the agency was placed within the new Department of Military, civil Defense and Veterans' Services, which, in 1974, was, redesignated the Department of defense and Veterans' Services. In 1998, the Department was renamed as Department of Defense, Veterans and Emergency Management.

The Maine Veterans' Small Business Loan Authority Board was established in 1973. In 1983, it was redesignated under the Finance Authority of Maine as the Maine Veterans' Small Business Loan Program.

MARYLAND DEPARTMENT of VETERANS AFFAIRS

SECRETARY Designee: Thomas Hutchins
MAILING ADDRESS 7 LOCATION:
   ROOM 110, FEDERAL BUILDING
   31 HOPKINS PLAZA
   BALTIMORE, MD 21201
TELEPHONE: (410) 962-4700
FAX: (410) 333-1071
FTS: (410) 922-4700
E-MAIL: md.veterans@erols.com

1. SERVICES PERFORMED.

The Maryland Veterans Commission is an independent State Agency with a service mission to:
A. Provide quality statewide assistance to veterans, their dependents and survivors in developing and present benefits claims to federal, state and local governmental agencies.
B. Manage and operate authorized Maryland State Veterans Cemeteries and a Civil War Cemetery.

C. Maintain and care for the Maryland Vietnam Veterans and the Korean War Memorials.

D. Provide staff support and assistance to other State Veterans Commissions.

2. STATE BENEFITS:

A. Apprentices: Service in the Armed Forces is credited in connection with time required for apprentice in, or in preparation for, any profession, trade or calling.

B. Assistance: Assistance and representation in developing and presenting veterans benefits claims to the U.S. Department of Veterans Affairs.

C. Auto Tag: Certain severely disabled veterans (amputees who have lost the use of one or more legs, hands, arms, blind veterans, and veterans who are totally disabled) may be issued a special license tag for a motor vehicle without charge. Also no fee placards for disabled persons entitling them to special parking privileges.

D. Bonus: The State of Maryland has not authorized a bonus to Maryland veterans from any war era, to include: World War I, World War II, Korean, Vietnam, or Persian Gulf.

E. Civil Rights: Absentee voting by service personnel and their spouse.

F. Discharge Papers: Military Separation Reports (DD 214's) may be recorded by the veteran in the County Court House of choice at no charge. The Maryland Veterans Commission maintains discharge reports from 1979 to present. Military installation will forward discharge report if (1) Maryland was the veteran home of record at time of entry into service; or (2) if veteran planned to relocate to Maryland after discharge from the service, and requested the record to be sent to Maryland.

G. Education (War Orphans): Aid for tuition and other educational expenses for children of Maryland veterans who are killed in action, die from service-connected causes, or are totally and permanently disabled due to service. The law includes children of POWs and MIAs as a result of the Southeast Asia Conflict. The child has to be born prior to or during the time the veteran was a POW or MIA.

H. Game Fishing License: Convalescent patients from veterans hospitals may obtain permit to fish without license.

I. Fishing and Hunting Licenses Fees for Disabled Veterans and Former Prisoners of War: Allows 100% service-connected disabled veterans and former Prisoners of War to obtain certain fishing and hunting licenses, and trout and deer stamps, without a fee.

J. Grave Care L Registration: Permanent registry of all persons who served in military service in time of war and who are buried in Maryland.

K. High School Certificates: Equivalent certificates may be issued to members of the Armed Forces, 17 years of age or older, upon examination in the usual high school subjects.

L. Inheritance Tax: Assets of certain estates of members of the Armed Forces dying during period of active service are exempt from inheritance tax.

M. Licenses: Renewal of professional, trade, etc., licenses within one year after release from military service.

N. Maryland Veterans Home Commission: Charlotte Hall Veterans Home is a 378-bed licensed long-term care facility governed by the Maryland Veterans Home Commission and operated under contract with DHS of Maryland, Inc. The facility provides a broad range of residential and therapeutic services. These include domiciliary care, comprehensive nursing care and special care services for residents with Alzheimer's disease or related disorders.

O. Property Tax: Exemption of taxes on dwelling house and lot of veterans with service-connected, 100% permanent and total disabilities. This exemption passes to the widow on the death of the veteran. The law provides an exemption of real and personal property tax for veterans organizations used exclusively for purposes of the organization.

P. Public Records: Copies furnished free of charge of birth, marriage, or death certificates required in connection with claims against the United States Government for benefits.

Q. Re-employment Rights: Application for reinstatement to former job in private or public sector must be made within 90 days of military discharge.

S. State Employees Retirement System: Military service credit for veterans.

T. Unemployment Insurance: Is payable to an honorably discharged veteran after release from active duty under the provisions of the federal law governing unemployment insurance.

U. Veterans Cemeteries: Any veteran who received an honorable discharge from the United States Armed Forces for full-time active duty, and meets certain residency requirements, shall be eligible for burial in a State Veterans Cemetery. The veterans' spouse and dependent children also qualify for interment. There are five veterans cemeteries statewide (Allegheny, Anne Arundel, Baltimore, Dorchester, and Prince George's Counties).

V. Veterans' Preference: Applicants for state employment shall be granted preference points on examinations; 10 points to certain service-connected disabled veterans; 5 points to non-disabled veterans. Certain minimum active duty standards apply. The spouse of a veteran will be granted preference points under certain circumstances.

3. USDVA REGIONAL OFFICE:

Baltimore Regional Office
Federal Building
31 Hopkins Plaza
Baltimore, MD 21201
Washington Regional Office
1120 Vermont Ave., N.W.
Washington, DC 20421

4. VETERANS ORGANIZATIONS, STATE HEADQUARTERS:

Military Order of Purple Heart
Federal Building, Room 114B
31 Hopkins Plaza
Baltimore, MD 21201
AMVETS
Federal Building, Room 114
31 Hopkins Plaza
Baltimore, MD 21201

Catholic War Veterans
War Memorial
Baltimore, MD 21202
Veterans of Foreign Wars
War Memorial Building
Baltimore, MD 21202

Disabled American Veterans
War Memorial Building
Baltimore, MD 21202
The American Legion
War Memorial Building
Baltimore, MD 21202

Jewish War Veterans
Federal Building, Room 114
31 Hopkins Plaza
Baltimore, MD 21201
Paralyzed Veterans of America
Federal Building, Room G-07C
31 Hopkins Plaza
Baltimore, MD 21201

MASSACHUSETTS DEPARTMENT OF VETERANS SERVICES

COMMISSIONER: THOMAS G. KELLEY
MAILING ADDRESS & LOCATION:
   DEPARTMENT OF VETERANS SERVICES
   239 CAUSEWWAY ST.
   SUITE 100
   BOSTON, MA 02114
TELEPHONE: (617) 727-3578
FAX: (617) 727-5903
E-MAIL: gpeterson@vet.state.ma.us

1. SERVICES PERFORMED

A. The Department of Veterans' Services (DVS) is the leading advocate for the more than half-million veterans of the Commonwealth and their families and survivors. DVS establishes policy, proposes legislation, and ensures adequate funding for veteran programs is included in the Governor's budget, and represents the interests of veterans in matters coming before the General Court.

B. DVS represents all state agencies and individual veterans before the federal Department of Veterans Affairs (VA) in securing federal compensation and other benefits that might be available.

C. The Department also administers the needs-based benefits program through Veterans' Service Officers (VSO) in each municipality of the Commonwealth.

D. Provides state funding and monitors contract performance to organizations offering homeless shelter, transitional housing, and outreach services to veterans.

E. DVS has a Women Veterans' Network Program whose mission is to provide women with information on benefits; expand awareness of the needs of women veterans and identify available health and human resources to meet those needs; and to advocate on behalf of women veterans.

2. STATE BENEFITS:

This program provides financial assistance with food, housing, clothing, employment, and medical and burial assistance to eligible veterans. Contact your VSO in your local City/Town Hall.

A. State Bonus:
Currently, the Persian Gulf Bonus is available through DVS to certain veterans who served during the period 08/02/90 and 04/11/91. There are other bonuses available through the Commonwealth's Treasury Office, One Ashburton Place, Boston, MA 02108.

B. Property Tax:
There are a number of exemptions available to certain disabled veterans or their survivors. Contact your VSO in your local City/Town Hall.

C. Motor Vehicle Sales & Excise Tax:
Certain disabled veterans are eligible for these exemptions. Contact the Department of Revenue at 617-887-6367 for the exemption.

D. Public Housing:
Veterans and their families are given preference for state-aided public housing through their local housing authority.

E. Employment: Veterans are given preference for employment on the eligibility list for civil service positions.

F. Educational Assistance: Veterans may be eligible to attend state colleges tuition free or discounted, on a space available basis. Contact the Veterans' Representative at the State College of your choice.

G. Annuity: There is a $1500 annuity, paid in two payments of $750, available for 100% service-connected disabled veterans; parents of a son or daughter whose death occurred as result of injury sustained or disease contracted during active service in time of war, insurrection, or combat; and, to an unremarried spouse whose husband or wife died as result of injury sustained or disease contracted during active service in time of war, insurrection, or combat.

H. Massachusetts Veterans' Memorial Cemetery: The first of two cemeteries is completed in Agawam. This cemetery will better serve the Commonwealth's veterans and their families in the western part of the

State. It is the first of two state veterans' cemeteries to be constructed in the Commonwealth. The second will be located in central Massachusetts, in Winchendon, with a projected opening date in the year 2003. Please contact the Cemetery at 413-821-9500.

I. Veterans' License Plates: A variety of veterans' license plates are available through the Registry of Motor Vehicles.

J. Soldiers Homes: The Soldiers' Homes provide a variety of services to veterans, such as, acute hospital, domiciliary, and long-term, physical and occupational therapy and more. Please call 413-532-9475 extension 126 for Holyoke or 617-884-5660 extension 210 for Chelsea.

K. Outreach and Housing: A network of 15 DVS-sponsored Outreach Centers and Housing facilities provide graduated levels of shelter, care, guidance, and counsel.

3. MILITARY DOCUMENTS, & VITAL STATISTICS:

[1]Adjutant Generals Office of Military War Records
239 Causeway Street
Boston, MA 02114
(617) 727-2964

[2]Registry of Vital Statistics and Research
Department of Public Health
150 Tremont Street, Rm. B-3
Boston, MA 02111
(617) 727-0036—Registrar's Office
(617) 727-0110—Records Section

---

1. DD-214, Certified Copy—no charge
2. Birth. Death, Marriages—(State Records) Certified Copy, $11.00 (No charge for veterans)

MICHIGAN VETERANS AFFAIRS DIRECTORATE
DEPARTMENT OF MILITARY AND VETERANS AFFAIRS

DEPUTY DIRECTOR: HUBERT B. HESS
MAILING ADDRESS & LOCATION:
  7109 W. SAGINAW
  LANSING, MI 48913
TELEPHONE: (517) 335-6523
FAX: (517) 241-0674
E-MAIL: hessh@michigan.gov

1. SERVICES PERFORMED

The Veterans' Affairs Directorate (Asst. Adjutant General for Veterans' Affairs) exercises executive supervision, on behalf of the Michigan Department of Military and Veterans Affairs, for all state supported/resourced veterans' programming.

A. State Veterans' Homes: The Grand Rapids Home for Veterans, established in 1886, has a capacity of 763 nursing and residential beds. The D.J. Jacobetti Home for Veterans, established in 1981 in Marquette, MI, has a capacity of 241 nursing and residential beds. The Homes' admissions and member governance are overseen by a seven-member gubernatorially appointed board of managers nominated by statutorily designated state veterans service organizations for staggered six-year terms. The Homes have an aggregate operating budget in excess of $45.5 million.

B. Michigan Veterans Trust Fund (MVTF): Created in 1946 from $50 million in postwar reserve funds, the MVTF, utilizing approximately $4 million of interest earnings from the trust, administers two grant programs—the Emergency Grant Program and the Tuition Grant Program. Emergency grants are available to war time veterans and their dependents during times of personal emergent need. This program is administered through local MVTF county committees appointed by the MVTF Board of Trustees. The Tuition Grant Program dates back to 1935 and has been administered by the MVTF since 1966. Tuition grants are available to sons and daughters of totally disabled or deceased service-connected veterans attending Michigan institutions of higher education. MVTF grant policies and adjudication, county committee appointments and expenditure from trust earnings are governed by a seven-member gubernatorially appointed board of trustees nominated by statutorily designated state veterans service organizations for staggered three-year terms. The MVTF also functions as the state central repository for DD-214s (copy 6) since 1979 and maintains separation documents of Michigan veterans granted state service bonuses from WWI, WWII, Korean Conflict, and the Vietnam War.

C. State Grants to Veterans Service Organizations: Since 1927, the State has provided grants to congressionally chartered veterans service organizations in Michigan supplementing their respective service officer programs providing accredited representation to eligible veterans. The Veterans' Affairs Directorate administers approximately $3 million annually in grants to Michigan's eleven designated active veterans' service organizations assisting them in generating over $135 million in recoveries (DVA benefits).

2. STATE BENEFITS:

A. Emergency Grants: For wartime veterans or their dependents in time of emergent personal need (see above).

B. Tuition Grants: For eligible sons and daughters of service connected deceased or 100% disabled for Michigan higher education toward and undergraduate degree.

C. Discharge Documents: Recorded with County Clerks in veteran's county of residence.

D. Headstone Placement/Burial Assistance: Soldiers/Sailors relief and/or county Veteran Affairs provide assistance for eligible veterans.

E. Rights to Employment Services: (Veteran Employment Bill of Rights) provides statewide access to employment and training, with equitable outreach to veterans for state and federal training funds.

F. Re-Employment Rights: Meets or exceeds Federal standards, with enforcement through the Michigan office of the U.S. Dept. of Labor.

G. Vocational Rehabilitation: Federal funds are available to train veterans throughout the Michigan Dept. of Education.

H. Civil Service Preference Points: Provides credit for service to veterans, and certain eligible spouses in public employment tests (rules depend on municipal jurisdiction).

I. Motor Vehicle Plates: Special designation at a nominal fee for various wartime eras, Ex-POW, Pearl Harbor Survivor, and National Guard/Reserves.

J. Service Credits: Available to purchase toward state retirement system.

K. Homestead Property Tax Credit: A credit available through the filing of state personal income tax, a portion of the property tax dependent on income level. Also hardship exemptions available through local assessing body.

L. Veteran Bonuses: (All have expired) for each WWI, WWII, Korea, Vietnam with MVTF or county agencies.

3. VETERANS SERVICE ORGANIZATIONS:

American Legion
212 N. Verlinden
Lansing, MI 48915
AMVETS
151 W. Jefferson Avenue
Detroit, MI 48226

Catholic War Veterans
151 W. Jefferson Avenue
Detroit, MI 48226
Disabled American Veterans
151 W. Jefferson Avenue
Detroit, MI 48266

Jewish War Veterans
16990 12 Mile Road
Southfield, MI 48076
Marine Corps League
11245 E. 14 Mile Road
Sterling Heights, MI 48312

Polish Legion of American Veterans
1280 McNamara Bldg.
Detroit, MI 48226
Vietnam Veterans of America
1231 McNamara Bldg.
Detroit, MI 48226

Paralyzed Veterans of America
405S0 Grand River
Novi, MI 48375
Military Order of the Purple Heart
1226 McNamara Bldg.
Detroit, MI 48226

Veterans of Foreign Wars
924 N. Washington Ave.
Lansing, MI 48901

4. U.S. DEPARTMENT OF VETERANS AFFAIRS:

Regional Office
477 Michigan Avenue
Detroit, MI 48266
VAMC
Southfield & Outer Drive
Allen Park, MI 48101

VAMC
5500 Armstrong Road
Battle Creek, MI 49015
VAMC
Iron Mountain, MI 4980

VAMC
1500 Weiss
Saginaw, MI 48602
VA Outpatient Clinic
850 N. Otsego
Gaylord, MI 49735

Vet Center
1766 Fort Street
Lincoln Park, MI 48146
Great Lakes Medical Regional Office
P.O. Box 1407
Ann Arbor, MI 48106

VAMC
2215 Fuller Road
Ann Arbor, MI 48105
VA Outpatient Clinic

3019 Coit St. NE
Grand Rapids, MI 49505

VAMC
4646 John R. Street
Detroit, MI 48201

5. OTHER VETERANS SERVICE CENTERS:

Vet Center
20802 Greenfield
Oak Park, MI 48237
Vet Center
1940 Eastern Avenue
Grand Rapids, MI 49507

Vets Center
942 Terrace
Muskegon, MI 49440
Vets Center
1231 Hastings
Traverse City, MI 49684

Vets Center
720 Lundington Street
Escanaba, MI 49829
Vets Center
14 S. Monroe Street
Monroe, MI 48161

Homeless Veterans Center
1122 E. Easterday Avenue
Sault Ste. Marie, MI 49783

6. MICHIGAN VETERANS FOUNDATION: (Homeless Veterans Program)

Post Office Box 15037
Lansing, MI 48901

MINNESOTA DEPARTMENT OF VETERANS AFFAIRS

COMMISSIONER: JEFFERY L. OLSON
MAILING ADDRESS & LOCATION:
   STATE VETERANS SERVICE BUILDING
   20 WEST 12TH STREET, 2nd FLR.
   ST. PAUL, MINNESOTA 55155-2079
TELEPHONE: (651) 296-2562
FAX: (651) 205-4208
E-MAIL: jolson@mdva.state.mn.us

1. SERVICES PERFORMED.

A. Office of the Commissioner: Provides technical supervision and training to Minnesota's system of county veterans service officers. These county veterans service officers are located in each of Minnesota's eighty-seven counties. Telephone (612) 296-2562.

B. Veterans Benefits Division: Administers the State Soldier's Assistance Program, a temporary financial assistance program, maintains bonus records, including copies of form DD 214, administers an educational grant program, provides referral services to other providers. Telephone (612) 296-2562.

C. Financial Guardianship Division: Provides financial management services to incompetent veterans and their dependents. Telephone (612) 296-2562.

D. Veterans Preference Division: Provides assistance to veterans seeking enforcement of state veterans preference statutes. Telephone (612) 296-2562.

E. Agent Orange Division: Provides information and referral services to veterans and their dependents regarding the agent orange issue. Telephone (612) 296-2562.

F. Claims Division: Provides accredited representative services to veterans and their dependents for the following organizations: Minnesota Department of Veterans Affairs, American Legion, Veterans of World War I, Jewish War Veterans, Regular Veterans of America, and the

Noncommissioned Officers Association of America and The Retired Enlisted Association
   Room 191, Bishop Henry Whipple Federal Building
   1 Federal Drive
   Fort Snelling, Minnesota 55111
   Telephone: (612) 725-3171
   FAX: (612) 296-8664

G. State Veterans Cemetery: Provides burial to eligible veterans and their dependents. Definition of eligibility is the same as for national cemeteries.
   State Veterans Cemetery
   Rt #5, Box 93B
   1 Memorial Drive
   Little Falls, MN 56345-9805
   (320) 632-3272

The Minnesota Department of Veterans Affairs operates a Branch Claims Office to serve veterans and their dependents in the portion of Minnesota served by the United States Department of Veterans Affairs (USDVA) Regional Office in Fargo, North Dakota.
   Department of Veterans Affairs
   Moorhead Branch Office
   USDVA Regional Office, Room 207
   2101 No. Elm Street
   Fargo, North Dakota 58102
   Telephone: (701) 237-2613
   FAX: (701) 237-2632

2. STATE BENEFITS:

A. The Department of Veterans Affairs Benefits Division manages the following veterans benefits programs.
1) State Soldiers Assistance Program: Provides limited emergency financial assistance to state veterans and their dependents while the veteran is disabled and unable to work;

2) Medical Assistance: May' be available to assist eligible veterans and their dependents with expenses of emergency hospitalization or medical, dental and optical needs. Applicants must meet strict low income requirements.

3) War Orphan and Veterans Education Assistance: Provides limited financial assistance to eligible children of veterans who were killed in action or who died in service-connected disabilities. Veteran applicants must meet strict program rules.

B. State Benefits for veterans, disabled veterans and former prisoners of war:

1) Veterans' preference in public employment: Hiring and dismissal.

2) Educational assistance: Dependents of those held as prisoners of war after August 1, 1958.

3) Bonus Records: Copies of discharges filed with applications for state war bonuses.

4) Exemption from registration taxes on motor vehicle: Certain disabled veterans only.

5) No fees: For certified copies of official records used in claims for veterans benefits from the USDVA, the Minnesota Department of Veterans Affairs or, when provided, to any congressionally chartered veterans' organizations.

6) Reduced property taxes: For disabled persons, including veterans.

7) No state or excise taxes: On motor vehicles purchased by a disabled veteran with the assistance of the USDVA.

8) Free fishing license: a free fishing license shall be issued to a Minnesota resident veteran, as defined by M.S. 197.447, who is rated as 100% service-connected disabled by the USDVA; a fishing license is not required for patients of the USDVA Medical Centers, with written consent of the hospital administrator. Free small game and deer license—same requirements.

9) State Veterans Cemetery: Located near Little Falls, and Camp Ripley, Minnesota.

10) Free License Plates: Are available to Ex-POWs and recipients of the Congressional Medal of Honor.

11) Special License Plates: For certain organizations, periods of war.

3. MINNESOTA VETERANS HOMES BOARD OF DIRECTORS:

State Veterans Service Building
St. Paul, Minnesota 55155-2079
Chair: Steve O'Connor
Telephone: (612) 296-2073

Provides skilled nursing care and domiciliary care to eligible veterans and widows or widowers and spouses of veterans if the widow or widower or spouse is 55 years of age or older. The Board operates veterans homes at the following locations in Minnesota:

Minneapolis
346 skilled care beds
Hastings
200 domiciliary beds

Silver Bay
89 skilled care beds
Luverne
83 skilled care beds

Fergus Falls
85 skilled care beds

4. VITAL STATISTICS:

Vital Records
Minnesota Department of Health
717 Delaware Street SE

Minneapolis, MN 55440
(612) 623-5121

5. USDVA REGIONAL OFFICE:

USDVA Medical Center—Minneapolis
One Veteran Drive
Minneapolis, MN 55417
Charles Milbrandt, Director
(612) 725-2000

USDVA Medical Center-St. Cloud
St. Cloud, Minnesota 56303
Barry Bahl, Director
(320) 252-1670

USDVA Regional Office and Insurance Center
Bishop Henry Whipple Federal Building
1 Federal Drive
St. Paul, Minnesota 55111 4050
Ronald J. Henke, Director

6. VETERANS ORGANIZATIONS, STATE HEADQUARTERS:

The American Legion and Auxiliary
Veterans' of Foreign Wars and Auxiliary
Disabled American Veterans
Military Order of the Purple Heart
Vietnam Veterans of America
AMVETS
State Council Headquarters

LOCATION:
State Veterans Service Building

20 West 12th Street
St. Paul, Minnesota 55155

MISSISSIPPI STATE VETERANS AFFAIRS BOARD

EXECUTIVE DIRECTOR: CHARLES E. BURNHAM
MAILING ADDRESS:
  P.O. Box 5947
  Pearl, MS 39208-5947
LOCATION:
  3466 HWY 80 East
  Pearl, MS 39208-5947
TELEPHONE: (601) 576-4850
FAX: (601) 576-4868
E-MAIL: cburnham@vab.state.ms.us

1. SERVICES PERFORMED.

A. SVAB furnishes representation to veterans, widows and dependent children by virtue of Power of Attorney made to one of the following:
  State Veterans Affairs Commission
  Military Order of the Purple Heart
  American Legion
  Veterans of Foreign Wars
  American Red Cross
  NCOA
  American Ex-POWS
  Blinded Veterans
B. State Approving Agency for veterans and war orphans.
C. Service organizations located in Jackson VARO, but not associated with SVAB:
  Disabled American Veterans
  AMVETS
  Paralyzed Veterans of America

2. STATE BENEFITS:

A. Tax Exemption: 100% service-connected disabled veterans have $6, 000 Ad Valorem tax exemption.

B. Licenses: Hunting and fishing license and $1 car tag for 100% disabled veterans. Ex-POWs and Medal of Honor recipients eligible for $1 car tag, free car tag for unremarried widow of serviceman killed in war or national emergency and a Veterans license plate which costs an additional $30, the proceeds of which benefit needy veteran residents of the State Veterans Nursing Home.

C. Employment: Veterans preference in hiring and layoffs. Retirement credit for wartime service.

D. Home Loan: Program administered under the direction of Veterans Home Purchase Board, PO Box 115, Jackson, MS 39205.

E. County Service Officer Program: Each county is authorized to hire CVSO to assist veterans and widows.

F. State Veterans' Homes: Four 150-bed State Veterans Nursing Homes located in Jackson, Oxford, Kosciusko and Collins, MS.

G. Veterans War Bonus: None

H. Income Tax Exemption: $7,500 exemption from income tax on federal and state retirements.

3. VITAL STATISTICS:

Administrative Officer
State Board of Health
P. O. Box 1700
Jackson. MS 39205

4. USDVA REGIONAL OFFICE:

1600 East Woodrow Wilson Ave.
Jackson, MS 39216

5. VETERANS ORGANIZATIONS, STATE HEADQUARTERS:

The American Legion
P.O. Box 688
Jackson, MS 39205
Veterans of WWI, USA, Inc.
War Memorial Building
Jackson, MS 39205

Disabled American Veterans
P.O. Box 10916
Jackson, MS 39205
Veterans of Foreign Wars
P.O. Box 2027
Jackson, MS 39205

6. GENERAL INFORMATION:

The duties of the State Veterans Affairs Board and Commission shall be to assist former and present members of the Armed Forces of the United States, and their dependents, in securing any benefit or privilege under any federal, state, or local laws or regulations to which they are entitled; and to advise the Governor and the Legislature on veterans' affairs. The State Veterans Affairs Board is designated as the "State Approving Agency" for the State of Mississippi. It shall be the duty of the Board to inspect, approve, and supervise schools, institutions, and establishments for war orphans and veterans' training.

The State Veterans Affairs Board consists of seven members appointed by the Governor, one from each congressional district as they existed on January 1, 1952, in the State of Mississippi Each member is appointed for a term of seven years, one member being appointed each year, staggered terms of appointments. . The State Veterans Affairs Board shall annually appoint an executive director (who shall also serve as Executive Secretary of the State Veterans Affairs

Board), a deputy director, three division directors and one management information specialist. The executive director, deputy director and division directors shall be honorably discharged or honorably released veterans of any war or police action in which the Armed Forces of the United States have been, or shall be committed for action.

The Board, and Commissioners of the State Veterans Affairs Board, shall cooperate fully with all congressionally chartered veterans organizations within the state, including serving as the powers of attorney for said congressionally chartered veterans organizations, upon the request of said organization, provided all Powers of Attorney to the State Veterans Affairs Board shall be processed first.

The Board is charged with the responsibility of operating the MS State Veterans Homes located in Jackson, Oxford, Kosciusko and Collins.

MISSOURI VETERANS COMMISSION

EXECUTIVE DIRECTOR: RONALD L. TAYLOR
MAILING ADDRESS:
   POST OFFICE DRAWER 147
   1719 SOUTHRIDGE DR.
   JEFFERSON CITY, MO 65102-0147
LOCATION:
   1719 SOUTHRIDGE DRIVE
   JEFFERSON CITY, MO 65109
TELEPHONE: (573) 751-3779
FAX: (573) 751-6836
E-MAIL: taylor@mvc.state.mo.us

1. SERVICES PERFORMED.

A. Provide information, counsel, and assistance to veterans and their dependents through a statewide network of Veterans Service Officers

B. Manage seven veterans homes, located strategically throughout the state. Administrators are licensed by the state, and report to the Executive Director through the Superintendent of Homes.

C. Manage two state veterans cemeteries.

2. STATE BENEFITS:

A. State Veterans Homes: Providing three levels of long-term skilled nursing care.

B. State Veterans Cemeteries: Two open in January 2000 at Higginsville, MO and Springfield, MO.

C. Free Automobile License Plates: Veterans who are rated 100% for service-connected disabilities, or in need of adaptive equipment, as well as Medal of Honor recipients, former POWs and widows of former POWs. Other veteran plates are available for a $15.00 fee.

D. Veterans' Preference: For employment, and when testing for any position with the state, a five-point preference, or ten points for a service-connected, disabled veteran.

E. Free Hunting/Fishing Licenses: For 60 percent or more rated service-connected veterans.

F. Agent Orange Settlement: Payments made from the Agent Orange Fund to a veteran or his dependents are exempt from state tax.

G. Priority: State agencies, which administer federally funded employment and training programs for veterans shall give priority to qualified veterans and other eligible persons.

H. Tuition-Free Scholarships: Legislation passed in 1991 provides that certain surviving widows and children of Vietnam Veterans may qualify to receive tuition-free scholarships to attend institutions of post-secondary education in Missouri. The Veteran's death must be attributable to illness that could possibly be a result of exposure to toxic chemicals such as "Agent Orange" during the Vietnam conflict in order for the survivor to qualify.

I. Veterans Memorial Renovation Grants: A Memorial Grant Program was established by the General Assembly through House Bill

1519 in 1998, authorizing the appropriation of up to $2,000,000 for matching grants to renovate dedicated veterans memorials in Missouri. The Commission accepted applications for this program from July 1, 1999 through June 30, 2000. A total of twelve applications were received with eleven being approved for total matching funds in the amount of $1,365,000. Legislation signed into law in 2000 revised the statute to include the construction of new veterans memorials as well as the continued grants for restoration of existing memorials and extended the program through 2004.

3. VITAL STATISTICS:

(Birth, Death, Marriage, Divorce)
   Department of Health
   Bureau of Vital Statistics
   920 Wildwood
   P.O. Box 570
   Jefferson City, MO 65102-0570
   (573) 751-6387

4. USDVA REGIONAL OFFICE:

   400 South 18th Street
   St. Louis, MO 63103-2271
   1-800-827-1000

5. USDVA MEDICAL CENTERS

   VA Medical Center
   915 North Grand
   St. Louis, MO 63106
   (314) 652-4100
   VA Medical Center—Jefferson Barracks
   Division
   St. Louis, MO 63125
   (314) 652-4100

Harry S. Truman Memorial
VA Medical Center
800 Hospital Drive
Columbia, MO 65201
(573) 814-6300
John J. Pershing VA Medical Center
Hwy. 67 North
Poplar Bluff, MO 63901
(573) 686-4151

VA Medical Center
4801 Linwood Boulevard
Kansas City, MO 63128
(816) 861-4700
1-800-525-1483
Gene Taylor VA Outpatient Clinic
600 North Main
Mount Vernon, MO 65712
(417) 466-4000

6. MISSOURI VETERANS HOMES:

MVH—St. James
620 North Jefferson
St. James, MO 65559-1999
(573) 265-3271
Patricia Faenger, Administrator
MVH—Mount Vernon
600 North Main
Mount Vernon, MO 65712
(417) 466-7103
Don Long, Administrator

MVH—Mexico
#1 Veterans Drive
Mexico, MO 65265
(573) 581-1088
Cheryl Goodwin, Administrator
MVH—Cape Girardeau
2400 Veterans Memorial Drive
Cape Giardeau, MO 63701
(573) 290-5870

MVH—St. Louis
10600 Lewis & Clark Boulevard
St. Louis, MO 63136
(314) 340-6389
Paulette Wright, Administrator
MVH—Cameron
1111 Euclid
Cameron, MO 64429
(816) 632-6010
Joanna Mooney, Administrator

MVH—Warrensburg
1300 Veterans Road
P.O. Box 1076
Warrensburg, MO 64093
(660) 543-5064
Stan Smith, Administrator

7. VETERANS ORGANIZATIONS, STATE HEADQUARTERS:

The American Legion
Lynn Dorrell, Adjutant
P.O. Box 179

Jefferson City, MO 65102
(573) 893-2353
Veterans of Foreign Wars
Don Watts, Adjutant
P.O. Box 26
Jefferson City, MO 65102
(573) 636-8761

Disabled American Veterans
Paul D. Pealer, Adjutant
P.O. Box 148
Portland, MO 65067
(573) 236-4478
AMVETS
Ben Haynes, Commander
3257 Pomme de Terre
Flemington, MO 65650
(417) 253-4463

8. VETERANS EMPLOYMENT REPRESENTATIVE:

Mick Jones, Director
Veterans Employment and Training Service
MO Dept. of Labor and Industrial Relations
P.O. Box 59
421 East Dunklin Street
Jefferson City, MO 65104-0059
(573) 751-3921

9. FEDERAL CEMETERIES:

Jefferson Barracks National Cemetery (Open)
101 Memorial Drive
St. Louis. MO 63125
(314) 263-8691 or 8692

Springfield National Cemetery
(Closed—*except for cremated remains only*)
1702 East Seminole Street
Springfield, MO 65804
(417) 881-9499

Jefferson City National Cemetery
(Closed)
1024 East McCarty Street
Jefferson City, MO 65101
(Call Jefferson Barracks National Cemetery, St. Louis, MO for information)

10. STATE CEMETERIES:

State Veterans Cemetery—Higginsville
20109 Business Highway 13
Higginsville, MO 64037
(660) 584-5252
Jess Rasmussen, Cemetery Director
State Veterans Cemetery—Springfield
5201 S. Southwood Road
Springfield, MO 65804
(417) 823-3944
Mike Robbins, Cemetery Director

MONTANA DEPARTMENT OF MILITARY AFFAIRS

ADMINISTRATOR: JOSEPH S. FOSTER
MAILING ADDRESS & LOCATION:
  POST OFFICE BOX 5715
  HELENA, MT 59604
TELEPHONE: (406) 324-3740
FAX: (406) 324-3745
E-MAIL: jofoster@state.mt.us

1. SERVICES PERFORMED.

The Montana Veterans Affairs Division represents veterans and widows and other dependents under Power of Attorney to the following:

Montana Veterans Affairs Division
Veterans of World War I, USA, Inc.
AMVETS
Military Order of the Purple Heart
The American Legion
Regular Veterans Association
Blinded Veterans Association
Vietnam Veterans of America

2. STATE BENEFITS:

A. Tax Exemption: Real Estate tax reduced for the 100% service-connected disabled wartime veteran and certain surviving spouses.

B. State Veterans Home: 22-bed domiciliary, 90-bed nursing home and 15-bed special care unit located in Columbia Falls, MT; 80 bed skilled/intermediate skilled nursing home facility with 10 of the 80 beds for special care residents located in Glendive, MT.

C. State Loan Program: None

D. State Bonus: Expired for World War I, World War II, Korean Conflict, and Vietnam.

E. License Plates: Free to 100% service-connected disabled wartime veterans for one automobile. Veteran license plates available in support of State Veterans Cemetery Program.

F. Burial Assistance: $250 paid by county of residence; county of residence provides $70 toward mounting of government grave marker; 2 State Veterans Cemeteries.

G. Educational Assistance: Tuition waivers are provided at the units of the University of Montana system for wartime veterans no longer eligible for VA educational benefits and who are Montana residents; children of resident of Montana who served with the armed forces of the United States in any of its wars and who were killed or died as a result of injury or disease, or other disabilities incurred while in the service of the armed forces of the United States; spouses or children of residents of Montana who have been declared to be prisoners of war or missing in action.

H. Discharges Recorded: Discharge papers are recorded without charge by the Clerk & Recorder of each county.

3. VITAL STATISTICS:

Records and Statistics Bureau
Department of Health & Environmental Services
Room C118
Cogswell Building
Helena, MT 59620

4. FEDERAL and STATE VETERANS FACILITIES:

VA Regional Office
Ft. Harrison, MT 59636
1-800-827-1000
Anaconda VA Outpatient Clinic
118 7th St., 2nd Floor
Anaconda, MT
(406) 563-6090

VA Medical Center
Ft. Harrison, MT 59636
(406) 442-6410
Kalispell Primary Care Clinic
66 Claremont St.
Kalispell, MT 59901
(406) 571-5980

Missoula Vet Center
500 N. Higgins

Missoula, MT 59803
(406) 721-4918
1-800-626-8686
VA Eastern MT Health Care System
Out Patient Clinic & Nursing Home
Miles City, MT 59301
(406) 232-3060
1-888-461-1000

Missoula VA Outpatient Clinic
900 N. Orange, Suite 101
Missoula, MT 59803
(406) 327-0912
Eastern Montana Veterans Home
2000 Montana Ave
Glendive, MT 59330
(406) 345-8855
(866) 887-3684

Billings Vet Center
1234 Avenue C
Billings MT 59102
(406) 248-8579
Montana Veterans Home
P.O. Box 250
Columbia Falls, MT 59912
(406) 892-3256

Billings VA Community Based Clinic
and VA Mental Health Clinic
2345 King Ave. W.
Billings, MT 59102
(406) 651-5670

1-888-461-5000
Glasgow Outpatient Clinic
621 3rd Street So.
Glasgow, MT 59230
(406) 228-4351

Sidney VA Primary Care Clinic
216 14th Ave. S.W.
Sidney, MT 59270
Montana State Veterans Cemetery
Helena, Montana
(406) 324-3740

Great Falls Primary Care Clinic
1417 9th St. S., Suite 200
Great Falls, MT 59405
(406) 761-0179
Eastern Montana State Veterans Cemetery
Miles City, Montana
(406) 324-3740

Bozeman VA Primary Care Clinic
300 N. Wilson, Suite 2004
Bozeman, MT 59715
(406) 522-8923

5. VETERANS ORGANIZATIONS, STATE HEADQUARTERS:

The American Legion
P.O. Box 6075
Helena, MT 59604
Disabled American Veterans

P.O. Box 777
Victor, MT 59875

Veterans of Foreign Wars
P.O. Box 6228
Helena, MT 59604

6. GENERAL INFORMATION:

The Veterans Welfare Act was passed by the Montana Legislature at its 1919 session. The purpose of the act was the encouragement, aid and assistance for soldiers in the United States military forces in the first World War. The assistance available was to help obtain employment, education, training, and comfort to those who had been in the military and naval service of the United States during the war.

The same act created a Veterans Welfare Commission to administer the Veterans Welfare Act. This Commission consisted of three members, appointed by the Governor. The Commission was given powers to employ such persons as necessary to assist in its work and expend such money appropriated by the act, as it deemed necessary to carry out the purpose of the act.

The Veterans Welfare Commission was reorganized by the 1945 Legislature. This act enlarged the membership of the Commission to five members who were appointed by the Governor. The members of the Commission were to be honorably discharged veterans from service in the military forces of the United States in any of its wars and must be residents of the State of Montana. The appointments were made for a five-year period. It was the duty of the Commission to establish a Statewide service for discharged veterans and their families. The Commission actively cooperated with State and Federal agencies having to do with the affairs of veterans and their families and promoted the general welfare of all veterans and their families.

In 1971, the State Legislature passed the Executive Reorganization Act. Under this act, the Veterans Welfare Commission was to be placed in a new department to be created. On November 1, 1971, the Department of Social and Rehabilitation Services (S.R.S.) was created by Executive Order. The Veterans Welfare Commission became the Board of Veterans Affairs and the agency became the Veterans Affairs Division. The Division was attached to S.R.S. for administrative purposes only. The duties, powers and term of appointments for the Board members remained the same.

In 1983, the Legislature passed a bill transferring the Board and the agency from S.R.S. to the Department of Military Affairs. This transfer was also for administrative purposes only.

At present, the Board employs an Administrator, Office Manager, Senior Service Officer and Program Assistant in the state office along with a Cemetery Sexton and part-time groundskeeper. The agency also has eight field Service Officers and six Veteran Service Technicians located throughout the State of Montana. These field officers have 56 counties to travel and assist veterans and their dependents.

The Administrator and the Senior Service Officer are accredited by the USDVA to represent claims before the agency. Powers of Attorney are taken by the Veterans Affairs Division in their own right and this agency also handles all claims for the American Legion, AMVETS, Veterans of World War I of the USA, Inc., the Military Order of the Purple Heart, Vietnam Veterans of America, the Regular Veterans Association and the Blinded Veterans Association.

On September 8, 1987, the state officially opened the Montana State Veterans Cemetery in Helena for veterans and their spouses. A new Eastern Montana State Veterans Cemetery opened in Miles City, MT on July 2, 2001.

NEBRASKA DEPARTMENT OF VETERANS' AFFAIRS

EXECUTIVE DIRECTOR: JOHN HILGERT
DEPUTY DIRECTOR: DANIEL L. PARKER
MAILING ADDRESS:
    STATE OFFICE BUILDING

PO BOX 95083
LINCOLN, NE 68509-5083
LOCATION:
301 CENTENNIAL MALL SOUTH
TELEPHONE: (402) 471-2458
FAX: (402) 471-2491
E-MAIL: jhilgert@mail.state.ne.us

1. SERVICES PERFORMED.

A. The Department administers state veteran benefits and provides representation by state veterans service officers for veterans and their dependents in claims before the VA.
B. The Department's state veterans service officers provide sole representation on behalf of the:
Nebraska Dept. of Veterans Affairs
The American Legion
Veterans of Foreign Wars
Military Order of the Purple Heart
American Ex-POWs
Vietnam Veterans of America
National Association of County Veterans Service officers
C. Nebraska has 87 county veteran service officers who work closely with the Department in the state-federal claims filing process and administer county veterans' aid and benefit programs.
D. Sponsors an annual School of Instruction for county, post and chapter service officers.

2. STATE BENEFITS:

A. Aid Funds: Nebraska Veterans' Aid Fund (NVA).
B. Veterans' Homes: Four locations (Grand Island, Norfolk Omaha, Scottsbluff).
C. Education:
(1) Waiver of Tuition

(2) Tuition Credit for Active Reservists
(3) Tuition Credit for National Guard
D. Burial:
(1) Grave registration
(2) Possible Assistance from NVA Fund
E. Discharges: DD 214: Nearly 700,000 documents of Nebraska veterans on file.
F. Tax Exemptions:
(1) Homestead
(2) Property Tax for paraplegics
G. Hunting and Fishing Permit exemptions.
H. State Bonus: None

3. VITAL STATISTICS:

Health and Human Services/Vital Records Office
P.O. Box 95044
Lincoln, NE 68509 5044

4. U.S. DEPARTMENT OF VETERANS AFFAIRS FACILITIES:

VA Medical Center
600 South 70th Street
Lincoln, NE 68510
VA Medical Center
2201 North Broadwell
Grand Island, NE 68803

U.S. Department of Veterans Affairs Regional Office
5631 South 48th Street
Lincoln, NE 68515
VA Medical Center
4101 Woolworth Avenue
Omaha, NE 68105

5. VETERANS ORGANIZATIONS, STATE HEADQUARTERS:

The American Legion
200 N. 56th Street
P.O. Box 5205
Lincoln, NE 68505
Disabled American Veterans
101 Crestridge Drive
Bellevue, NE 68005

Veterans of Foreign Wars
2431 North 48th Street-or-P. O. Box 4552
Lincoln, NE 68504
Paralyzed Veterans of America
Great Plains Chapter
7612 Maple Street
Omaha, NE 68134-6502

Vietnam Veterans of America
Nebraska State Council
847 West Military
Fremont, NE 68025
American Ex-POWs
3711 South 117th
Omaha, NE 68144

Military Order of the Purple Heart
1024 "K" Street
Lincoln, NE 68508
AMVETS
P.O. Box 4263
Lincoln, NE 68504

6. VIETNAM VETERAN'S OUTREACH CENTERS:

920 "L" Street
Lincoln, NE 68508
2428 Cuming Street
Omaha, NE 68131-1600

7. GENERAL INFORMATION:

The NVA Fund was established in 1921. This is a temporary emergency aid fund to assist veterans, their spouses, and dependents in time of need when an unforeseen emergency occurs. County or post veterans' service officers submit applications to the department.

Tuition may be waived by the University of Nebraska, state colleges, and community colleges on behalf of any child, spouse, widow, or widower, resident of Nebraska who meets specified eligibility requirements.

The Department of Veterans Affairs shall preserve, by counties, a permanent registry of the graves of all persons who shall have served in the Armed Forces of the United States at the time of war and whose mortal remains rest in Nebraska.

Enlisted members of the Army National Guard or Air Guard and the active selected reserve (Army, Marine, or Naval Reserve) meeting requirements may be eligible for tuition credit at a state supported university, college, or community college.

Nebraska has four veterans' homes: Grand Island, Norfolk, Omaha, and Scottsbluff. The homes provide care for Nebraska veterans who served in the Armed Forces during a period of war. Dependent spouses, Gold Star Mothers and Gold Star Fathers, and widows have basic entitlement for admission.

NEVADA COMMISSION FOR VETERANS' AFFAIRS

EXECUTIVE DIRECTOR: CHARLES W. "Chuck" FULKERSON
MAILING ADDRESS & LOCATION:
1201 TERMINAL WAY, ROOM 221

RENO, NV 89502
TELEPHONE: (775) 688-1653
FAX: (775) 688-1656
FTS: (775) 470-5238

DEPUTY EXECUTIVE DIRECTOR: STEVE LONG
MAILING ADDRESS:
  c/o VA AMBULATORY CARE CENTER
  1700 VEGAS DR., #1719
  LAS VEGAS, NV 89106
TELEPHONE: (702) 636-3070
FAX: (702) 636-3079
E-MAIL: cfulkers@govmail.state.nv.us OR ovsinlv@hotmail.com

1. SERVICES PERFORMED

A. Represents veterans, widows and dependents in their pursuit of benefits offered by the U.S. Dept. of Veterans Affairs.
B. Represents veterans and their dependents under power of attorney made to the following organizations:
  The American Legion
  Veterans of World War I, USA, Inc.
  Military Order of Purple Heart
  Nevada Commission for Veterans Affairs
  Jewish War Veterans
  Fleet Reserve Association
  California Dept. of VA
  Regular Veterans Association
  Ex-POWs
  Marine Corp League
  Catholic War Veterans of USA
  Blinded Veterans Association
C. Service organizations having their own service officers:
  Disabled American Veterans

AMVETS

Veterans of Foreign Wars

D. Administers guardianship program for incompetent veterans, widows and children of deceased veterans. Operates two state veterans' cemeteries.

2. STATE BENEFITS:

A. Tax Exemption: The State of Nevada offers to honorably discharged veterans with wartime service a tax exemption, which may be applied to either real or personal property (vehicle). The exemption, to the extent of $1000 assessed valuation, may be used only once during a 12 month period. Application for exemption is made by filing an annual affidavit with the County Assessor's Office.

B. Hunting & Fishing License: A free hunting and fishing license is available to honorably discharged veterans with a 50% or higher service-connected disability.

C. License Plates: 100% service-connected disabled veterans may register one vehicle with a license plate with words Disabled Veteran for a fee of $1. Other special veterans; plates are available by calling the nearest Dept. of Motor Vehicles and Public Safety Office for specific information.

D. State Tax: Nevada has no State Income Tax.

E. Veterans Home: Pending.

F. State Bonus: None

G. Guardianship: For incompetent veterans, widows and children of deceased veterans.

H. Loan Program: None

I. Burial Plot: Free to veterans in either State Cemetery. Spouse or minor dependent is $350.

J. Employment Preference: Upon successfully obtaining a passing score on a City, County or State examination, up to five bonus points may be added to the scores of:

(1) Honorably discharged veterans or widows of veterans;

(2) Disabled veterans; and

(3) Nevada residents.

3. VITAL STATISTICS:

State Department of Health (Birth & Death Records)
Division of Vital Statistics
Carson City, NV 89710
(702) 687-4481
Marriage and divorce records may be obtained in county in which license was purchased or divorce was obtained, at County Recorder or County Clerk.

4. USDVA REGIONAL OFFICE:

1201 Terminal Way
Reno. NV 89502
1-800-827-1000

5. VETERANS ORGANIZATIONS, STATE HEADQUARTERS:

The American Legion
737 Veterans Memorial Dr.
Las Vegas, NV 89101
(702) 382-2353
Veterans of Foreign Wars
P. O. Box 2562
Fallon, NV 89407-2562
(775) 423-8663

Disabled American Veterans
National Service Officer
1201Terminal Way, Suite 107
Reno, NV 89502
(775) 784-5239

AMVETS
National Service Officer
1201 Terminal Way, #109
Reno, NV 89502
(775) 329-9833

6. GENERAL INFORMATION:

The Nevada Commission for Veterans Affairs was created by an Act of the Nevada State Legislature on March 29, 1943. The Office of the Commissioner and Deputy Commissioner are responsible for helping veterans and their families obtain all the services, compensation and government benefits to which they may be entitled; for managing veterans' funds who the Court declare as unable to handle their own financial matters; for supervising the operation and maintenance of two State Veterans' Cemeteries; and for developing and establishing a State Veterans' Home in Nevada. The Commissioner's Office manages the fiscal matters for the entire division.

NEW HAMPSHIRE STATE VETERANS COUNCIL

DIRECTOR: DENNIS J. VIOLA
MAILING ADDRESS & LOCATION:
   STATE VETERANS COUNCIL
   275 Chestnut Street
   Room 321
   Manchester NH 03101-2411
TELEPHONE: (603) 624-9230
TOLL FREE: 1-800-622-9230 (in state only)
FAX: (603) 624-9236
E-MAIL: nhviold@vba.va.gov

1. SERVICES PERFORMED.

A. Assist veterans who are residents of this state or their dependents to secure all benefits or preferences to which they may be entitled under any state or federal laws or regulations.

B. A director and three veteran service officers who provide assistance in the application and development of claims or related services at seventeen sites throughout the stale. These sites are visited on a routine, published schedule.

2. STATE BENEFITS:

A. Tax Exemption: Property tax exemption to eligible veterans and widows. Additional exemption if total permanent service-connected disability or paraplegic.

B. N.H. Veterans Home: Located at Tilton, with 150 beds in Nursing Home Care.

C. State Bonus: Deadline for World War I, World War II, and Korean Conflict has passed. Vietnam Conflict remains open. Persian Gulf War Bonus of $100 began in October 1997 and expires in October 2002. To be eligible, applicant must have entered service from New Hampshire and must have been awarded the Southwest Asia Service Medal.

D. Licenses: Free automobile license registration and parking for service-connected amputee or blind. Exemption of registration fee for Ex-POWs. Free hunting and fishing licenses for service-connected total disability. Service-connected veterans and their unmarried widows exempt from payment of fees for Peddler's License.

E. Education: Free tuition at vocational-technical college and state educational institutions of secondary college grade for certain children of missing veterans or veterans who died of service-connected disability.

F. Burial Allowance: For certain veterans.

G. Employment Preferences: Reemployment rights and veterans' preference in employment.

3. VITAL STATISTICS:

Bureau of Vital Records
Health and Human Services Building
6 Hazen Drive
Concord, NH 03301

4. USDVA DEPARTMENT OF VETERANS AFFAIRS:

Norris Cotton Federal Building
275 Chestnut Street
Manchester, NH 03101
VA Medical Center
718 Smyth Road
Manchester, NH 03104

Vietnam Veterans Outreach Center
103 Liberty Street
Manchester, NH 03104

5. VETERANS ORGANIZATIONS, STATE HEADQUARTERS:

The American Legion
Norris Cotton Federal Building
275 Chestnut Street
Manchester, NH 03101
(603) 666-7658
Disabled American Veterans
Norris Cotton Federal Building
275 Chestnut Street
Manchester, NH 03101
(603) 666-7664

Veterans of Foreign Wars
Norris Cotton Federal Building
275 Chestnut Street
Manchester, NH 03101
(603) 666-7653
AMVETS
Norris Cotton Federal Building
275 Chestnut Street
Manchester, NH 03101
(603) 666-7969

NEW JERSEY DEPARTMENT OF MILITARY AND VETERANS' AFFAIRS

DEPUTY COMMISSIONER FOR VETERANS' AFFAIRS: Emil H. Philibosian, Colonel, USAR
MAILING ADDRESS:
  P.O. BOX 340
  TRENTON, NJ 08625-0340
LOCATION:
  101 Eggert Crossing Road
  Lawrenceville, NJ 08648
TELEPHONE: (609) 530-7062
Toll-free information: 1-800-624-0508 (in state only)
FAX: (609) 530-7109
E-MAIL: Emil.Philibosian@njdmava.state.nj.us

1. SERVICES PERFORMED.

A. Division of Veterans Healthcare Services provides long-term care and respite care for veterans, National Guard and reserve components of the Armed Forces of the United States. Three long-term care homes are conveniently located in north, central and southern New Jersey. Veterans Memorial Home at Paramus is located at 1 Veterans Drive, P.O. Box 608, Paramus, NJ 07653-0608. Veterans Memorial Home at

Menlo Park is located at 132 Evergreen Road, P.O. Box 3013, Edison, NJ 08818-3013. Veterans Memorial Home at Vineland is located at 524 North West Boulevard, Vineland, NJ 08360.

B. Division of Cemeteries, Memorials, Monuments, and Museums encompasses free interment and perpetual care in the Brigadier General William C. Doyle Veterans Memorial Cemetery; maintains the State's Memorials: Vietnam Veterans Memorial and Education Center, Korean War Memorial; preserves and displays historical documents and artifacts honoring and memorializing the service of New Jersey's Veterans to the Nation and the State: Militia Museum at Sea Girt and Lawrenceville.

C. Division of Veterans Programs is responsible for administering all requests for assistance pertaining to federal and state veterans' benefits, as well as overseeing a "Transitional Housing Program" for homeless veterans. There are Veteran Service Officers located in 17 sites throughout the state; Trenton, Brick, Paterson, Lawrenceville, Atlantic City, Mt. Laurel, Thorofare, Asbury Park, Vineland, Hackensack, Elizabeth, Jersey City, New Brunswick, Newton, Port Murray, Dover (1 day/week), Newark (Liaison Office). Other responsibilities are Civil Service Veterans Preference and Pension Status Claims, Distinguished Service Medals, Vietnam Service Medals.

2. STATE BENEFITS:

A. Real Estate Tax Deduction: Eligible veterans may annually deduct $200 in 2002 and $250 in 2003 and every year thereafter.

B. Real Estate Tax Exemption: Eligible veterans rated 100 percent permanent service-connected by the U.S. Department of VA may apply for 100 percent property tax exemption.

C. Catastrophic Entitlement: Eligible veterans may receive $750/year [monthly entitlement of $62.50] if in receipt of a 100% permanent service-connected disability rating from the U.S. Department of Veterans Affairs that resulted from wartime service. (The seven catastrophic disabilities are: loss of sight; amputation of both hands, both feet or one hand and one foot; hemiplegia and permanent paralysis of one leg and one are or either side of the body; osteochondritis and permanent loss of use of both legs; multiple sclerosis and the loss of use of both feet or both legs; Quadriplegia.

D. Medals: Distinguished Service Medal (DSM): Eligible veterans of the Armed Forces of the United States who served in time of war or national emergency and meet certain criteria may apply.

Vietnam Service Medal: Eligible veterans of the Armed Forces who served in the South East Asia Theatre of Operations from 1960 to 1975 and meet certain criteria may apply.

Meritorious Service Medal: Eligible combat veterans who were not a resident of New Jersey when they entered the military service, but whom currently reside and have been a resident in the state for the previous five years.

E. Education: The U.S. Department of Veterans Affairs and State Veterans Services Offices sponsor programs that offer veterans, reservists, and their dependents access to educational benefits.

Through the New Jersey Department of Military and Veterans Affairs and the Department of Education, a program **"Operation Recognition"** was launched to honor World War II era veterans who left school to join the military and never received a high school diploma.

Free undergraduate college tuition **"POW-MIA Tuition Benefit Program"** is available to any child born or adopted before, during or after the period of time his or her parent was officially declared a prisoner of war (POW) or person missing in action (MIA) after January 1, 1960.

Children of those service personnel who died while in the military or due to service-connected disabilities, or who are officially listed as missing in action by the U.S. Department of Defense may claim **War Orphans Tuition Assistance** [$500 per year for four years of college or equivalent training].

F. Veterans Tuition Credit Program: provides additional education benefits [$400 annually or $200/semester/full-time and $100/semester/part-time] to veterans eligible for federally funded education programs and who served on active duty from December 31, 1960 to May 7, 1975 and who were legal residents of New Jersey at the time of induction into the Armed Forces or at the time of discharge from active service or for a period not less than one year prior to making application.

G. Civil Service Benefits: War period veterans who pass state civil service examinations are given absolute **"veterans preference"** over non-veterans when applying for state, county, and municipal employment. A veteran retirement **"Civil Service Pension Plan"** is available to qualified veterans.

H. Licenses: Honorably discharged veterans can obtain a no-fee license to vend any goods, wares or merchandise, or solicit trade within the state. There is no charge to a veteran obtaining a license for real estate brokers, agents and solicitors.

Free hunting and fishing licenses are available through the Division of Fish and Wildlife to qualified disabled veterans.

I. Transportation: to VA Medical Centers, clinics, hospitals, private physicians, VA Regional Office and local veterans' service offices is available through the state veterans' service offices.

J. Post Traumatic Stress Disorder (PTSD) and Readjustment Counseling: through contracted clinicians, experienced in PTSD counseling, determine the best course of treatment for a veteran and their family.

3. VITAL STATISTICS:

For Birth, Death, Marriage Certificates:
New Jersey Department of Health and Senior Services
Vital Statistics Registration
P. O. Box 370
Trenton, NJ 08625-0370

For Divorce Decree:
Years 1900-1989

Clerk of the Superior Court
Superior Court of NJ
Public Information Center
171 Jersey Street
P.O. Box 967
Trenton, NJ 08625-0967

For Divorce Decree:
Years 1989 to present
The county court that issued decree

4. VETERANS ORGANIZATIONS-DEPARTMENT OF NEW JERSEY:

The American Legion
135 West Hanover St., 4th Floor
Trenton, NJ 08618
(609) 394-1532
Disabled American Veterans
135 West Hanover St., 4th Floor
Trenton, NJ 08618
(609) 396-9562

Veterans of Foreign Wars
135 West Hanover St., 4th Floor
Trenton, NJ 08618
(609) 393-1929

5. USDVA REGIONAL OFFICE:

20 Washington Place
Newark, NJ 07102
1-800-827-1000

NEW MEXICO VETERANS SERVICE COMMISSION

DIRECTOR: John Garcia
MAILING ADDRESS & LOCATION:
 POST OFFICE BOX 2324
 SANTA FE, NM 87503
TELEPHONE: (505) 827-6300
FAX: (505) 827-6372
E-MAIL: johnm.garcia@state.nm.us

1. SERVICES PERFORMED.

A. Represents veterans, widows and dependents by virtue of Power of Attorney made to one of the following organizations:
 The American Legion
 Military Order of the Purple Heart
 Veterans of Foreign Wars
 Disabled American Veterans
 Paralyzed Veterans of America
 AMVETS

B. There are no county service officers. The Department has seventeen field service officers stationed in areas where demand for service justifies their employment.

2. STATE BENEFITS:

A. Tax Exemption: $2,000 tax exemption program for eligible veterans and widows with certain residence requirements.

B. License: Free motor vehicle license plates for amputee veterans. Special registration plates for Medal of Honor recipients, Prisoner of War veterans, 100 percent service-connected disabled veterans, and Pearl Harbor survivors.

C. Hunting and Fishing License: Free lifetime hunting and fishing license for 100 percent service-connected disabled veterans.

D. Public Records: Free public records for U.S. Department of Veterans Affairs (USDVA) purposes.

E. Education:
1. The Commission nominates war orphans for state scholarships
2. Vietnam Veterans scholarship for veterans who were residents of
NM at time of entry and who are in receipt of the Vietnam Campaign
Medal.
F. Guardianship/Consevatorship: Administers program for incompetent veterans, widows, and children of deceased veterans.

3. VITAL STATISTICS:

Vital Statistics Bureau
Harold Runnels Building
Santa Fe, NM 87503

4. USDVA REGIONAL OFFICE:

500 Gold Avenue, S. W.
Albuquerque, NM 87102

5. VETERANS ORGANIZATIONS, STATE HEADQUARTERS:

The American Legion
1215 Mountain Road, N.E.
Albuquerque, NM 87102
Disabled American Veterans
P.O. Box 3097, Station D
Albuquerque, NM 87190

AMVETS
P.O. Box 1283
Albuquerque, NM 87102
Veterans of Foreign Wars
P.O. Box 8411, Station C
Albuquerque, NM 87198

Paralyzed Veterans of America
833 Gibson Blvd., SE
Albuquerque, NM 87102
Military Order of the Purple Heart
1310 Ridgecrest Drive, SE
Albuquerque, NM 87103

6. GENERAL INFORMATION:

The 1927 New Mexico State Legislature created a state agency called the Disabled Soldier's Relief Commission, consisting of three members as appointed by the Governor. A 1929 amendment provided that the New Mexico State Senate consent to the appointment of the Commission members and also defined the powers and duties as herein described. The name of the Commission was changed by the Legislature in 1937 to its present name, "The New Mexico Veterans' Service Commission". The Legislature appropriates funds for the operating expenses of the Commission from the General Fund. The Commission is headed by a director, appointed by the Commission with approval of the Governor. The Commission consists of five members who shall be veterans and who shall be appointed by the Governor by and with the consent of the Senate.

The Commission carries out five programs to implement the agency objectives

Veterans Assistance Program

To render service to all veterans, widows and dependents of veterans residing in New Mexico, through a staff of well-trained and experienced field service officers stationed in areas of New Mexico where demand for such service justifies their employment. Specific functions performed by our service officers in the field are:
1. To furnish an explanation of all laws granting benefits to veterans or their dependents, and the regulations incident thereto, which will clearly present in understandable terms the issues involved.

2. Provide assistance to claimants in the proper preparation of their claims.

3. Advise and assist claimants in the procurement and preparation of documentary or other evidence when required.

4. Explain decisions rendered by the USDVA or other agencies, and advise dissatisfied claimants of their right of appeal and assist in the development of such an appeal.

5. Assist veterans when applying for regular or emergency admission to USDVA Medical Centers for treatment of service-connected disabilities.

6. Maintain liaison with local offices or governmental agencies and all veterans organizations.

7. Be available to address and/or discuss related problems of any group interested in veterans affairs.

Guardianship Program

In 1937, the New Mexico Legislature authorized the Commission to act as guardian, administrator or executor of the estate of deceased veterans or of the estate of incompetent veterans and, by later laws, as guardian of the estate of the minor children of veterans. Today this service is one of the most important of the Commission's responsibilities. Furthermore, the law provides that this service shall be rendered without cost to the estates, except for the pro-rated share of the cost of the blanket guardianship bond.

State Scholarship Program

Chapter 170, New Mexico Laws of 1949 provides authority for the Commission to nominate eligible war orphans for tuition-free state scholarships in any New Mexico state-supported education institution of secondary or college grade.

Tax Exemption and License Program

Chapter 169, New Mexico Laws of 1957 places upon the Commission the responsibility of issuing Certificates of Eligibility to all persons who are entitled to the veteran's tax exemption benefits in New Mexico. Motor vehicles license plates are now being issued to those veterans who meet the eligibility criteria.

Administrative Program

Many basic services are required to support the benefits program of this agency. These include: office operations, personnel administration, and financial management. Under this program we maintain liaison with all state agencies, USDVA agencies and other veteran service commissions throughout the United States.

Rural Outreach Programs

Due to the vast land mass and large number of rural communities the NMVSC provides daily service to twenty-two Native American tribal areas as well as many small rural towns throughout the state.

NEW YORK DIVISION OF VETERANS AFFAIRS

DIRECTOR: GEORGE P. BASHER
MAILING ADDRESS & LOCATION:
  5 EMPIRE STATE PLAZA
  SUITE 2836
  ALBANY, NY 12223-1551
TELEPHONE: (518) 474-6114
FAX: (518) 473-0379
E-MAIL: GBasher@veterans.state.ny.us

1. SERVICES PERFORMED.

The Division of Veterans Affairs provides counseling services and advocacy through a network of field offices across New York State.

Nearly 60 professionally trained state veteran counselors render specialized counseling and assistance to veterans, their families and survivors in applying for a vast array of federal, state and local veterans benefits. In addition, state veteran counselors (all are veterans) are dedicated veterans advocates who serve as liaison in providing advice and direction to those with social, medical and economic problems. The counseling service also provides assistance to active duty military personnel and their families.

2. STATE BENEFITS:

A. Tax Exemption: Partial real property tax exemption provided qualified wartime veterans and spouses.

B. State Bonus: World War II veterans' bonus terminated April 1, 1965; persons, however, may still apply if they can prove they were incapable of making application prior to the termination date because of physical or mental incapacity.

C. Blind Annuity: $1,000 is paid annually to eligible blind veterans and certain widows with approximately 3,800 currently being assisted.

D. Education: Educational grants are provided for eligible children of deceased or seriously disabled veterans, prisoners of war, or servicemen listed as missing in action; tuition assistance awards are available for Vietnam Era veterans and Persian Gulf War veterans who served in Indochina and enroll in a college within New York state.

E. Loan Program: None.

F. Burial: Benefits provided indigent veterans and wives, minor children and widows.

G. Licenses: Certain disabled veterans are eligible for reduced fees for hunting and fishing license permits and use of state parks and camping facilities; peddler's licenses issued without charge; special motor vehicle plates recognizing Medal of Honor, Purple Heart, disabled veterans former POWs, survivors of Pearl Harbor, Gold Star Mothers, and members of various veteran's organizations.

H. Civil Service Preference: Additional credit is given wartime and disabled veterans on competitive appointment exams and promotional exams. Job retention rights are applicable to veterans and spouses of totally disabled veterans.

I. Veterans Nursing Homes: New York State Veterans Home at Oxford with 242 beds for nursing care services. Provides comprehensive health care program designed to meet the needs of all residents. All persons admitted to the home must require health related or skilled nursing care, except for spouses who may accompany medically qualified applicants. New York State also operates a 350-bed long-term health care facility on the campus of the State University of New York at Stony Brook Long Island; and a 250-bed facility in St. Albans, Queens. A 126-bed nursing home is located in Batavia, Genesee County to serve the veterans of western New York. A fifth veterans home is located on the grounds of the VA Medical Center at Montrose in the lower Hudson Valley.

J. Motor Vehicle: Auto registration and Thruway permits (E-Z Pass) provided free-of-charge for certain seriously disabled veterans. Permit allows toll-free travel on New York State Thruway.

3. VITAL STATISTICS:

If birth, death or marriage occurred in New York State outside the City of New York write to:
New York Department of Health
Bureau of Vital Statistics
Albany, NY 12237

If birth, death or marriage occurred in the City of New York write to:
Birth and Death Certificates:
Marriage, Divorce & Discharge Certificates:

Department of Health
125 Worth Street

New York, NY 10013
Manhattan: (New York County)
City Clerk
Marriage License Bureau
Municipal Building
New York, NY 10007

Department of Health
1926 Arthur Avenue
(161st St.)
Bronx, NY 10452
Bronx: (Bronx County)
City Clerk's Office
851 Grand Concourse
Bronx, NY 10457

Department of Health
295 Flatbush Ave. Ext.
Brooklyn, NY 11201
Brooklyn: (Kings County)
Kings County Clerk
360 Adams Street
Brooklyn, NY 11201

Department of Health
90-37 Parks Blvd.
Jamaica, NY 11432
Queens: (Queens County)
City Clerk's Office/Queens Marriage Records
120-55 Queens Blvd.
Kew Gardens, NY 11424

Department of Health
51 Stuyvesant Place
Staten Island, NY 10301
Staten Island: (Richmond County)
City Clerk's Office
Boro Hall
Staten Island, NY 10301

4. USDVA REGIONAL OFFICE:

111 West Huron Street
Buffalo, NY 14202
245 W. Houston Street
New York, NY 10014

5. VETERANS ORGANIZATIONS, STATE HEADQUARTERS:

The American Legion
112 State Street
Albany, NY 12207
Disabled American Veterans
200 Atlantic Ave., Studio #1
Lynbrook, NY 11563

Catholic War Veterans
346 Broadway
New York, NY 10038
Veterans of Foreign Wars
1044 Broadway
Albany, NY 12204

Jewish War Veterans
346 Broadway
New York, NY 10013

6. GENERAL INFORMATION:

The New York State Division of Veterans' Affairs was created to assist returning servicemen and women in transitioning from military to civilian life following the end of World War II. The Division is an agency of the Executive Department of New York State. The responsibility of administering the veterans programs of New York State has been placed in the hands of the State Director of Veterans' Affairs.

Currently, there are 1.25 million living veterans in New York state, and with their dependents and survivors added this sector of the state represents a constituency of an estimated four million New Yorkers.

The heart of the state's veterans' program is in the Division's counseling service through a network of nearly 70 field offices across the state. The counselors are professional civil servants and are required to be veterans. They are under the direct supervision of the area deputy directors. It is the goal of the Division, through its counseling services, to help the veteran, his or her family and survivors to obtain benefits, the nation, state and community provide for them.

State veterans counselors are continually trained through regularly scheduled in-service training conferences and distribution of bulletins, manuals, instructional memoranda and periodic news releases. Many of them have increased their formal education by obtaining advanced degrees in related fields.

The Division works closely with other state, federal and local agencies to obtain constituents all available medical, economic and social benefits within their communities. The Division has worked hard to make other agencies aware and sensitive to the needs of veterans and their families, particularly the unique experiences and problems encountered by many combat veterans—such as Post Traumatic Stress Disorder and exposure to Agent Orange—and how it can impact their readjustment and their family lives.

In addition to counseling services, the New York State Division of Veterans' Affairs administers a Blind

NORTH CAROLINA DIVISION OF VETERANS AFFAIRS

ASSISTANT SECRETARY: CHARLES F. SMITH
MAILING ADDRESS & LOCATION:
  ALBEMARLE BUILDING, SUITE 1065
  1315 MAIL SERVICE CENTER
  325 N. SALISBURY STREET
  RALEIGH, N.C. 27699-1315
TELEPHONE: (919) 733-3851
FAX: (919) 733-2834
E-MAIL: Charlie.Smith@ncmail.net

1. SERVICES PERFORMED.

Represents veterans and dependents in obtaining all rights and benefits to which they may be entitled by virtue of the veteran's military service. Also cooperates with other states and recognized national veterans organizations.

2. STATE BENEFITS:

A. Tax Exemption: Provisions are made for certain types of tax relief relating to income tax, inheritance tax, license taxes and fees, and property tax. For specific information, contact the North Carolina Department of Revenue, Raleigh, North Carolina.
B. Veterans Home: None.
C. Nursing Home: State Veterans Nursing Home, Fayetteville, NC.
D. Loan Program: None
E. State Bonus: None.
F. State Cemeteries: Black Mountain, NC, Jacksonville, NC and Spring Lake, NC.
G. Scholarships: The Division administers an extensive program of state scholarships for eligible children of certain deceased, disabled and POW/MLA veterans.
H. Guardianship: Provision is made in State Law for management of U.S. funds payable to incompetent veterans and minor dependents.

I. Auto License Plates: Certain disabled and POW/MIA veterans may obtain free license plates. Other veterans license plates available, which require a $10.00 special fee.

J. Records: Copies of discharges, state and local public records may be obtained by Division representatives free of charge.

K. Employment: War veterans, their widows and wives of disabled veterans receive preference in state government employment.

L. Lifetime Hunting and Fishing Licenses: Certain disabled veterans may obtain a lifetime license upon payment of a statutory fee.

3. VITAL STATISTICS:

Division of Health Services
Vital Records Branch
225 N. McDowell Street
Raleigh, NC 27602

4. USDVA REGIONAL OFFICE:

Federal Building
251 N. Main Street
Winston-Salem, NC 27155

5. VETERANS ORGANIZATIONS, STATE HEADQUARTERS:

The American Legion
P. O. Box 26657
Raleigh, NC 27611
Disabled American Veterans
P. O. Drawer 28146
Raleigh, NC 27611

Veterans of Foreign Wars
P. O. Box 25337
Raleigh, NC 27611

AMVETS c/o VARO
Federal Building
251 N. Main Street
Winston-Salem, NC 27155

Marine Corps League
3500 Mintwood Dr.
Charlotte, NC 28227
American Ex-Prisioners of War
107 Circle Dr.
LaGrange, NC 28551

6. GENERAL INFORMATION:

The State of North Carolina first signified its official concern for war veterans in 1925 when the General Assembly made it the duty of the Commissioner of Labor "to aid veterans of the World War in securing the adjustment of claims against the Federal Government."

In 1945, the General Assembly created the North Carolina Veterans Commission as an independent state agency specializing in service to veterans. In 1967, the agency name was changed to the North Carolina Department of Veterans Affairs and, in 1977, under the State government Reorganization Act; the Department became a Division of North Carolina Department of Administration.

The Veterans Affairs Commission serves in an advisory capacity to the Governor. The Commission is composed of twelve members appointed by the Governor for four-year terms. The state commanders of congressionally chartered veterans' organizations operating in North Carolina serves as an Advisory Committee to the Veterans Affairs Commission.

The agency is directed by the Assistant Secretary for Veterans Affairs, who is approved by the Secretary of the Department of Administration. The agency is composed of a state service office, fifteen district veterans service offices, affiliated county veterans service offices in most of the state's 100 counties and two, state veterans cemeteries.

Annuity Program for some 3,800 veterans and certain widows.

The Division oversees the Bureau of Veterans Education, which serves as the state's approving agency, which approves and supervises institutions offering programs for veterans and other eligible persons.

A toll-free information and referral hotline—1-888-VETS-NYS (838-7697)—enables veterans from across the state to receive information and assistance immediately from the nearest state veterans counselor for more thorough counseling and help when necessary.

NORTH DAKOTA DEPARTMENT OF VETERANS' AFFAIRS

COMMISSIONER: RAY HARKEMA
MAILING ADDRESS:
    POST OFFICE BOX 9003
    FARGO, ND 58106-9003
LOCATION:
    1411 32nd STREET SOUTH
    FARGO, ND
TELEPHONE: (701) 239-7165
FAX: (701) 239-7166
E-MAIL: rharkema@state.nd.us

1. SERVICES PERFORMED.

The duties and purposes of the agency are to coordinate agencies or instrumentalities of the State set up to render service and benefits to returning veterans; to have charge of and implement programs and benefits authorized by statute, to assist or represent veterans or their widows, administrators, executors, guardians, or heirs in processing claims; to assist, supervise, advise and direct of work of County Veterans Service Officers. The Department takes Power of Attorney in their own name and furnishes representation to veterans through accreditation of other veterans' organizations only for Veterans of World War I, USA, Inc., AMVETS, Military Order of the Purple Heart, Blinded Veterans Association, American Legion, and Regular Veterans Association.

2. STATE BENEFITS:

A. Licenses: Special license plates for disabled veterans with loss of use and former prisoners of war veterans (POW) are issued by the motor vehicle department upon the payment of five dollars.

B. Tax Exemptions: Property Tax Exemptions granted to paraplegic veterans up to net assessed valuation of $10,000 and lesser exemption to other service-connected veteran (or their unremarried spouse) if veteran has over 50% service-connected disability and meets income limitation.

C. State Veterans Home: The extended care nursing home facility at the North Dakota Veterans Home, Lisbon, North Dakota 58054, was completed October 1991. The total bed capacity is 150 (domiciliary bed capacity of 112 and special care bed capacity of 38).

D. Loan Program: Loans to eligible resident veteran for temporary financial emergencies may be granted to honorably discharged veterans in amounts up to $2,000.00. Ten percent interest is charged. One-half of the interest is refunded if the loan is repaid within the period the loan was granted. The loan can be granted for periods of 6 to 48 months. Unremarried Widow or Widower of eligible veterans and National Guard members who meet certain active duty requirements are also eligible for a loan.

E. Job Reinstatement: Officers and employees of the State or any of its political subdivisions have reinstatement rights relative to their former position if they apply for such position within ninety days after release from active service.

F. Emergency Hardship Assistance Program: The purpose of this assistance is to provide monies taken from earned interest of the Veterans Post War Trust Fund to give aid and comfort to veterans that are in an emergency need of dental work, eye glasses, hearing aid, or transportation for medical treatment and who cannot afford this type of anatomical care or transportation because of low income.

G. Veterans Transportation System: The Veterans Transportation System is designed to aid veterans in transportation to a Veterans Hospital. Currently', there are approximately 5 vans on scheduled routes transporting veterans to Fargo, North Dakota and Miles City, Montana. County Veterans Service Officers have the schedules and routes.

H. North Dakota Veterans Cemetery: This cemetery is located on a 35 acre tract of land in the southwest corner of Fort Abraham Lincoln State Park south of Mandan, ND.

3. VITAL STATISTICS:

State Department of Health
Vital Records
Capitol Building
Bismarck, North Dakota 58505

4. USDVA REGIONAL OFFICE:

2101 North Elm
Fargo, North Dakota 58102

5. VETERANS ORGANIZATIONS, STATE HEADQUARTERS:

The American Legion
P.O. Box 2666
Fargo, ND 58108
Veterans of Foreign Wars
P. O. Box 2186
Fargo, ND 58108

Disabled American Veterans
P. O. Box 2047

Williston, ND 58802-2047
AMVETS
3238 16 Avenue SW
Fargo, ND 58103

Vietnam Veterans of America
823 6th Avenue NE
Minot, ND 58701

6. GENERAL INFORMATION:

The Administrative Committee on Veterans Affairs was created and is responsible for organization, policy, and general administration of all veterans affairs in the State of North Dakota. The committee shall consist of three ex officio non-voting members and fifteen voting members. The Adjutant General, the Center Director of the USDVA, and the Executive Director of Job Service North Dakota, shall be the ex officio non-voting members who shall serve in an advisory capacity to the Committee. The voting members are appointed by the Governor from names submitted by the American Legion, Disabled American Veterans, Veterans of Foreign Wars, AMVETS and Vietnam Veterans of America. They appoint and set the salary of the Commissioner of Veterans Affairs and Commandant of the North Dakota Veterans Home. Within the Committee are two subcommittees. One member shall be chairman of the Committee. One seven-member subcommittee is responsible for supervision of the Department of Veterans Affairs, and a seven member subcommittee is responsible for the supervision of the North Dakota Veterans Home.

North Dakota has 53 County Veterans Service Officers who work under the supervision of the Department of Veterans Affairs. The Department of Veterans Affairs has 6 people on staff. They are: Commissioner Loan Officer, 3 Veterans Specialists, Administrative Secretary, and Administrative Clerk Service Officers are located in every county in the State. Training conferences are held each year for

County Service Officers and others interested in the veterans' benefit program.

The population of living veterans in North Dakota is approximately 64,000. Nationally recognized veterans organizations in the State are: The American Legion; AMVETS; Catholic War Veterans; Disabled American Veterans; Military Order of the Purple Heart; Veterans of Foreign Wars; Veterans of World War I, USA, Inc.; EX-POW's; and Vietnam Veterans of America.

DIVISION OF VETERANS AFFAIRS COMMONWEALTH OF THE NORTHERN MARIANA ISLANDS

DIRECTOR: JESUS C. MUNA
MAILING ADDRESS:
  P.O. BOX 3416 CK
  SAIPAN, MP 96950-3416
TELEPHONE: (670) 664-2650/2651
FAX: (670) 664-2660
E-MAIL: NOT AVAILABLE
UPDATED INFORMATION NOT AVAILABLE

OHIO OFFICE OF VETERANS AFFAIRS

DIRECTOR: RONALD EDWARDS
MAILING ADDRESS & LOCATION:
  77 S. High Street
  Columbus, Ohio 43215
TELEPHONE: (614) 644-0898
FAX: (614) 466-9354
E-MAIL: redwards@gov.state.oh.us

1. SERVICES PERFORMED.

A. Coordinate 88 county veterans service offices.
B. Accredit service officers.
C. Office of advocacy for veterans.

D. Provide copies of discharge for wartime veterans who received state bonuses (WWII, Korea, Vietnam).

E. Work with legislature to promote veterans' issues.

F. Work with other state offices to assure legal and employment benefits for veterans.

G. Research war records for information (Civil War, Spanish American War, WWI, some from 1812).

2. STATE BENEFITS:

A. Veterans' Bill of Rights in employment.

B. War Orphans' scholarships for those who qualify.

C. Special auto license plates for former Prisoner of War, Purple Heart, Pearl Harbor survivor, Ohio National Guard (some free of charge).

D. Hunting, fishing, and boating licenses free to special categories of veterans.

3. VITAL STATISTICS:

Obtain birth, death, or marriage certificates for other State Directors of Veterans' Affairs.

4. USDVA REGIONAL OFFICE:

Regional Office
Federal Building
1240 East Ninth Street
Cleveland, OH 44199

5 medical centers, 4 clinics
2 benefits centers
5 vet centers
1 national cemetery

5. STATE FACILITIES:

Ohio Veterans Home—Sandusky

6. VETERANS ORGANIZATIONS, STATE HEADQUARTERS:

American Legion
P. O. Box 8007
Delaware, OH 43015
740/362-7478

AMVET S
1395 E. Dublin Granville Road
Suite 222
Columbus, OH 43229
614/431-6990
Fax: 614/431-6991
1-800-OH-AMVET

Disabled American Veterans
35 E. Chestnut Street, 4th Floor
Columbus, OH 43215
614/221-3582
Fax: 614/221-4822

Veterans of Foreign Wars
35 E. Chestnut Street, 4th Floor
Columbus, OH 43215
614/224-1838
Fax: 614/224-3861

Vietnam Veterans of America
Buckeye Council
35 E. Chestnut Street, 4th Floor
Columbus, OH 43215
614/228-0188
Fax: 614/228-2711

**American Ex-Prisoners of War
Department of Ohio**
35 E. Chestnut Street, 4th Floor
Columbus, OH 43215
614/469-4725

Army and Navy Union USA, Inc.
2002 Tallmadge Road
Kent, OH 44240
330/673-9373
Fax: 330/673-8371

Catholic War Veterans
35 E. Chestnut Street, 4th Floor
Columbus, OH 43215-2541, Suite 402
Office: 614/221-7601
Fax: 614/221-0278

Jewish War Veterans
7847 Meadowlark Lane,
Reynoldsburg, OH 43068
614/866-2460

Herman Rosen, State Service Officer
1145 College Avenue, Apt. 512
Columbus, OH 43209
614/231-1708

Korean War Veterans Association, Inc.
582 Wiltshire
Columbus, OH 43204
614/279-8630

Marine Corps League
35 E. Chestnut Street, 4th Floor
Columbus, OH 43215
(419) 836-3315
(440) 255-0189

Military Order of the Purple Heart
35 E. Chestnut Street, 4th Floor
Columbus, OH 43215
614/228-8250
Fax: 614/228-7290

37th Division
35 E. Chestnut Street, 4th Floor
Columbus, OH 43215
614/228-3788
614/846-3536

World War I Veterans
35 E. Chestnut Street, 4th Floor
Columbus, OH 43215
614/221-1839

Rainbow Division Veterans Association
4143 Karl Road, Unit 111
Columbus, OH 43224

Air Force Association
1616 Sienna Lane, N
Columbus, OH 43229

Air Force Sergeants Association
703 North Road
Niles, OH 44446
330/544-3363

American Merchant Marine Veterans
Ohio Valley Chapter
P. O. Box 62563
Cincinnati, OH 45262-2563
Contact: Bert Hinds
49 Twin Lakes Drive
Fairfield, OH 45014
513/874-5606

Association of Naval Aviation, Inc.
5597 Birkdale Court
Columbus, OH 43232-3021
614/861-4974

Blinded Veterans Association
477 H Street, Northwest
Washington, DC 20001-2694
202/371-8880

Blue Star Mothers of America, Inc.
Department of Ohio
1809 N. Metcalf
Lima, OH 45801
419/228-1146

Buckeye State Disabled Veterans
14701 Detroit Road
Suite 369

Lakewood, OH 44107
216/228-1223

China-Burma-India Veterans Association
Columbus Basha
3125 Bembridge Road
Columbus, OH 43221-2203

China-Burma-India Veterans Association
825 Brookfield Road
Kettering, OH 45429

Cleveland Lutheran Veterans Club
2226 Lincoln Avenue
Parma, OH 44134

Coalition of Retired Military Veterans
P.O. Box 13064
Akron, OH 44334
330/668-2205

Coast Guard Combat Veterans Association
2295 Haviland Road
Columbus, OH 43220

Combat Infantrymen's Association, Inc.
Columbus, OH 43223
P. O. Box 23351

Desert Shield/Desert Storm Association
3349 Wilbur Drive
Lima, OH 45805-4504
419/227-0200

Destroyer Escort Sailors Association
Ohio Chapter
1108 Jackson Street
Greenville, OH 45331-1190

32nd Airborne Division Association
259 Washington Boulevard
Northfield, OH 44067

Fleet Reserve Association
1007 Stevenson Road
Erlanger, KY 41018
606/341-1934

Gold Star Wives of America, Inc.
5024 Oakridge Drive
Toledo, OH 43623-2305

Governor's Advisory Committee on Women Veterans
77 South High Street, 30th Floor
Columbus, OH 43215
614/644-0898

Italian American War Veterans of the US, Inc.
Capt. Charles M. Marino, Post #3
115 S. Meridian Road
Youngstown, OH 44509
216/788-2931

Legion of Valor
2266 Adner Court
Columbus, OH 43220

Lithuanian Veterans Organizations (RAMOVE)
17706 Crestland
Cleveland, OH 44119
216/481-4199

NAM-POWS, Inc.
Capt. Robert Doremus, USN, Ret.
2757 Elm Avenue
Bexley, OH 43209
614/237-9908

Navy League of the United States
P. O. Box 09531
Columbus, OH 43209-9531
614/451-6025

Navy Seabee Veterans of America
3818 Skyview Drive
Brunswick, OH 44212-1237
330/220-5040

**Non-Commissioned Officers Association
of the United States of America**
583 Kyle Lane
Fairborn, OH 45324-6403
513/878-6934

Ohio Chapter MIA/POW
P. O. Box 14853
Columbus, OH 43214
614/451-2405

Ohio Chapter of The Eighth Air Force Historical Society
568 Colima Drive
Toledo, OH 43609
419/382-8595
Fax: 419/382-4242

Ohio Council of Fraternal, Veterans and Service Organizations, Inc.
P. O. Box 883
Lancaster, OH 43130-0883

Ohio LST Association
14360 London Road
Orient, OH 43146
614/877-0865

Ohio Military Veterans Partnership
7057 Pineview Drive
Huber Heights, OH 45424
937/236-6724

Ohio National Guard Association
P. O. Box 8070
Columbus, OH 43201

The Ohio Veterans Coalition
P. O. Box 493
Barberton, OH 44203-0493

Ohio Veterans Home
3416 Columbus Avenue
Sandusky, OH 44870
419/625-2454

101st Airborne Division Association
P. O. Box 101
7698 State Route 41
Bentonville, OH 45105
330/867-5445

Paralyzed Veterans of America
Buckeye Chapter
25100 Euclid Avenue, Suite 117
Cleveland, OH 44117
216/731-1017 or 1-800/248-2548

Pearl Harbor Survivors Association
Lake Erie Chapter 127
690 Pendley Road
Willowick, OH 44094

Pearl Harbor Survivors Association
709 French Drive
Columbus, OH 43228
Phillip E. Mills
614/279-4778

Pearl Harbor Survivors Association
04370 Poppe Road
St. Marys, OH 45885
419/753-2749

Pearl Harbor Survivors Association
1332 Cedarcliff Drive
Beavercreek, OH 45434-6739
937/426-7920

Polish Legion of American Veterans
6005 Fleet Avenue
Cleveland, OH 44105
216/341-9556
330/650-1681
216/641-8791
216/888-8407

The Rakkasans
187th Airborne R.C.T.
Buckeye Chapter
3027 Queen City Avenue
Cincinnati, OH 45238-2432
513/481-4045

Rangers Battalions World War II
Ohio Valley Chapter 6
Box 15
Boscom, OH 44809
419/937-2383

The Retired Officers Association of the United States
4294 Janwood Drive
Copley, OH 44321-1304
330/836-7526

Seabee Veterans of America
Ohio Department, Island X-1
1 Wooster Place
Oxford, OH 45056
513/523-8842

17th Infantry Regiment
1280 N. Cole Street
Lima, OH 45801
419/228-4421

Sons of Union Veterans
6917 Avon Drive
Darbydale, OH 43123

Third Armored Division Association
306 Pinney Drive
Worthington, OH 43085
614/885-8796

Tuskegee Airmen
1870 Greenway Avenue
Columbus, OH 43219
614/252-1992

Ukrainian American Veterans
1881 Jacqueline Drive
Parma, OH 44134
216/884-1673

Underage Veterans of the USA
1765 Coonpath Road, NW
Lancaster, OH 43130
614/653-4721

USS Columbus Veterans Association
1163 Manor Drive
Columbus, OH 43232-1640
614/575-2110

Veterans of the Vietnam War, Inc.
1267 U. S. 42
Ashland, OH 44805
419/289-0154

WAVES National
2024 Leisure Road, NW
Minerva, OH 44657-8806
330/868-7634
330/628-3295

West Point Society of Central Ohio
7620 Olentangy River Road, Ste #201
Columbus, OH 43235
614/848-7620

Women's Army Corps Veterans Association
5441 Walshire Drive
Columbus, OH 43232
614/863-5237

Women Veterans (WIMSA)
44 Pocono Road
Worthington, OH 43235
614/846-7866

World Federation of Hungarian Veterans
9391 Hilo Farm Drive
Kirtland Hills, OH 44060
216/842-6431
(Some American veterans, some veterans of the Hungarian national
forces)

OKLAHOMA DEPARTMENT OF VETERANS' AFFAIRS

DIRECTOR: PHILLIP L. DRISKILL
MAILING ADDRESS & LOCATION:
  POST OFFICE BOX 53067
  OKLAHOMA CITY, OK 73152
TELEPHONE: (405) 521-3684
FAX: (405) 521-6533
E-MAIL: pdriskill@odva.state.ok.us

1. SERVICES PERFORMED

A. The Department has its own veterans service officers strategically located throughout the state.
B. Power of Attorney accepted in the name of all accredited veterans organizations.
C. Emergency/Disaster grants for needy veterans and their dependents.
D. Maintain an office at the U.S. Department of Veterans Affairs (USDVA) Regional Office and USDVA medical centers and out-patient clinics.

2. STATE BENEFITS:

A. Tax Exemption: Additional on personal property.
B. State Veterans Centers:
Ardmore: Nursing care for 175 and domiciliary care for 10.
Clinton: Nursing care for 145.
Norman: Nursing care for 301.
Sulphur: Nursing care for 132 and domiciliary care for 10.
Talihina: Nursing care for 184.
Claremore: Nursing care for 250.
C. Loan Program: None
D. State Bonus: None
E. Emergency Financial Assistance Program.
F. Reduced fee auto tags for certain veterans.

G. Free Hunting and Fishing License: For 60% disabled resident veterans

3. VITAL STATISTICS:

State Commissioner of Health
1000 N. W. 10th Street
Oklahoma City, OK 73104

4. USDVA REGIONAL OFFICE:

125 South Main
Muskogee, OK 74401

5. VETERANS ORGANIZATIONS, STATE HEADQUARTERS:

The American Legion
P.O. Box 53037
Capitol Station
Oklahoma City, OK 73152
Disabled American Veterans
P.O. Box 53503
Capitol Station
Oklahoma City, OK 73152

Veterans of Foreign Wars
P.O. Box 53275
Capitol Station
Oklahoma City, OK 73152

6. GENERAL INFORMATION:

The state veterans program administered by the Oklahoma Department of Veterans Affairs, under the direction of the War Veterans Commission as the controlling board, provides a complete service to the State's veterans. This service includes nursing and domiciliary care, financial assistance in emergencies, and field service counseling in the filing of claims for U.S. Department of Veterans Affairs and state benefits.

Oklahoma leads all other states in the number of Veterans Centers providing intermediate to skilled nursing care and domiciliary care for its wartime veterans. These centers are located in Ardmore, Claremore, Clinton, Norman, Sulphur, Talihina and a new center is currently under construction in Lawton.

The Oklahoma Department of Veterans Affairs also has a Claims and Benefits Division. This division has offices at the V.A. Regional Office in Muskogee; V.A. Medical Center, Oklahoma City; V.A. Medical Center, Muskogee; V.A. Outpatient Clinic, Tulsa; V.A. Outpatient Clinic, Lawton; and the ODVA Central Office, Oklahoma City. For further convenience of Oklahoma's veterans, the Claims and Benefits Division has Veterans Service Officers who travel on an itinerant basis offering assistance in all counties throughout the state. Schedules may be obtained by calling 1-888-655-2838.

OREGON DEPARTMENT OF VETERANS' AFFAIRS

DIRECTOR: JON A. MANGIS
MAILING ADDRESS & LOCATION:
   700 SUMMER STREET NE
   SALEM, OR 97310-1201
TELEPHONE: (503) 373-2388 or (800) 692-9666
FAX: (503) 373-2362
E-MAIL: mangisj@odva.state.or.us

1. SERVICES PERFORMED.

A. Provides claims assistance to veterans and their dependents and is accredited to represent:
   Veterans of World War I of the USA
   Jewish War Veterans
   AMVETS

Military Order of the Purple Heart
Non-Commissioned Officers Association
Blinded Veterans Association
American Red Cross
B. Financially assists the following organizations with their service and rehabilitation programs:
AMVETS
The American Legion
Disabled American Veterans
Veterans of Foreign Wars
C. Coordinates with counties, financially assists county veteran service officer programs and provides for their training.
D. Provides itinerant claims service at state hospitals, state correctional facilities, private nursing homes and residences.

2. STATE BENEFITS:

A. Loan Program: The Oregon Veterans' Loan Program assists eligible veterans buy homes at a below market rate. State Law limits the amount of money ODVA may loan to $143,000.

B. Conservatorship: Administers a conservatorship program for incompetent and minor beneficiaries of the USDVA.

C. Education: Provides educational aid benefits up to $50 a month to Oregon veterans of Korean Conflict, and recipients of Armed Forces Expeditionary Medal or Vietnam Service Medal.

D. Property' Tax Exemption: For veterans 40% or more disabled, to widows up to $11,000 of assessed value on property tax.

E. State Home: The 1993 Legislature passed authority to build a Veterans' Home to be managed by ODVA. Oregon's first Veterans Home is located in The Dalles, Oregon and opened in October 1997.

F. Employment: Five and ten point civil service preference to war veterans for state, county, city, and political subdivision employment. May only be used once and must be used within 15 years of discharge. Promotional preference for 30 percent disabled veterans. Reemployment rights to veterans who leave a position for the purpose of entering the Armed Forces.

G. Licenses: Free angling and hunting licenses to 30% disabled veterans. Free vehicle licenses for severely disabled veterans.

H. Special Veteran License Plates: The 1993 Legislature passed a bill that allows certain groups to apply to DMV for plates that represent their group.

3. VITAL STATISTICS:

Oregon Slate Health Division
Vital Records
800 N.E. Oregon Street
Portland. OR 97232

4. USDVA REGIONAL OFFICE:

1220 SW Third Avenue
Portland, OR 97204

5. VETERANS ORGANIZATIONS, STATE HEADQUARTERS:

American Ex-Prisoners of War
13055 Peachvale St.
Tigard, OR 97224
AMVETS
1220 SW Third Ave., Rm. 1586
Portland, OR 97204

Veterans of Foreign Wars
1220 SW Third Ave., Rm. 1589
Portland, OR 97204
Veterans of WWI, USA
700 Summer St. NE
Salem, Oregon 97310

The American Legion
1220 SW Third Ave., Rm. 1510
Portland, Oregon 97204
Military Order of the Purple Heart
1220 SW Third Ave., Rm. 1509
Portland, Oregon 97204

Disabled American Veterans
1440 Federal Building
1220 SW Third Avenue
Portland, OR 97204

6. GENERAL INFORMATION:

The Oregon Department of Veterans' Affairs, a separate agency of the State of Oregon, was created by the 1945 Legislature to administer certain benefits to war veterans. The agency is headed by a Director who receives advice from a nine-member Advisory Committee which meets at least four times a year and reports to the Governor annually concerning the administration of the Department.

The broad powers extended to the Director are contained in the following brief section of the Oregon law: "The Director, in the performance of his duties, shall organize and coordinate the administration of all present and future Federal and State laws pertaining to war veterans and their dependents in this State." Since the program started in 1945, veterans have obtained almost 300,000 loans in the amount of over $7,000,000.000.

Educational aid payments ranging up to $50.00 per month have gone to over 16,000 veterans since 1945.

The Claims and counseling sections completed 18,542 actions during the 1996-97 fiscal year. These actions included counseling interviews, rating board and claims reviews, filing claims and appeals, attending personal hearings and handling requests from other offices.

The Conservatorship program obtains maximum benefits for living and health care needs for veterans and their dependents who are legally determined to be unable to provide for themselves and when no one else will. The average number of conservatorship cases for fiscal year 1996-97 was 322 and the average amount of federal dollars brought into Oregon, through the program per month, was approximately $498,000.

Oregon has approximately 368,000 veterans according to 1996 estimates provided by the USDVA.

PENNSYLVANIA DEPARTMENT OF MILITARY AND VETERANS' AFFAIRS

DIRECTOR: CECIL B. HENGEVELD
MAILING ADDRESS & LOCATION:
  FORT INDIANTOWN GAP
  BUILDING P-O-47
  ANNVILLE, PA 17003-5002
TELEPHONE: (717) 861-8901
FAX: (717) 861-8589
E-MAIL: chengeveld@state.pa.us

The Bureau for Veterans' Affairs, Department of Military Affairs coordinates with all departments and agencies of the Commonwealth in regard to programs affecting Pennsylvania's eligible veterans, their widows and orphans that are mandated by legislative act. To accomplish its myriad of missions, the Bureau has two divisions and operates three field offices, co-located at the U.S. Department of Veterans Affairs (USDVA) offices in Philadelphia, Pittsburgh, and Wilkes-Barre.

Veterans' Assistance Division:

The Veterans' Assistance Division has the responsibility for administering all requests for assistance pertaining to federal and state veterans' benefits except those requests concerning state-operated Veterans' homes.

The three field offices function under the staff supervision of the Veterans' Assistance Division. Their function is to assist eligible veterans and their family members and survivors to obtain any benefit and/or advantage due them under the laws of the United States, the Commonwealth of Pennsylvania, or any other state or governmental agency. The field offices act as liaison between the Bureau for Veterans' Affairs and the USDVA concerning federal benefits available to veterans and their family members and survivors. They provide federal and state veterans' benefits including Outreach, Counseling, Financial Counseling and referrals to services for financial assistance on an emergency and temporary basis.

Veterans' Homes Division:

Veterans' Homes Division is responsible for the operation of the five (soon-to-be six) state-operated veterans' homes. Serves as the point of contact for the Veterans' Homes Advisory Councils. The Division operates a central control office for receipt of applications to the homes. Establishes and maintains application files and waiting lists for each level of care provided by the Homes. Acts as the point of contact for county directors of veterans affairs, veterans organizations, and the legislature concerning all aspects of admissions and operation of the Homes.

2. STATE BENEFITS:

A. Veterans Emergency Assistance: Provides aid in an emergency and temporary basis (not to exceed three months) to veterans, their widows, infant children or dependents that reside in Pennsylvania for the necessities of life (food, dairy, shelter, fuel, and clothing).

B. Educational Gratuity: Payments of educational gratuities for children of honorably discharged veterans who have been certified by the USDVA has having wartime service-connected disabilities rated as totally and permanently disabled or children of veterans who die or have died of war service-connected disabilities or died in service during a period of war or armed conflict.

C. Real Estate Tax Exemption: Any honorably discharged veteran who is a resident of the Commonwealth shall be exempt from the payment of all real estate taxes levied upon any building, including the land upon which it stands, occupied by him as his principal dwelling, provided that as a result of war-time military service the veteran has a 100% service-connected disability rating by the USDVA; that such dwelling is owned by him solely or jointly with his spouse (an estate by the entirety), and the NEED for the exemption from the payment of real estate taxes has been determined by the State Veterans' Commission. Upon decease of veteran, tax exemption passes on to unremarried surviving spouse.

D. State Veterans' Homes: Veteran must have served in the Armed Forces of the United States or Pennsylvania Military Forces, released from service under honorable conditions. Veteran must be a bona fide resident of this Commonwealth upon making application. Applications are processed on a 'first come, first serve" basis.

3. OTHER STATE BENEFITS:

A. Educational grants for veterans and POW/MIA dependents.
B. Scotland School for Veterans' children.
C. Civil Service preference.
D. Free certified copies of birth and death records.
E. Special vehicle registration plates for severely disabled/disabled veterans.
F. Special registration plates for Purple Heart recipients and Ex-Prisoners of War.
G. Special parking placards for disabled veterans.
H. Free fishing license for certain disabled veterans.
I. Free hunting licenses for certain disabled veterans.
J. Antlerless deer license for qualified disabled veterans.

K. State retirement credit for Honorable Military Service.
L. Veterans' employment assistance.
M. Blind Veterans Pension.
N. Paralyzed Veterans Pension.

4. GOVERNOR'S VETERANS OUTREACH & ASSISTANCE CENTERS:

600 Rugh Street
Greensburg, PA 15601
Tel: (724) 837-7988 or 1-800-432-9735
Center Director: William "Bill" Kish
Pittston Career Link
300 Kennedy Blvd
Pittston, PA 18640
Tel: (717) 654-9589 or 1-800-432-9735
Center Director: Ronald Faust

25 Moser Road
Pottstown, PA 19464
Tel: (610) 326-5233 or 1-800-247-2323
Center Director: Ronald F. Pennypacker
15 East 12th Street
Erie, PA 16501
Tel: (814) 453-5719 or 1-800-352-0915
Center Director: Elmer C Smith, Jr.

3525 N. Sixth Street
Harrisburg, PA 17110-1469
Tel: (717) 234-1681 or 1-800-932-0930
Center Director: William E. Woodman

RHODE ISLAND DIVISION OF VETERANS AFFAIRS

ACTING ASSOCIATE DIRECTOR: DANIEL EVANGELIATA

MAILING ADDRESS & LOCATION:
  480 METACOM AVENUE
  BRISTOL, RI 02809
TELEPHONE: (401) 462-0324
FAX: (401) 254-2320
E-MAIL: devangelista@gw.dhs.state.ri.us

1. SERVICES PERFORMED.

A. Information and advisory services to veterans and their dependents regarding benefits, or compensation to which they may be entitled under federal or state laws.

B. Counseling and referral services to veterans and their dependents in matters involving compensation, pension, hospitalization, insurance, out-patient treatment, loans, education and training

C. Applications for the Rhode Island Veterans' Home are processed by and admissions are arranged through this unit.

D. Applications for the Rhode Island Veterans' Cemetery are processed by and arranged through this unit. Telephone: (401) 884-7482.

2. STATE BENEFITS:

A. Tax Exemption: Veterans of wartime service and Gold Star parents are eligible for a $1,000 to $5,000 property tax exemption. Additional exemptions are also available for the blind veterans and disabled veterans requiring "specially adapted housing".

B. State Veterans' Home and Nursing Care Facilities: 339-bed facility with 260 beds for long-term convalescent and skilled nursing care for chronically ill veterans and 79 beds for domiciliary self-care veterans, located at Bristol, Rhode Island.

C. Burial: Eligible veterans at the Rhode Island Veterans' Cemetery in Exeter, Rhode Island.

D. Veterans Grave Registrations: are maintained upon notification as to his or her death noting place of interment. Historical cemeteries and all burial sites throughout the state are located and marked. This unit processes applications for federal headstones and Rhode Island state war markers.

E. Civil Service Preference: 5 points for veterans, 10 points for disabled veterans.

F. Veterans' Bonus: World War II, Korean and Vietnam. Dates expired. Requires eligible veterans to secure legislative approval for payment.

G. Free License Plates: for former Prisoners of War.

3. VETERANS ORGANIZATIONS, STATE HEADQUARTERS:

The American Legion[3]
Veterans Memorial Building
83 Park Street
Providence, RI 02903
Veterans of Foreign Wars[3]
Veterans Memorial Building
83 Park Street
Providence, RI 02903
Disabled American Veterans[3]
Jewish War Veterans[3]
AMVETS[3]

4. GENERAL INFORMATION:

Rhode Island Veterans Affairs is a division within the Department of Human Services.

Rhode Island Veterans' Cemetery interments are arranged only after a death occurs when:

1. The veteran was honorably discharged.

---

3. Service organizations have their own service representative located in the USDVA Regional Office, Providence, Rhode Island.

2. Entered service while a legal resident of Rhode Island or lived in Rhode Island as a legal resident for two (2) continuous years prior to time of death.

3. Last period of service terminated honorably and had a period of active service during wartime.

The mission of Veterans Affairs is to facilitate the coordination of all veterans programs of the state, primarily through professional staff with services to veterans of all wars, their dependents, members of the Armed Forces, other state agencies, veteran organizations, and other interested parties.

Veterans are assisted directly with processing applications to the local VARO for compensation and pension benefits. The Rhode Island state veteran population is approximately 111,000.

SOUTH CAROLINA OFFICE OF VETERANS AFFAIRS

DIRECTOR: JIMMIE RUFF
MAILING ADDRESS & LOCATION:
  BROWN STATE OFFICE BUILDING
  1205 PENDLETON STREET, STE. 226
  COLUMBIA, SC 29201
TELEPHONE: (803) 734-0200
FAX: (803) 734-0197
E-MAIL: JRuff@govoepp.state.sc.us

1. SERVICES PERFORMED

A. Represents veterans and dependents by virtue of accreditation made to one of the following veterans' organizations:
  AMVETS
  Non Commissioned Officers Assoc.
  The American Legion
  South Carolina Dept. of Veterans Affairs
  Veterans of Foreign Wars

Military Order of the Purple Heart
American Red Cross
Vietnam Veterans of America
Fleet Reserve Association
The Retired Enlisted Association
Blinded Veterans Association

B. Service Organizations not associated with the Office of Veterans Affairs in the USDVA Regional Office in South Carolina are:

Disabled American Veterans
Paralyzed Veterans of America

2. STATE BENEFITS:

A. Tax Exemption: The first $3000 of military retirement pay for longevity. Property tax exemption for permanently and totally disabled veterans.

B. State Veterans Home:

1. C.M. Tucker Center, 90 beds, Columbia, SC.

2. Richard Michael Campbell State Nursing Home, 220 beds, Anderson, SC.

C. Loan Program: None

D. State Bonus: None

E. Education: Free tuition at any state-supported institution of higher learning, including colleges, universities, and technical schools for children of war veterans who died of a service-connected disability, or if the veteran is permanently and totally disabled from any condition. This law also includes free tuition to children of ex-prisoners of war and missing in action, and recipients of the Congressional Medal of Honor.

3. VITAL STATISTICS:

Bureau of Vital Statistics
Department of Health & Environmental Control
2600 Bull Street Columbia, SC 29201

4. USDVA REGIONAL OFFICE:

1801 Assembly Street
Columbia, SC 29201

5. VETERANS ORGANIZATIONS, STATE HEADQUARTERS:

The American Legion
PO Box 11355
Columbia, SC 29201
Disabled American Veterans
VARO, 1801 Assembly Street
Columbia, SC 29201

AMVETS
VARO, 1801 Assembly Street
Columbia, SC 29201
Veterans of Foreign Wars
VARO, 1801 Assembly Street
Columbia, SC 29201

6. GENERAL INFORMATION:

Act No. 78, Acts of the General Assembly of South Carolina, approved March 15, 1927, authorized the establishment of this office "for the purpose of assisting ex-servicemen in securing the benefits to which they are entitled under the provisions of Federal legislation and under the terms of insurance policies issued by the Federal Government for their benefit."

The Act, among other things, authorized and directed the Governor to appoint a Director of Veterans' Affairs, who shall be charged with the duty of assisting all ex-servicemen, regardless of the wars in which their service may have been rendered, in filing, presenting and prosecuting to final determination all claims which they have for monetary compensation, hospitalization, training and insurance benefits under the terms of Federal Legislation relative thereto.

The General Assembly, during the 1945 session, passed an Amendatory Act, approved by the Governor on March 22, 1945, providing for the establishment of a county veterans affairs officer in each county in the state and the methods of appointment of a county veterans affairs officer. This Act increased the total appropriation to the Department of Veterans Affairs to partially pay for the operation of these local offices. The 46 counties supplement the amount received from the state.

The Act further ensured a stabilization and coordination of the service work for, and in behalf of, the war veterans and ex-servicemen and women, in order that they may be guaranteed the maximum benefits granted by laws enacted by Congress. The Director of Veterans' Affairs is authorized and directed to establish uniform methods and procedure for the performance of service work among the several county officers, to maintain contact and close cooperation with them, to provide assistance, advice and instructions, with respect to changes in law and regulations and administer procedures in relation to the application of such laws; and he is authorized to require from time to time, reports from such county service officers, reflecting the character and progress of their official duties.

Among the duties of our whole organization are those relating to advisement and assistance in reference to the preparation of the necessary applications and the development of supporting evidence required by the Government. The programs with which we are concerned deal with claims for service-connected disability compensation; pension benefits on account of permanent and total disability; death benefits payable in certain instances to the widows and minor children of deceased veterans; many phases of National Service Life Insurance and Indemnity Insurance such as original applications, applications for reinstatement, conversion to permanent plans, death claims, etc.; education and training; advisement in connection with the Home Loan

Guaranty Program; hospitalization of veterans; claims for reimbursement of burial expenses, grave markers, discharge changes, etc. Service is rendered in assisting dependents of active servicemen in connection with family allotment, allowances, etc. Our personnel, by request of the U.S. Department of Labor, are designated as advisors in connection with the administration of the Veterans Reemployment Rights Program.

The Director of Veterans Affairs and staff members are not only advisors (legal and otherwise) to the various county officers on questions involving the interpretation of all laws and regulations, but also represent claimants before USDVA rating agencies when formal hearings are held in connection with contested claims.

SOUTH DAKOTA DIVISION OF VETERANS' AFFAIRS

DIRECTOR: DENNIS G. FOELL
MAILING ADDRESS & LOCATION:
    SOLDIERS & SAILORS
    WAR MEMORIAL BUILDING
    500 EAST CAPITOL AVENUE
    PIERRE, SOUTH DAKOTA 57501-5070
TELEPHONE: (605) 773-3269
FAX: (605) 773-5380
E-MAIL: dennisf@mva.state.sd.us

1. SERVICES PERFORMED

A. Furnishes representation to veterans, widows, and other dependents of deceased veterans by virtue of Power of Attorney made to one of the following:
    Veterans of World War I, USA, Inc.
    Non-Commissioned Officers Assoc.
    The American Legion
    Military Order of the Purple Heart
    Veterans of Foreign Wars

American Ex-Prisoners of War, Inc.
South Dakota Division of Veterans Affairs
AMVETS
The Retired Enlisted Association
B. Service organizations not associated with the Division in the USDVA Regional Office in South Dakota:
Disabled American Veterans
Paralyzed Veterans of America

2. STATE BENEFITS:

A. Tax Exemption: For paraplegics.
B. State Veterans Home: Located at Hot Springs.
C. Loan Program: Not to exceed $500.
D. State Bonus: Paid to World War I, World War II, Korean, Vietnam, and Persian Gulf War Veterans—filing dates have expired
E. Education: War orphans education and assistance to POW/MIA.
F. Burial Allowance: Up to $100 and headstone setting-$40.
G. Free Tuition: To state universities in South Dakota for undergraduate or extension courses to veterans who served in the time period 25 June 1950, through 7 May 1975.
H. Veterans' Preference for state employment.

3. VITAL STATISTICS:

Director of Public Health Statistics
Department of Health
Joe Foss Building
c/o 500 East Capitol Avenue
Pierre, South Dakota 57501-5070

4. USDVA REGIONAL OFFICE:

2501 West 22nd Street
P. O. Box 5046
Sioux Falls, South Dakota 57117-5046

5. GENERAL INFORMATION

The Division of Veterans Affairs became a part of the Department of Military and Veterans Affairs by reorganization of state government and works in conjunction with a six-member veterans commission

County and tribal veterans service officers are county and tribal employees, employed and paid by the count" or tribe. Though not under our jurisdiction, the Division of Veterans Affairs by statute confirms and approves their appointments. The Division is, however, responsible for training all county and tribal veterans service officers.

The War Veterans Emergency Loan Program is funded by a revolving fund, from which loans not to exceed $500 are made to veterans for emergency purposes; repayment without interest is required within two years of the loan approval.

The State Veterans' Home has a total capacity of 180, which includes two domiciliaries and a nursing home facility.

The State provides retirement credit to members of the Armed Forces while on active duty if a public employee immediately preceding entrance into service and returning within one year of discharge.

A supplement salary program is also in effect for county and tribal service officers. The state provides 25% of the service officer's salary providing the county or tribe meets certain requirements, mainly that of salary schedule and training criteria.

TENNESSEE DEPARTMENT OF VETERANS AFFAIRS

COMMISSIONER: JOHN A. KEYS
MAILING ADDRESS:
   215 EIGHTH AVENUE NORTH
   NASHVILLE, TN 37243-1010
LOCATION:
   The American Legion Building
TELEPHONE: (615) 741-2930
FAX: (615) 741-4785
E-MAIL: donald.samuels@state.tn.us

1. SERVICES PERFORMED.

A. The Department (TDVA) represents Veterans and their families through Power of Attorney granted by individual Veterans and the below Organizations:

American Red Cross
Military Order of the Purple Heart*
American Ex-Prisoners of War
Noncommissioned Officers Assoc.
Blinded Veterans Association
The Retired Enlisted Association
AMVETS*
The American Legion
Fleet Reserve Association
Veterans of Foreign Wars of the U.S.
Marine Corps League
Veterans of World War I of the USA, Inc
Vietnam Veterans of America

B. Through our service delivery network of 11 departmental field offices, approximately 90 county-employed service officers and 21 Veterans service organizations, TDVA assists Tennessee Veterans in obtaining the care, support, earned benefits and recognition they earned in service to our Nation.

C. The Claims Office is under the direction of Donald L. Samuels, Assistant Commissioner, Room A-310, Federal Building Annex, 110 Ninth Avenue South, Nashville, TN 37243-5000, telephone: 615/741-1863.

D. The Field Services Division is under the direction of John Furgess, Assistant Commissioner, 215 Eighth Avenue North, Nashville, TN 37243-1010, telephone: 615/741-4988.

E. Service organizations not associated with this Department located in the USDVA Regional Office, Nashville, are:

Disabled American Veterans
Federal Building Annex

Room A-308
110 Ninth Avenue South
Nashville, TN 37203
Telephone: 615/736-5735

AMVETS
Federal Building Annex
Room A-307
110 Ninth Avenue South
Nashville, TN 37203
Telephone: 615/736-5900

F. State Veterans Cemeteries are located in Knoxville, Nashville and Memphis.

G. The Tennessee State Veterans Homes Board operates State Veterans Homes in Murfreesboro (615/895-8850) and Humboldt (901/784-8405).

2. STATE BENEFITS:

A. State Veterans Cemeteries

B. State Veterans Homes

C. Free license plates for 100% service connected disabled Veterans, Ex-Prisoners of War, and recipients of the MOH, DSC, NC or AFC

D. Property tax relief for combat related 100% totally disabled Veterans and/or their surviving spouses

E. Free hunting and fishing licenses for Veterans with 30% or more war service connected disabilities

F. Parking privileges for free license plate holders

G. Veterans preference in State employment

H. Credit for military service in State employment

I. Scholarships for eligible dependent children

J. Motor vehicle privilege tax exemption for 100% disabled Veterans

K. Special/Memorial license plates for certain Veterans

L. Reemployment rights of public employees

M. Discounts in State Parks

N. Registration of discharges by county registrar at no fee

3. VITAL STATISTICS:

Vital Records
421 Fifth Avenue, North
2nd Floor, Central Services Building
Nashville, TN 37247-0450

4. USDVA REGIONAL OFFICE:

Federal Building Annex
110 Ninth Avenue South
Nashville, TN 37203

5. VETERANS ORGANIZATIONS, STATE HEADQUARTERS:

The American Legion
215 Eighth Avenue North
Nashville, TN 37203
Telephone: 615/254-0568
Disabled American Veterans
G-22 War Memorial Building
Nashville, TN 37243-0163
Telephone: 615/242-7328

Veterans of Foreign Wars
G-21 War Memorial Building
Nashville, TN 32719
Telephone: 615/242-5851
AMVETS
844 S. Germantown Road, Suite E
Chattanooga, TN 37412
Telephone: 423/624-9835

TEXAS VETERANS' COMMISSION

EXECUTIVE DIRECTOR: JAMES NIER
MAILING ADDRESS:
  POST OFFICE BOX 12277
  AUSTIN, TX 78711
LOCATION:
  10TH & COLORADO
  E.O. THOMPSON BLDG., SIXTH FLOOR
TELEPHONE: (512) 463-5538
FAX: (512) 475-2395
E-MAIL: info@tvc.state.tx.us

1. SERVICES PERFORMED.

A. Represents veterans and dependents: This agency furnishes representation to veterans, widows and dependents by Power of Attorney made to the Texas Veterans Commission or one of the following veterans organizations:
  The American Legion
  Veterans of Foreign Wars
  Veterans of World War I, USA
  Fleet Reserve Association
  AMVETS
  Military Order of the Purple Heart
  Vietnam Veterans of America
  Blinded Veterans Association
  American Ex-POWs of America, Inc.
  Non-Commissioned Officers Association
  Retired Enlisted Association
  American Red Cross
B. County Service Officers are trained and certified by the Commission, but are not Commission employees.

2. STATE BENEFITS:

A. Tax Exemption: Property tax exemption for service-connected disabled veterans.

B. State Veterans Home: Four Texas State Veterans Homes have been established for the care and treatment of eligible Texas veterans and is offered through the Texas Veterans Land Office. For further information, call 1-800-252-VETS (Texas only); 512/463-9592

C. Loan Program:

Texas Veterans Land Program: (loans to Texas veterans residents to purchase a minimum 5 acre tract of land.)

Texas Veterans Housing Assistance Programs: (Loans to veteran residents to purchase a home.)

Texas Veterans Home Improvement Loan Program: (Loans to veteran residents to make a variety of home improvements.) These programs are offered through the Texas General Land Office.

D. State Bonus: None

E. License Plates: Disabled veterans, former POW's Medal of Honor, Purple Heart, and Pearl Harbor Survivors.

F. Education: Tuition exemption for eligible Texas veterans at state-supported schools (Hazlewood Act).

3. VITAL STATISTICS:

Bureau of Vital Statistics
Department of Health
1100 West 49th Street
Austin. TX 78756

4. USDVA REGIONAL OFFICE:

Houston, Texas
6900 Almeda Road
Houston, TX 77030-4200
Waco, Texas
One Veterans Plaza

701 Clay
Waco, TX 76799

5. VETERANS ORGANIZATIONS, STATE HEADQUARTERS:

The American Legion
P. O. Box 789
Austin, TX 78767
Disabled American Veterans
P.O. Box 20906
Waco, Texas 76702-0906

Veterans of Foreign Wars
P. O. Box 14468
Austin, TX 78761
AMVETS
2641 Windswept Lane
Mesquite, Texas 75181

Vietnam Veterans of America
P.O. Box 7621
The Woodlands, Texas 77387
Military Order of the Purple Heart
217 LaJolla Drive
San Antonio, Texas 78233-2515
American Ex-POW's of America, Inc.
11418 Mile Drive
Houston, Texas 77065-1802
Desert Shield/Desert Storm Assn.
P.O. Box 1712
Odessa, Texas 79760

6. GENERAL INFORMATION:

The Texas Veterans Commission (TVC), which is composed of six members who are appointed by the Governor, was established in 1927. The purpose of the Texas Veterans Commission is to assist and counsel Texas veterans, their dependents or survivors in all matters pertaining to veterans' entitlements. It is the designated agency of the State of Texas to represent the state and its veterans before the United States Department of Veterans Affairs (USDVA) or any other agency handling matters relating to the interests of rights of the veteran.

The Commission maintains a comprehensive statewide veterans assistance program and its chief aim is to assist veterans and their families in obtaining benefits to which they are entitled. The Commission employs a staff that assists veterans in filing claims and following them through to a successful adjudication. These services are provided through two regional offices located at Houston and Waco, and twenty-eight VA Medical Centers and field offices located throughout Texas. There are also 243 veterans county service officers in the State of Texas.

Assistance in filing for USDVA benefits is given to dependents and survivors of veterans who are in state schools, institutions, orphanages and homes. Awarding of benefits to these eligible dependents and helpless children makes it possible for them to have a more satisfactory life, correlated with a lesser financial burden on the community and state.

The Commission is furnished a record of death of all veterans who die in the State of Texas. The Commission also receives the DD214 of each veteran who lists Texas as his home of record. These documents are mailed to the local veterans county service officer who contacts the veteran or survivor concerning entitlement to benefits based on the veteran's military service.

The Commission produces a number of publications. The TVC Journal keeps interested parties and service officers informed of veterans' programs, USDVA decisions, new rules and regulations, legislation, laws and procedures relating to veterans benefits as well as other items of informative value to veterans. Pamphlets for service officers dealing with the more technical aspects of laws, procedures and related benefits are published. Compilations of state benefits and public information pamphlets are also published.

A statewide service officers training conference is sponsored annually by the TVC. The conference brings the nation's experts together with the service officers of Texas for discussion and instruction relating to laws regulations and procedures applied in connection with veterans' claims. Also, a series of area conferences are held annually to update service officers on latest procedures and regulations relating to veterans' benefits.

The Military Contact Program enables the Commission to assist members of the armed services. TVC counselors offer guidance and information to servicemen who are hospitalized and are undergoing examination for medical board proceedings preparatory to processing for medical discharge. The goals of this program are accomplished by Commission representation at all military installations in Texas.

The State of Texas provides low interest loans to veterans for the purchase of land, the purchase of a home, and for home improvements. Currently, the maximum loan for land is $40,000; a home is $150,000; and for home improvement $25,000. Any amount in excess of the maximum must be provided by the veteran or through a commercial lending institution. These programs are offered through the Texas General Land Office. For further information, call 1-800-252-VETS (Texas only); 512/463-9592

All of these activities are predicated on the underlying philosophy of the Commission that every Texas veteran deserves and should receive every benefit to which he/she is entitled.

GOVERNMENT OF THE VIRGIN ISLANDS OF THE UNITED STATES
DIVISION OF VETERANS' AFFAIRS

DIRECTOR: GREGORY FRANCIS

ASST. DIRECTOR: JOHN D. MATARANGAS, Sr.
MAILING ADDRESS:
   OFFICE OF VETERANS AFFAIRS
   1013 ESTATE RICHMOND
   CHRISTIANSTED, ST CROIX VI 00820-4349
TELEPHONE: (340) 773-6663
FAX: (340) 692-9563
E-MAIL: NONE AVAILABLE

1. LOCAL BENEFITS:

A. Homestead Tax Exemption of $20,000 of the valuation of real property.
B. G. I. Loans up to $95,000 at a low interest rate (6%).
C. Tuition free education at public schools and the University of the Virgin Islands for veterans who entered the armed forces while residing in the Virgin Islands.
D. Free out-patient medical care for service connected veterans at the Veterans Administration Community Base Clinic.
E. Decedent's estates and fiduciary relations (Veterans Guardianship).
F. Veterans 10-point preference (added to score) on local civil service careers examinations.
G. Administrative leave for veterans for burial attendance.
H. Administrative leave for Reserve Military Service.
I. Free burial plot in local cemeteries to veterans who are residents and entered the armed forces while residing in the Virgin Islands.
J. Up to $2,000 reimbursement to next of kin for burial expenses of local veterans who entered the armed forces while residing in the Virgin Islands.

2. USDVA REGIONAL OFFICE:

   U.S. Dept of Veterans Affairs
   Community Based Clinic/Vet Center
   District of St. Croix

RR 2, Box 12 Kingshill
St. Croix, VI 00850
Medical Director: Dr. Wilma Colon
340-778-5553
340-778-9497

U.S. Dept of Veterans Affairs
Community Based Clinic/Vet Center
District of St. Thomas/St. John
9800 Buccaneer Mall, Suite 8
Charlotte Amalie, St Thomas, VI 00802
Medical Director: Dr. Carlton Alexis
340-774-6674
340-774-2069

NO OTHER INFORMATION AVAILABLE

UTAH DIVISION OF VETERANS AFFAIRS

DIRECTOR: TERRY SCHOW
MAILING ADDRESS & LOCATION:
    UTAH DIVISION OF VETERANS AFFAIRS
    550 Foothill Blvd Room 206
    Salt Lake City, Utah 84108
TELEPHONE:
(801) 326 2372
1 (800) 894 9497
FAX: (801) 326 2369
E-MAIL: tschow@utah.gov

STATE BENEFITS

A. PROPERTY TAX ABATEMENT

A Utah permanent place-of-residence property tax exemption equivalent to the military service-connected disability rating percentage is provided for disabled veterans or for their unremarried widows or minor orphans. Veteran's disability rating must be at **least** 10%, max. property tax exemption at 100% military service-connected disability rating: $82,500. Example: 10% disability X $82,5000=$8,250 tax abatement. (Utah Code Vol 3, Section 59)

Note: To apply for Utah Disabled Veterans Property Tax Exemption, request VA Form 20-5455 from U.S. Dept. of Veterans Affairs (VA) at 800-827-1000, then file VA Form 20-5455, along with a copy of the veteran's U.S.military active duty release/discharge certificate or other satisfactory evidence of eligible military service, and the tax exemption application, **on or before September 1st**, to the applicable county treasurer, tax assessor or clerk/recorder located in the county courthouse or county government building of each county seat

B. DRIVERS LICENSE PRIVILEGES

Driver licenses possessed by persons on U.S. military active duty shall be valid 90 days after active duty discharge, unless driver licenses are suspended or revoked for cause by a police department or other judicial entity. (Utah Code Vol 2, Section 41)

C. VETERANS LICENSE PLATES

Utah veterans license plates may be purchased for an initial $25.00 voluntary contribution for the Utah State Division of Veterans Affairs, plus a $10.00 plate transfer fee, in addition to normal registration and property tax fees, at Utah Tax Commission/Motor Vehicle. Proceeds from the sale of these plates help to fund veteran programs within the state. Utah veteran's license plates display colored decal emblems of the U.S. military branch in which served (Air Force, Army, Coast Guard, Navy and Marines) and are further inscribed "UTAH HONORS VETERANS". Utah special group license plates for Purple Heart recipients, Pearl Harbor Survivors or former POW's are exempt of application and renewal fees: however, regular registration and property tax fees still must be paid. Proper evidence to present for special group plates includes Military Order of the Purple Heart or Pearl Harbor Survivors Association membership cards, or DD-214 (& equivalent WD AGO 5355) military discharge certificates.

NOTE: You need not wait until renewal time to purchase the license plates. (Utah Code Vol 2 Section 41: Utah State Tax Commission/ Motor Vehicle regulations)

D. DISABLED LICENSE PLATES/WINDSHIELD PLACARDS

Disabled license plates having the blue & white international symbol of accessibility decal may be obtained by submitting a TC 842 application form, accompanied by licensed physician certification stating: (1) the disability limits or impairs ability to walk as defined in the 1991 Federal Uniform System for Handicapped Parking, and (2) the time period the physician determines the disability will continue. Disabled veterans applying for Utah disability license plates especially should note that veteran disability letters from the VA Regional Office are not acceptable evidence to Tax Commission/Motor Vehicle offices. However, licensed physician certifications by VA doctors are acceptable evidence, provided the following is stated in the letter: (1) the disability limits or impairs ability to walk as defined in the 1991 Federal Uniform System for Handicapped Parking, and (2) the time period the physician determines the disability will continue. Normal fees for plate transfer, registration, and property taxes still must be paid upon initial application and renewal of disability license plates. Upon request, one additional disability windshield placard may be issued to disabled persons applying for or already possessing disability special group license plates. For more information, telephone toll-free 800-DMV-UTAH. (Utah Code vol 2 Section 41.)

E. DISABLED PARKING PRIVILEGES: Disabled persons (including disabled veterans) may park an appropriately marked vehicle for reasonable periods without charge in metered parking zones or in restricted parking areas (spaces clearly identified by the international symbol of accessibility as reserved for disabled persons.) Only vehicles appropriately marked with disability special group license plates or disability windshield placards hung from the front windshield rearview mirror attachment may legally park in accessible (disabled) parking spaces. (Utah Code Vol 2, section 41)

F. VETERANS JOB REPRESENTATIVES: Local Veterans Employment Representatives (LVER) and Disabled Veterans Outreach Person (DVOP) are located statewide in the larger employment offices of the Utah Dept. of Workforce Services. They provide intensive employment related services for targeted veterans: referral to job opportunities, resume writing, referral letters, veteran's preference, employment counseling, etc. (Utah Code Vol 2 Section 35

G. VETERANS JOB PREFERENCE: Eligible veterans or unremarried spouses are granted either 5 or 10 points, as applicable, for employment preference, added to the results of any written &/or oral exam or other related qualifying technique, by any Utah government entity (state, county, municipality, special district or other political subdivision or administration.) The U.S. Dept. of Labor will protect the veteran's rights to the Veterans Job Preference. (Utah Code Vol 3, Section 71)

H. VETERANS HIRING PRIORITY: Any officers, agents or representatives of the state, or any contractor performing work for Utah state government, who willfully fails to hire a military veteran shall be guilty of a misdemeanor. (Utah Code Vol 3, Section 71)

I.MILITARY LEAVE: Utah state, county or municipal government employees, who are members of the organized reserve/national guard, are allowed full pay for 15 days of military leave per year for annual military encampment. Military leave is in addition to and distinguished from annual accrued vacation leave with pay. (Utah Code Vol 3 Section 67 & USERRA federal Uniformed Services Employment & Reemployment Rights Act.)

J. VETERANS REEMPLOYMENT RIGHTS: Veterans and members of the National Guard and Reserves may be eligible for reemployment with their civilian employers it they meet certain requirements under the Uniformed Services Employment & Reemployment Rights Act (USERRA). USERRA also provides protection against discrimination in employment because of service in the uniformed services (Title 38, chap 43 USC). Inquiries regarding reemployment rights should be directed to the U.S.D.L., Veterans Employment & Training Services (801-524-5703) (Utah Code Vol 3, Section 67 & USERRA federal Uniformed Services Employment & Reemployment Rights Act, as amended.)

K. UTAH STATE DIVISION OF VETERANS AFFAIRS: The Utah State Division of Veterans Affairs is currently located in the Wallace F. Bennett Federal Building, 125 S. State St. Rm 5223, Salt Lake City, Utah 84138-1102. By mid-year 2002, it is anticipated that the Division of Veterans Affairs office will be relocated to a new building located at 550 Foothill Blvd. Salt Lake City, Utah 84158, On the VA Medical Center Campus. The mission of the office is to provide counsel, assisting veterans and dependents in claims processing and establishing rights to state and federal benefits, along with providing information and advisory services. An outreach assistance program to rural Utah veterans is provided by veteran service officers of the Utah Department of American Legion, Disabled American Veterans, and Veterans of Foreign Wars, under contract with the Utah State Division of Veterans Affairs. DD-214's U.S. active duty military service discharge certificates are on file in the office for the previous five years, only for veterans with Utah residency (home of record) or with a Utah forwarding address at the time of release from active duty. DD-214's older than the previous five years are located at the State Archives, 801-538-3013. New legislation in 2000 changed the office to the Utah State Division of Veterans Affairs, effective 01 July 2000. (Utah Code Vol 2, Section 39 & Utah Code Vol 3, Section 71.) As of July 2001, the Utah State Veterans Cemetery & Memorial Park came under the direction of the Utah State Division of Veterans Affairs. As of July

2002, the Utah State Veterans Nursing Home will also come under the Utah State Division of Veteran Affairs.

L. UTAH STATE VETERANS NURSING HOME: The first Utah State Veterans Nursing Home, located by the VA SLC Healthcare System (veterans hospital), phone 801-584-1900; fax 801-584-1960, address, 700 Foothill Blvd, SLC, UT 84113-1104, was dedicated on 22 April 1998 and became operational in May 1998. Quality nursing and health care services are provided for Utah veterans with U.S. military service during peacetime or wartime. While wartime service is not a requirement for admission to the nursing home, wartime veterans with one day or more of wartime service, as recognized by state and federal laws, have top priority. A veteran's spouse or surviving spouse may also qualify for admittance to the Utah State Veterans Nursing Home, providing the marriage to the veteran occurred at least one year before the application. (Utah Code Vol 2, Section 26)

M. UTAH STATE VETERANS CEMETERY & MEMORIAL PARK: Located at 17111 Camp Williams Road in Bluffdale, phone number, 801-254-9036, fax number 801-254-5756. This states veteran's cemetery generally follows the eligibility requirements of VA National Cemetery System, including: any U.S. Armed Forces active personnel dying while performing duty or after having served during wartime. Reservist and National Guard retired personnel with 20 years of service are eligible for burial also. Surviving spouses and dependent children also are eligible to be buried in the Utah State Veterans Cemetery & Memorial Park, under rules established by the state of Utah. Authorized in 1988 by act of the Utah State Legislature, dedication occurred on Memorial Day, 1990. Veterans are not to be buried in any portion of any cemetery or burial ground used for paupers; cities, towns, counties or other political subdivisions of the state of Utah may provide proper sites for burial of veterans. (Utah Code Vol 3, Section 71)

N. MILITARY DISCHARGE RECORDS: Utah State Archives has military discharge records for Utah veterans from territorial times

(1849-1895) through 31 December of the year prior to the previous five years, (which are kept in our office) phone (801-538-3013) U.S. military service records on file will be copied by Utah State Archives for a small fee. Utah State Division of Veterans Affairs has active duty U.S. military service DD-214's for Utah Veterans for the previous five years. DD-214 certified copies are provided free of charge; toll free 800-894-9497. Utah National Guard Headquarters at Draper, Utah maintains file copies of National Guard bureau NGB 22 "record of separation" certificates for completed service in the Utah Army National Guard & Utah Air National Guard (1950-present). NGB 22 certified copies are free of charge; phone 801-523-4534.

NOTE: For many years, veterans were encouraged to place their DD-214 on file with their local county recorders office. We no longer recommend this practice because of security issues. (Utah Code Vol 1, Section 17 & Vol 3, Section 71)

O. FREE USE OF ARMORIES: Organizations of war veterans are entitled to have free use of state of Utah armories as meeting places, provided such use shall not interfere with the use of armories by the National Guard or organized militia of Utah. (Utah Code Vol 3, Section 71)

P. PROFESSIONAL LICENSE FEES: Veterans previously licensed in Utah for a profession may be reinstated by paying the current annual renewal fee plus a $10.00 reinstatement fee. An exam for many professional licenses is an original requirement. (Utah Code Vol 3, Section 58)

Q. FISHING LICENSE PRIVILEGES: Blind, paraplegic, or otherwise permanently disabled persons including disabled veterans meeting the strict qualifying criteria, will be issued Utah Handicapped Fishing Licenses free of charge by the Utah Division of Wildlife Resources (DWR). Free Utah Disabled Veterans Fishing Licenses are no longer offered, due to a 1999 Utah state law change, which repealed this provision. Previously, disabled veterans with a 10% or greater military-service connected disability rating could receive Utah Disabled Veterans

Fishing Licenses. Currently, disabled veterans qualifying for Utah Handicapped Fishing Licenses are only those with obvious physical handicaps, such as, permanently confined to wheelchairs, paraplegic, minus at least one limb, permanently requiring crutches, blind, or otherwise permanently disabled. (Utah Code Vol 1, Section 23)

R. SPECIAL FUN TAGS: Free of charge to disabled veterans, other disabled persons, and persons 62 & over are Utah Special Fun Tags, which allow free admission to most of the 44 state-controlled parks, campgrounds and other recreation areas throughout Utah. The Utah Special Fun Tags also allows a $2.00 camping fee discount Monday through Thursday, excluding holidays. Utah Special Fun Tags are available to disabled veterans upon application to the Utah Division of Parks and Recreation, along with a VA letter documenting 10% or greater military service-connected disability rating. (Utah Code Vol 1, Section 23)

S. BUS/TRAX REDUCED FARE CARDS: Greatly discounted fares (65% reduced) to ride Utah Transit Authority (UTA) busses and TRAX light rail system are available for veterans meeting these criteria: Forty percent (40%) or greater military service-connected disability rating by VA or Eligibility for VA non-service connected pension: or Regardless of disability pct. Rating for veterans & others with transportation disabilities causing either: difficulty boarding or alighting from a bus/light rail system, difficulty standing in a moving but/light rail system, difficulty reading bus/light rail system schedules & understanding information signs, difficulty hearing announcements by bus/light rail system, or difficulty hearing announcements by bus/light rail systems operators. Persons receiving Social Security Disability benefits, SSI, or Medicare also my get UTA Reduced Fare Cards. Elderly persons age 65 and over qualify for Senior Passes at the same price as Reduced Fare Cards. To obtain UTA Reduced Fare Cards for .50 cents regular fares or $18.00 monthly fares, do the following: 1. Go to either UTA location at 167 S. Main St. or 3600 S. 700W. In SLC, 2. Complete UTA Reduced Fare Card application form, 3. Present evidence (a VA letter verifying service connected disability rating or non service connected pension, 4. pay $2.00 for UTA photo identification to incorporate on UTA Reduced Fare Card. (Utah Code Vol 4 Section 72, Utah Transit Authority Regulations & U.S. Transportation Regulations)

T. GOLDEN ACCESS PASSPORT: A lifetime entrance pass to most national parks, monuments, historic sites, recreation areas, and national wildlife refuges that charge an entrance fee. The Golden Access Passport admits the pass holder and any accompanying passengers in a private vehicle. Where entry is not by private vehicle, the passport admits the pass holder, spouse, and children. The Golden Access Passport also provides a 50% discount on federal use fees charged for facilities and services such as camping, swimming, parking, boat launching, and cave tours. It does not cover or reduce special recreation permit fees or fees charged by concessionaires. A Golden Access Passport must be obtained in person at any federal area where an entrance fee is charged or at one of the agencies administering the Golden Access Passport. It is available to citizens or permanent residents of the United States who are medically determined to be blind or permanently disabled. Veterans may obtain a passport by showing proof of a medically determined permanent disability or eligibility for receiving benefits under federal law. A letter from the Department of Veterans Affairs stating the veteran's disability rating will suffice. Agencies administering the Golden Access Passport are Bureau of Land Management, Fish and Wildlife Service, Bureau of Reclamation, Army Corps of Engineers, National Park Service, and Forest Service.

U. COMMUNITY BASED OUTPATIENT CLINICS: Following is a list of the clinics that provide medical treatment to veterans. It is recommended that you contact the clinic to ascertain the requirements of the clinic. **Ogden,** 982 Chambers St., S. Ogden, UT, 84405 801-479-4105.. **Roosevelt,** 210 W. 300 N. Roosevelt, UT. 84066, 435-722-3971, **Orem,** 740 W. 800 N. Ste. 440, Orem, UT. 84057 801-235-0953, **St. George,** 1067 E. Tabernacle, St. George, UT. 84770, 435-634-7608, **Nephi,** 48 W. 1500 N., Nephi, UT. 84648,

435-623-3129, **Fountain Green,** 300 W. 300 S., Fountain Green, Ut., 435-623-3129, **Milford,** 451 N. Main, Milford, UT, 435-623-3129. For further information on the clinics, please contact the VA Hospital at 1-800-613-4012.

GENERAL INFORMATION

The Veterans Administration Regional Office (VARO) is located at 125 S. State St., Salt Lake City, UT. 84138. They are located on the fifth floor of the Wallace F. Bennett Federal Bldg. However, by mid-year 2002, VARO will re-locate to a new building on the campus of the VAMC (VA Hosp.) in Salt Lake City, UT. VARO's new address will be, 550 Foothill Blvd., SLC. UT. 84158. You will still be able to contact the VA by calling 1-800-827-1000.

VA HOSPITAL

The VA-SLCHCS, (VA Hospital) is located 700 Foothill Blvd, Salt Lake City, UT. They can be reached by calling 801-582-1565 or toll free from within Utah, at 1-800-613-4012. By calling either number, you will be able to access any department that you may need.

    The Salt Lake City "Vet Center" is located at 1354 E. 3300 S., SLC, UT. They can be reached at 801-584-1294, or toll free from within Utah at 1-800-281-1294.

    The Provo "Vet Center" is located at 750 N. 200 W., Provo, UT. They can be reached at 801-377-1117 or toll free from within Utah at 1-800-246-1197.

    Both centers provide counseling and referral services especially designed for "war era" veterans. They also provide an extensive "out-reach" program aimed at helping the men and women who proudly served their country.

    HOMELESS VETERANS FELLOWSHIP: The Homeless Veterans Fellowship is located at 541 23rd St. Ogden, UT. They can be reached at 801-392-7662. HVF provides transitional housing for up to eighteen months for veterans. They can also provide emergency food bags and personal hygiene items. Coffee and donuts provided during open hours.

VALOR HOUSE: Located on the campus of the VA Hospital, in Salt Lake City, UT, the Valor House provides transitional housing for homeless veterans for up to two years. There will be a total of 60 beds available, after the 2002 Olympics. For more information regarding this program, please contact Rich Landward at 801-582-1565 ext 42703, or Danica Richins at 801-582-1565 ext 42614. You can also access the Hospital by calling 1-800-613-4012.

VETERANS UPWARD BOUND: Located on the campus of Weber State University in Ogden, UT. They provide a valuable service to veterans in that they assist veterans in obtaining admission to post secondary schools. All of the services provided by VUB are free to the veteran. They will provide tutors to veterans in Ogden and Salt Lake City. For more information, please contact James Kopecky, Director, VUB at 801-626-7173

NO OTHER INFORMATION AVAILABLE

VERMONT STATE VETERANS' AFFAIRS

DIRECTOR: CLAYTON CLARK
MAILING ADDRESS & LOCATOIN:
    118 STATE STREET
    DRAWER 20
    MONTPELIER, VT 05620-4401
TELEPHONE: (802) 828-3379
IN STATE (888) 666-9844
FAX: (802) 828-5932
E-MAIL: cclark@VA.STATE.VT.US

1. SERVICES PERFORMED

To represent service personnel, veterans and their dependents and acquaint them with all federal, state and local benefits to which they may be entitled.

A. MATERIAL KEPT AT THE OFFICE: DD214/Discharge for World War II, Korean Conflict, Vietnam Era, and all peacetime service since World War II. National Guard 201 Personnel Files from 1946 through 1986. PLEASE USE MAILING ADDRESS ABOVE FOR REQUESTED ITEMS.

B. NATIONAL GUARD 201 PERSONNEL FILES: Military Dept., Green Mountain Armory, Military Personnel Records, Camp Johnson, Colchester, VT 05446-3004. We do have some microfilm at our office. Camp Johnson's phone number is: (802) 654-0135

2. STATE BENEFITS:

A. State Veterans Home: Bennington, Vermont, with domiciliary capacity of 24 beds (Level III). Telephone (802) 442-6353.

B. State Home Nursing Care: Bennington, Vermont, with capacity of 185 beds (Levels I & II).

C. Education: Each Department of Employment and Training Office has professionals dedicated to finding employment and job training for veterans.

D. Maintain Records: of war service from Revolutionary War to present. Contact the State Veterans Affairs Office for information.

E. Bonus: Vietnam Era. Contact the State Veterans Affairs Office for information.

F. License Plates: The Department of Motor Vehicles offers the following plates for veterans: U.S. Veteran; Combat Wounded Veterans; Ex-Prisoner of War; Vietnam Veterans of America; Pearl Harbor Survivor; and Nation Guard.

G. Disabled and Needy Veterans Fund: This fund provides temporary assistance to veterans and their dependents that need financial assistance. Contact the State Veterans Affairs Office for information.

H. Hiring Preference: Honorably discharged veterans will receive preference in hiring for state positions; disabled veterans receive additional preference.

I. Veterans Cemetery: The state operates a veterans cemetery in scenic Randolph, Vermont. Contact the State Veterans Affairs Office for information.

3. VITAL STATISTICS:

(Birth, death & marriage for years 1760—1979) (Divorce for years 1861—1984)
Public Records
General Services, Rt. #3
Middlesex, Vt. 05633
Telephone: (802) 828-3286

(Birth, death & marriage for years 1980 to present) (Divorce for years 1985 to present)
Vermont Dept. of Health
Vital Records Division
P.O. Box 70
Burlington, VT 05402
Telephone: 1-800-439-5008

4. USDVA REGIONAL OFFICE:

White River Junction, VT 05009-0001
Telephone: 1-800-827-1000 or
(802) 295-9363

5. VETERANS ORGANIZATIONS, STATE HEADQUARTERS:

The American Legion
126 State Street
Montpelier, VT 05602

Veterans of Foreign Wars
126 State Street
Montpelier, VT 05602

Disabled American Veterans
c/o VA Center
White River Junction, VT 05009-0001
Vermont Vietnam Veterans
P.O. Box 103
Williston, VT 05495

Vietnam Veterans of America, Inc.
Vermont Chapter
Robert Hannan, President
WA Chapter #601
P.O. Box 4146
Bennington, VT 05201

6. GENERAL INFORMATION

In 1945, the Vermont State Veterans Board was created by act of legislation. Its members were the adjutant general and two members appointed by the Governor.

An executive secretary was also authorized, the first being Colonel Alexander J. Smith, a former president of the National Association of State Directors of Veterans Affairs. The duties of the executive secretary are to acquaint himself and his assistants and employees with all federal, state and local benefits to which service personnel, veterans discharged under conditions other than dishonorable, their families and heirs may be entitled; assist them in filing claims; and to represent them in such activities where necessary; provide information concerning services and facilities relative to these benefits, to all federal, state and local organizations and agencies requesting same; and cooperate in any way possible in service to the service personnel, veterans and dependents.

In addition to the aforementioned activities, the State Veterans Board was given the approving authority for all practical on-the job training in Vermont as associated with the veterans vocational rehabilitation and educational program. They were also delegated the administrative activities of the Military State.

Pay or bonus or World War II and the Korean Conflict In 1970, this office was delegated the responsibility of administering Military State Pay for the Vietnam Era.

Vietnam Bonus is paid to honorable service of enlisted personnel of the Armed Forces, who were residents of the State of Vermont at the time of entry into service. Dates included are: 5 Aug. 1964 1 April 1973, inclusive. Bonus pays $10.00 for each month of service, not exceeding 12 months, maximum of $120.00. $120.00 is paid survivors. Officers are not entitled.

The responsibility of maintaining records of war service of those who served from Vermont from the Revolutionary War to present is delegated to this office.

In 1960, the Legislature dispensed with the Veterans' Board and delegated the duties and responsibilities to the adjutant general, which brings us to the present. The State Veterans Affairs is a section of the Military Department and is composed of a Veterans Services Coordinator, The Veterans Cemetery Director, two clerks, and an outstanding volunteer.

VIRGINIA DEPARTMENT OF VETERANS' AFFAIRS

DIRECTOR: Bert Boyd
MAILING ADDRESS & LOCATION:
    POFF FEDERAL BUILDING RM. 503
    270 FRANKLIN RD. SW
    ROANOKE, VA 24011-2215
TELEPHONE: (540) 857-7104

FAX: (540) 857-7573
E-MAIL: bboyd131@worldnet.att.net

1. SERVICES PERFORMED.

A. Assists veterans, their widows, orphans and dependents in obtaining their benefits, rights and privileges under federal, state and local laws, enacted for their benefit. Disseminates statewide public service announcements through the various local and regional newspapers, TV and radio networks.

B. The Department is the accredited representative of the following organizations:

American Ex-Prisoners of War
American Legion
American Red Cross
AMVETS
Commonwealth of Virginia
Fleet Reserve Assoc.
Jewish War Veterans
Marine Corps League
Military Order of the Purple Heart
Non-Commissioned Officers Assoc.
Regular Veterans Assoc.
Veterans of Foreign Wars
Veterans of World War I, USA
Vietnam Veterans of America

C. Administers the Virginia War Orphans Education Program.

2. STATE BENEFITS:

A. Service to 110 cities and towns.
B. Claims counseling and forwarding for non-accredited organizations.
C. Strong advocacy for veterans before the USDVA and the State Legislature.

D. War Orphans Education: All children of wartime service-connected deceased or permanently and totally disabled veterans are provided free tuition in state-supported colleges and universities.

E. Special Automobile Tags: Special automobile license plates for disabled veterans, or former POW's are provided without fee. Other special plates designating the organization are available for a ten dollar fee.

F. Special Hunting and Fishing Licenses: Lifetime hunting and fishing licenses are available for disabled veterans.

G. State Home and State Cemetery: State veterans home opened in November of 1992. State cemetery scheduled to open in the Fall of 1995.

H. Vietnam Veterans Outreach Centers: Hampton, Richmond, Roanoke, and Springfield.

I. CJSDVA Facilities: Hospital and domiciliary in Hampton; McGuire Medical Center in Richmond; Salem Medical Center in Salem; VA Regional Office in Roanoke; service area for USDVA Regional Office, Washington, D. C.; and National Cemeteries at Culpepper, Quantico, and Arlington (under jurisdiction of the Army).

3. NATIONAL SERVICE ORGANIZATIONS:

Virginia is the national home of various veterans organizations including: Army Mutual Aid Association, Catholic War Veterans, Legion of Valor, Marine Corps League, Military Order of the Purple Heart, National Association of Uniformed Services, and the Non-Commissioned Officers Association.

4. Military INSTALLATIONS:

Home of the Norfolk Naval Base, Oceana Naval Air Station, Langley Air Force Base, Quantico Marine Base, Little Creek Amphibious Base, Camp Elmore, Fort Belvoir, Fort Eustis, Fort A.P. Hill, Fort Lee, Fort Monroe, Fort Myer, Fort Pickett, and Fort Story.

5. GENERAL INFORMATION:

The Department of Veterans' Affairs was created in 1942, as the Division of War Veterans' Claims, and in 1950 was placed under the Office of the Attorney General. In 1988, the General Assembly approved reorganization and the Division of War Veterans' Claims became the Department of Veterans' Affairs reporting to the Secretary of Administration, under the Governor.

Currently, the Department employs 57 full-time employees, located in nineteen offices throughout the state. Service is provided to 110 separate locations through agent travel.

In addition to the above, the Department administers the Virginia War Orphans Education Program, providing free tuition at state-supported colleges/universities to the children of wartime service-connected deceased veterans, wartime permanently and totally disabled veterans, and the children of servicemen either missing in action or prisoners of war.

The field offices generally consist of a Veterans' Claims Agent and an Office Services Specialist, except in the larger metropolitan areas where there are additional agents and staff. From the field offices, the agent travels to regularly scheduled itinerant points where they work with veterans and their dependents, representatives of all veterans' organizations, and social organizations in the preparation and presentation of claims. All positions of the Department are totally funded by the state. Certain localities do provide free or rent-assisted office space.

There are approximately 715,000 veterans in Virginia, with approximately l, 700,000 dependents.

The Department maintains service contact points at all USDVA Medical Centers in Virginia and at the VARO in Washington, D. C. Service is also provided to the VAMC's in Martinsburg, West Virginia, and Mountain Home, Tennessee, and at many military installations in Virginia.

The Department maintains a part-time staff at the Board of Veterans' Appeals to represent veterans from Virginia appealing claims denied at the Regional Office level.

WASHINGTON DEPARTMENT OF VETERANS' AFFAIRS

DIRECTOR: JOHN M. KING
MAILING ADDRESS:
  POST OFFICE BOX 41150
  OLYMPIA, WA 98504-1150
LOCATION:
  1011 PLUM ST
  OLYMPIA WA 98504
TELEPHONE: (360) 725-2151
TDD: (360) 725-2199
FAX: (360) 725-2197
E-MAIL: johnk@dva.wa.gov

1. SERVICES PERFORMED.

A. Coordinates closely with veterans ' service organizations throughout the state to ensure that every possible resource at the state and national level is available to serve veterans and their families. WDVA contracts with several organizations to operate service offices. The American Legion, Veterans of Foreign Wars, and Disabled American Veterans staff these offices. They assist veterans, family members and survivors in filling claims for benefits.
B. Operates fiduciary and protective payee programs for veterans and family members who have been rated incompetent to handle their financial affairs. By assuming custody of the individual's finances, the Department provides management services to ensure that basic needs are met. This program is open to individuals referred to WDVA by the US Department of Veterans Affairs and the Social Security Administration.

C. In addition to the outreach provided by the Veterans Community Service Coordinators, the Department targets segments of the veteran population, which have been traditionally underserved. The department participates in programs that address minority veterans issues.

D. The Department serves as an information resource for veterans who were exposed to Agent Orange and other herbicides used in Vietnam. WDVA stays abreast of legislation and regulations, which impact this area to ensure that the information reaches the state's 670,628 veterans.

E. The Department has been a national leader in providing Post Traumatic Stress Disorder (PTSD) counseling services since 1984. WDVA's professional counselors provide group and individual therapy sessions for veterans and family members. Veterans are referred to specialized or inpatient care on an as needed basis.

F. WDVA operates a Homeless Veterans Reintegration Project (HVRP) funded through the US Department of Labor VETS. HVRP provides homeless veterans with outreach, case management services and employment and training opportunities in Puget Sound.

G. WDVA offers a complete referral service at their central office to provide veterans with accurate and current information on the entire range of issues associated with veterans' benefits and entitlements. It is staffed with Veterans Benefits Specialists Monday through Friday from 8 a.m. to 5 p.m. A voice mail system takes messages during non-business hours. Veterans can call toll-free within the state of Washington at 1-800-562-2308. The office also offers walk-in services.

2. STATE BENEFITS:

Honorably discharged veterans who have served in any branch of the armed forces or who have service-connected disabilities MAY be entitled to one or more of the following state benefits:

A. Residency in the Washington Veterans Home in Retsil, the Washington Soldiers Home in Orting, or the Spokane Veterans Home.

B. Educational benefits.

C. Veterans assistance fund.

D. Burial benefits.

E. Employment preference; reemployment and layoff rights.

F. Military retirement credit.

G. Motor vehicle license plates.

H. Fishing/hunting license.

I. State park pass.

J. Documents and public records access.

3. GENERAL INFORMATION:

The Washington State Department of Veterans Affairs (WDVA) is a full-service state agency that assists veterans, their family members and survivors. The Department is an advocate for veterans and their families and aggressively pursues all federal and state benefits and entitlements on their behalf.

The Washington Department of Veterans Affairs provides services and outreach across the state through Veteran Community Service Coordinators (VCSCs), Veteran Service Offices and by training local post and chapter service officers to assist veterans obtain benefits

Veteran Community Service Coordinators network with local service providers in an assigned service delivery area to streamline and insure the quality of delivery of services to veterans and their families. VCSCs also work closely with Veteran Service Organizations to develop quality claims, reduce adjudication time and decrease appeals.

In conjunction with the Federal VA, WDVA also holds Community Information and Assistance Fairs to provide veterans and their families the opportunity to learn more about service-connected disability, vocational rehabilitation, VA healthcare enrollment and other services. VCSCs and Veteran Service Offices are located throughout the state. Community Information and Assistance Fairs are held periodically in all corners of the state. To locate a VCSC or Veteran Service Office—or to learn more about a Community Information and Assistance Fair—please call 1-800-562-2308.

The Department also operates the Washington Soldiers Home in Orting, the Washington Veterans Home in Retsil, and the Spokane Veterans Home which provide high quality long-term nursing care for honorably discharged veterans and eligible family members who meet certain financial requirements.

For more information on admission to a State Veterans Home call, 1-877-VETS-R-US (1-877-838-7787)

WEST VIRGINIA DIVISION OF VETERANS' AFFAIRS

DIRECTOR: Joe Martin
MAILING ADDRESS & LOCATION:
 1321 PLAZA EAST, SUITE 101
 CHARLESTON, WV 25301-1400
TELEPHONE: (304) 558-3661
FAX: (304) 558-3662 (call first)
E-MAIL: WVVETAFF@AOL.COM

ORGANIZATION

In addition to 16 area field offices throughout the state, the Department maintains claims offices at Huntington VARO, West Virginia, and Pittsburgh VARO, Pennsylvania.
 Michael Craig, Claims Manager
 640 Fourth Avenue
 Huntington, WV 25701
 Room 432-A, Federal Building
 1000 Liberty Avenue
 Pittsburgh, PA 15222

1. SERVICES PERFORMED.

A. This Division furnishes representation to veterans, their dependents and survivors by virtue of Power of Attorney vested in:
 Veterans of WWI of USA, Inc.
 The American Legion

American Red Cross
Vietnam Veterans of America
Non-Commissioned Officers Association
Veterans of Foreign Wars
West Virginia Division of Veterans Affairs
AMVETS
Military Order of the Purple Heart
Marine Corps League

B. Service organizations having their own service representatives in the Huntington West Virginia Regional Office:

Disabled American Veterans
Paralyzed Veterans of America

2. STATE BENEFITS:

A. Tax Exemption: There is provided for a partial examination of military retirement pay and certain other types of retirement or annuity benefits from the federal adjusted gross income for the purpose of computing state income tax.

B. Homestead Exemption: For certain eligible veterans. Specific information is available through the local county assessor's office.

C. State Bonus: Deadline expired For World War I, World War II, Korean Conflict and Vietnam Era. Desert Storm Bonus expired June 30, 1994.

D. Veterans State Loan Program: None

E. State Veterans Home (domiciliary): located in Barboursville, West Virginia

F. Free Vehicle Registration: For veterans who are drawing 100% service-connected compensation from USDVA, in receipt of an auto grant from the USDVA, a former POW. Free license for recipients of Purple Heart and Pearl Harbor Survivors. Free hunting and fishing privileges for 100% service-connected veterans or those in receipt of USDVA auto grant.

3. VITAL STATISTICS:

Director, Vital Statistics/Health Services
350 Capitol Street, Room 165
Charleston, WV 25301

4. USDVA REGIONAL OFFICE:

640 Fourth Avenue
Huntington, WV 25701

5. VETERANS ORGANIZATIONS, STATE HEADQUARTERS:

The American Legion
P.O. Box 3191
Charleston, WV 25332
Veterans of Foreign Wars
P. O. Box 9431
South Charleston, WV25309

Disabled American Veterans
P. O. Box 605
Elkview, WV 25071

All other organizations utilized the residential address of the current department commander.

6. GENERAL INFORMATION:

The West Virginia Division of Veterans Affairs is a department of State Government. It is under the supervision of a seven-member Veterans Council, whose members are appointed by the Governor for six-year terms, by and with the consent of the State Senate. The Director of the Division is also appointed by the Governor, by and with the consent of the State Senate, to serve at the will and pleasure of the Governor. All other positions within the Division are appointed by the Director under the rules and regulations of the State Civil Service.

The West Virginia Division of Veterans Affairs was created by an Act of the 1945 State Legislature and has continued to operate as an independent division of State Government since that time. Since the Division was organized, four additional field offices have been added to the original twelve.

The Division was created for the specific purpose of "aiding, assisting, counseling, advising and looking after the rights and interests of all persons known as veterans...and their widows, dependents and orphans, who are or have become citizens and residents of this state." The mission is to assist in every possible way those veterans and their dependents of the State of West Virginia to obtain all benefits to which they may be entitled under state and federal laws.

The Division performs claims work having a claims office located in the U.S. Department of Veterans Affairs (USDVA) Regional Office, Huntington, West Virginia. It is also necessary for this Division to maintain a claims office in the USDVA Regional Office in Pittsburgh, Pennsylvania, to service claims for those veterans of the four northern panhandle counties, whose records are located there because of geographic proximity. The Division also maintains field service with an office in sixteen different locations throughout the state. Each office has under its jurisdiction several counties maintains itinerant service. The Division is active in the field of training for service officers with a statewide service officers conference, which is conducted during May each year, as well as various conferences for its own personnel.

The veteran population of West Virginia, according to the latest figures, is estimated to be 184,000. The American Legion, Veterans of Foreign Wars, Disabled American Veterans, and Veterans of World War I of the USA, have active organizations within the state. Approximately 70,000 veterans are members of these various veterans organizations.

The Division also administers the State War Orphans Education Program on an annual appropriation of $3,500 all of which is expended for direct benefits to children attending school under this program. Tuition for the students under this program, attending state-supported schools is waived.

A domiciliary type State Veterans Home was opened on November 8, 1981, at Barboursville, West Virginia, with an initial capacity of 47 residents, which was increased to its full capacity of 195 residents in the late summer of 1982, when renovation of the existing physical facility was completed.

WISCONSIN DEPARTMENT OF VETERANS' AFFAIRS

SECRETARY: RAYMOND G. BOLAND
MAILING ADDRESS:
 POST OFFICE BOX 7843
 MADISON, WI 53707-7843
LOCATION:
 30 W. MIFFLIN STREET
 MADISON, WI 53707
TELEPHONE: (608) 266-1311
FAX: (608) 267-0403
E-MAIL: ray.boland@dva.state.wi.us

1. SERVICES PERFORMED.

A. Administer a comprehensive program of state veterans benefits, which are provided to qualified Wisconsin military veterans under the Wisconsin Statutes. Major benefits include loan and grant programs, admittance to the Wisconsin Veterans Homes and interment at state veterans cemeteries.
B. The Department maintains continual contact with 72 county veterans services officers, and coordinates its efforts with various intergovernmental agencies and more than 20 statewide veterans organizations.

2. STATE BENEFITS

A. Tax Exemption: No state income tax on military retirement pay.

B. Soldiers Home: The Wisconsin Veterans Home at King, Wisconsin, was established in 1887 by the Grand Army of the Republic, and has been in continuous operation since then. The Department of Veterans Affairs has operated the Home since 1945. The facility has four nursing care buildings with a total bed capacity of 749 beds. The Home provides complete care, including skilled nursing care, in a community setting. The modern facilities include: pharmacy, outpatient treatment, x-ray and laboratory, physical therapy and other therapy services. The Wisconsin Veterans Home at Union Grove opened in 2001 and provides community based residential facilities for veterans and spouses. A residential care apartment facility will open in 2003 and a skilled nursing facility will be added in 2005.

C. State Bonus: None since World War I.

D. Loan Programs:

(1) Primary Mortgage Loan Program: An annual percentage rate determined by the cost of the general obligation bonds sold to finance the program (somewhat lower than conventional rates and often lower than VA and FHA rates) applied for through an authorized conventional lender. (Investment: Nearly $23 billion in more than 55,000 veterans home loans since 1974)

(2) Personal Loan Program: Low interest rate loans of up to $15,000 with 10 years to repay.

E. Education:

(1) Part-time Study Grants: To reimburse for tuition and textbooks upon satisfactory completion of courses taken at high school, vocational school, state-supported college or university, and most private colleges or universities.

(2) Tuition Reimbursement: Veterans who have been out of military service ten years or less may be reimbursed up to 85 percent of the cost of tuition and fees at most schools in Wisconsin.

(3) Retraining Grants: This grant provides up to $3,000 per year to recently unemployed veterans who demonstrate financial need while being retrained for employment. The applicant must have been laid off or dismissed within the year preceding the date that the application is received by WDVA.

F. Burial Allowance: None by the Department. Counties may spend up to $300 in addition to VA burial allowance for burial of an indigent veteran and/or his or her spouse. Guardianship: No special provisions for veterans.

G. Emergency Medical and Dependency Grants: The Department makes Emergency Medical Care Aid Grants and Subsistence Aid Grants to relieve a veteran of "want and distress." There is a $5,000 maximum grant for medical care.

H. Graves Registration: Wisconsin Statutes provide for Department maintenance of a Graves Registration File of deceased veterans.

I. Veterans Museum: The Department maintains three veterans museums: The Wisconsin Veterans Museum, 30 W. Mifflin St., Madison, Wisconsin, the Wisconsin National Guard Museum at Volk Field, and the Veterans Museum at the Wisconsin Veterans Home, King, Wisconsin.

J. The Department operates three state veterans cemeteries—the Southern Wisconsin Veterans Memorial Cemetery near Union Grove, the Northern Wisconsin Veterans Memorial Cemetery near Spooner and a cemetery at the Wisconsin Veterans Home at King.

K. Military Funeral Honors Program: The Department operates a Military Funeral Honors Program that coordinates the provision of funeral honors at veterans' funerals through veterans service organizations, reserve and active duty members of the armed forces, and Military Funeral Honors Teams.

3. VA REGIONAL OFFICE:

P.O. Box 6
Milwaukee, WI 53295

4. VETERANS ORGANIZATIONS, STATE HEADQUARTERS:

The American Legion
2930 American Legion Dr.
P.O. Box 388
Portage, WI 53901-0388
Disabled American Veterans
c/o VA Regional Office
Building 6, Room C-231
Milwaukee, WI 53295

AMVETS
c/o VA Regional Office
Building 6
Milwaukee, WI 53295
Veterans of Foreign Wars
214 N. Hamilton
P.O. Box 1623
Madison, WI 53701

5. GENERAL INFORMATION:

The Department is headed by the Board of Veterans Affairs, consisting of seven members appointed by the Governor with the advice and consent of the State Senate for terms of six years. All members must be veterans. The powers and duties of the Board are regulatory, advisory and policy-making in nature, but not administrative.

The administrative powers and duties of the Department are vested in the Secretary who is appointed by, and serves at the pleasure of, the Board of Veterans Affairs.

The Department, with central offices in Madison, maintains a separate claims office in Milwaukee, which is co-located with the VA Regional Office there. The claims office acts in an advocate capacity for the veteran when attempting to resolve problems relating to VA pension, compensation and other VA benefits, or problems arising out of the veteran's military service records. The claims office also maintains liaison with the national service officers for the American Legion, AMVETS, the Disabled American Veterans, and the Veterans of Foreign Wars, which maintain service offices also co-located with the VARO.

Each Wisconsin county has a county veterans service officer (CVSO). The CVSO provides the veteran and his or her dependents with current information on federal, state and county veterans benefits. The CVSO is a county employee, but he or she acts as an agent of the Department of Veterans Affairs when processing applications for state veterans benefits. With one exception, the CVSO also similarly acts as an agent for the VA when processing a veteran's application for federal benefits. The Department maintains constant contact with the CVSOs, through the CVSO Association, the CVSO Advisory Council and through the department's Regional coordinators, who maintain individual associations with the service officers. The Department also holds workshops twice annually during CVSO Association conferences, and conducts 3-day initial orientation and training sessions for all newly-appointed CVSOs.

The museum, located at the Wisconsin Veterans Home at King near Waupaca, Wisconsin, is a popular attraction and features displays of memorabilia from the two World Wars. The Wisconsin Veterans Museum in Madison on the Capitol Square opened in June 1993. It depicts the contributions made by Wisconsin veterans of all wars and other armed conflicts. The veterans museum also operates the Wisconsin National Guard Museum at Volk Field.

Veterans organizations in the state of Wisconsin include: The American Legion, AMVETS, American Ex-POW's, Army-Navy Union, Catholic War Veterans, Disabled American Veterans, Jewish War Veterans, Marine Corps League, Military Order of the Purple Heart, National Association for Black Veterans, Navy Clubs of the U.SA, Polish Legion of American Veterans, Veterans of Foreign Wars, Vietnam

Veterans of America, Wisconsin Vietnam Veterans, U.S. Submarine Veterans of WWII, United Women Veterans and Wisconsin Association of Concerned Veterans Organizations.

WYOMING VETERANS AFFAIRS COMMISSION

DIRECTOR: Don Ewing
MAILING ADDRESS & LOCATION:
   WYOMING VETERANS AFFAIRS COMMISSION
   LTC HARDY V. RATCLIFF NATIONAL GUARD ARMORY
   Room 101
   5905 CY AVENUE
   CASPER, WY 82604
TELEPHONE: (307) 265-7372
FAX: (307) 265-7392
E-MAIL: wvac@trib.com

1. SERVICES PERFORMED

The Commission keeps informed on issues affecting Wyoming Veterans and makes appropriate recommendations to the Governor and Legislature. The Commission's duties include:

   a. Review State and Federal legislation affecting veterans;
   b. Act as liaison between veterans and government agencies;
   c. Inform veterans of benefits available;
   d. Meet quarterly.

The Commission established the Oregon Trail State Veterans Cemetery and works in cooperation with the Adjutant General who has charge of operation and maintenance.

2. STATE BENEFITS:

A. Veterans Preference: Under the law, eligible veterans (separated from the Armed Services under conditions other than dishonorable) are entitled to receive preference over non-veterans in selection and referral to job opportunities, and disabled veterans are entitled to priority over other veterans for such services.

B. Veterans Reemployment: Wyoming meets or exceeds federal law in providing reemployment rights. If all requirements are met, veterans can return to former jobs with all accrued seniority status, and rate of pay that would have been received if military service had not been entered.

C. Tax Exemptions: Veterans who qualify are eligible to receive county tax exemptions. Maximum exemption is $800.00. Maximum yearly deduction is approximately $60.00 per year on license plates and $150.00 per year for property taxes. Surviving spouses of qualified veterans may reopen exemption, and it becomes a lifetime benefit with no maximum limit, except for the yearly limit.

D. Educational Benefits for Vietnam Veterans: Wyoming Enrolled Act No. 61. Tuition waiver for not more than 10 semesters of credit classes on a full or part time basis at any of Wyoming's Community Colleges or the University of Wyoming; no expiration date; no requirement of continuous enrollment.

E. State Veterans Cemetery: Any veteran who received any discharge, other than a dishonorable discharge, from the Armed Forces of the United States is eligible for burial in the Oregon Trail State Veterans Cemetery. The spouse, handicapped or minor child of an eligible veteran may also qualify for burial in the State Veterans Cemetery, providing that the internment of the qualifying family member is in the same burial plot as that provided for the veteran.

3. VETERANS HOME

Wyoming veterans, or dependents of a veteran, who qualify may be admitted to the Veterans Home of Wyoming, located in Buffalo, Wyoming. Resident maintenance fees are based on their ability to pay with a monthly maximum charge of $1,150.00. Veterans receive a reduction of $328.00 from payments received on their behalf from the VA, and this results in a monthly maximum payment of $822.00. A resident with assets less than $10,000.00 is charged according to a formula that is applied to the resident's gross monthly income as follows: a resident pays 85% of total monthly income reduced by $65.00 for personal use.

4. CHEYENNE VA MEDICAL AND REGIONAL OFFICE:

The center provides primary and secondary in-patient services in medicine, surgery as well as outpatient services in medicine, surgery and psychiatry. Presently, the Center has an operating bed level of 86 care beds. The medical center also supports a 50 bed Nursing Home Unit located within the main hospital.

5. SHERIDAN VA CENTER:

A 292 bed non-affiliated neuropsychiatric facility providing high quality private and secondary medical and psychiatric care. Included in the bed compliment are 30 acute medical, 4 intensive care/coronary care unit, 48 intermediate care, 50 nursing home care, and 103 psychiatric beds along with a 57 bed alcohol dependence treatment unit.

6. VITAL STATISTICS:

Veterans may, and are strongly recommended to file their DD form 214s at their County Clerk's Offices. The filing is free of charge.

7. VETERANS ORGANIZATIONS, STATE HEADQUARTERS:

The American Legion
Dept. of Wyoming
Robert Nab, Adjutant
P.O. Box 545
Cheyenne, WY 82001
Phone: (307) 634-3035
Fax: (307) 635-7093

Veterans of Foreign Wars
Dept. of Wyoming
Roland Thomas, State Quartermaster
P.O. Box 6678
Cheyenne, WY 82003
Phone: (307) 634-1005

Disabled American Veterans
Dept. of Wyoming
Floyd Watson, Jr., Adjutant
219 S. Ames Ave.
Cheyenne, WY 82007
Phone: (307) 632-2338

WY Assoc. of Vietnam Veterans
Terry McCollum, Contact
1170 Bretton Drive
Phone: (307) 265-2870

Marine Corps League
Dept. of Wyoming
Gabriel Salazar, Adjutant
1508 E. 15th Street
Cheyenne, WY 82001
Phone: (307) 635-6702

United Veterans Council of WY
Todd E. White, President
P.O. Box 832
Worland, WY 82401
Phone: (307) 347-2716

The Retired Enlisted Association, Inc.

Chapter 46
Albert R.Buss, President
P. O. Box 5366
Cheyenne, WY 82003-5366
Phone: (307) 634-8237

8. GENERAL INFORMATION:

Wyoming created its Veterans Affairs Council, later renamed the Council of Veterans Affairs, by act of the legislature adopted March 5, 1975. Ostensibly, the primary purpose for its founding was to enable Wyoming, in cooperation with the Veterans Administration (now the U.S. Department of Veterans Affairs (VA)), to build the Oregon Trail State Veterans Cemetery at Evansville, Wyoming. It is the first and only veterans cemetery in the state and is part of the national veterans cemetery system.

The duties of the Wyoming Veterans Affairs Commission are spelled out in the statute to (1) study all federal and state legislation affecting veterans, their spouses, dependents and beneficiaries; (2) establish liaison with agencies dealing with veterans; affairs; and (3) make recommendations to the legislature and to the governor concerning veterans.

A primary function of the Veterans Affairs Commission has been to disseminate information regarding programs, benefits and matters of general interest to more than 53,000 veterans who live in Wyoming (approximately one-eighth of the state's entire population). To this end it participates in publishing and distributing a booklet describing benefits available to veterans. Also, it maintains a telephone veterans information service that can be accessed by dialing 1-800/832-1959, extension 5059 (Cheyenne callers telephone 772-5059). In addition, it provides information through the Wyoming World Wide Web pages accessed through either the Wyoming Information and Library Link (WILL) or by using one's web browser at HTTP://www.state.wy.us/governor/boards/veterans/veterans.html.

The Commission has been placed by statute in the state Department of Employment. By executive order of Governor Jim Geringer last year, however, it was transferred into the Adjutant General's Military Department and is expected to remain there after appropriate legislative action is taken next year. It works with the Adjutant General in the supervision and control of the Oregon Trail State Veterans Cemetery.

Attempts are presently being made to obtain a reliable source of funding to establish a staffed office for the Commission in order to provide more and better services for Wyoming's veterans and improve lines of communication with them and the veterans service organizations in the state. Until a permanent office is established, the business of the Commission is conducted out of the homes and private offices of the five members of the Commission. Chairman R. Stanley Lowe's home address is: 97 Primrose, Casper, WY 82604-4018, and his telephone number there is (307) 266-0315 and his direct line office number is (307) 266-0315.

The Governor appoints the five members set by statute to serve on the Veterans Affairs Commission for two year terms. The chairman is elected from the Commission by its members and serves for two years. In addition to Chairman Lowe, members of the Commission are: Evelyne E. Francis Ezell, Secretary, Ralins; Larry J. Bourret, Laramie; Barry D. Gasdeck, Laramie; and Arthur L. Rymill, Torrington.

The statute requires a meeting of the Commission be held at least once each year. Those meetings are convened on call by the Chairman, and information regarding the date, time and place of each meeting is given the press for publication. Intercommunication among the Commission members occurs regularly by telephone and correspondence and at meetings of veterans organizations they attend.

About the Author

Michael Riedel is an honorably discharged staff sergeant of the United States Air Force and a former Veterans Service Representative and Benefits Counselor of the U.S. Department of Veterans Affairs (VA). Mike has over 17 years experience, education and research in military and veterans issues and is a service-connected disabled veteran. Mike's father is an Air Force veteran of the Korean War, his grandfather is a World War II Navy veteran, and Mike's great-uncle is an Army veteran who received a purple heart for injuries sustained during campaigns in France and England during World War II while defeating the Nazis.

Mike served over four years on active duty and 18 months in the Air Force Reserve. He graduated in the top three percent of his Air Training Command Class. Mike worked as NCOIC of Information Management in communications, civil engineering, air weather service and air transportation squadrons.

Military awards and decorations include: U.S. Army Commendation Medal, Air Force Achievement Medal, Navy Meritorious Unit

Commendation, Air Force Good Conduct Medal, Air Force Longevity Service Award Ribbon, Air Force Outstanding Unit Award, Air Force Overseas Long Tour Ribbon, and the Air Force Basic Ribbon.

While serving with the U.S. Department of Veterans Affairs, Mike received the National Performance Award from the Office of the Vice President of the United States, seven Special Service Awards, and two Outstanding Performance Awards.

Mike worked nine years with the Federal VA as a Benefits Counselor and Veterans Service Representative, and then went on to work three years in a veteran's advocate role as a State Veterans Representative before leaving to work as a writer and a publisher.

0-595-29537-1

Made in the USA
Lexington, KY
04 August 2012